# THE ENVIRONMENT

## PATRON

Dato' Seri Dr Mahathir Mohamad

## SPONSORS

*The Encyclopedia of Malaysia* was made possible thanks to the generous and enlightened support of the following organizations:

DRB-HICOM GROUP

GEC-MARCONI PROJECTS (MALAYSIA) SDN BHD

MALAYAN UNITED INDUSTRIES BERHAD

MALAYSIA NATIONAL INSURANCE BERHAD

PERNAS INTERNATIONAL HOLDINGS BERHAD

PETRONAS BERHAD

RENONG BERHAD

SUNGEIWAY GROUP

TENAGA NASIONAL BERHAD

UNITED OVERSEAS BANK GROUP

YAYASAN ALBUKHARY

YTL CORPORATION BERHAD

*Note for Readers*
*The dates in this book are followed by the letters CE or BCE, which mean 'Common Era' and 'Before Common Era', respectively. These terms are synonymous with AD Anno Domini (in the year of our Lord) and BC, which means 'Before Christ'.*

## ACKNOWLEDGMENT

*The Encyclopedia of Malaysia* was first conceived by Editions Didier Millet and Datin Paduka Marina Mahathir. The Editorial Advisory Board, made up of distinguished figures drawn from academic and public life, was constituted in March 1994. The project was publicly announced in October that year, and eight months later the first sponsors were in place. By 1996, the structure of the content was agreed; later that year the appointment of Volume Editors and the commissioning of authors were substantially complete, and materials for the work were beginning to flow in. By late 1998, five volumes were completed for publication, and the remaining ten volumes fully commissioned and well under way.

The Publishers are grateful to the following for their contribution during the preparation of the first five volumes:
Dato' Seri Anwar Ibrahim,
who acted as Chairman of the Editorial Advisory Board;
and the following members of the Board:
Tan Sri Dato' Dr Ahmad Mustaffa Babjee
Prof. Dato' Dr Asmah Haji Omar
Puan Azah Aziz
Dr Peter M. Kedit
Dato' Dr T. Marimuthu
Tan Sri Dato' Dr Noordin Sopiee
Tan Sri Datuk Augustine S. H. Ong
Ms Patricia Regis
the late Tan Sri Zain Azraai
Datuk Datin Paduka Zakiah Hanum bt Abdul Hamid

## SERIES EDITORIAL TEAM

PUBLISHER
**Didier Millet**

GENERAL MANAGER
**Charles Orwin**

PROJECT COORDINATOR
**Marina Mahathir**

EDITORIAL DIRECTOR
**Timothy Auger**

PROJECT MANAGER
**Noor Azlina Yunus**

EDITORIAL CONSULTANT
**Peter Schoppert**

EDITORS
**Alice Chee**
**Chuah Guat Eng**
**Elaine Ee**
**Irene Khng**
**Sharaad Kuttan**
**Jacinth Lee-Chan**
**Nolly Lim**
**Kay Lyons**
**Premilla Mohanlall**
**Wendy (Khadijah) Moore**
**Alysoun Owen**
**Amita Sarwal**
**Tan Hwee Koon**
**Philip Tatham**
**Sumitra Visvanathan**

DESIGN DIRECTOR
**Tan Seok Lui**

DESIGNERS
**Ahmad Puad bin Aziz**
**Lee Woon Hong**
**Theivanai A/P Nadaraju**
**Felicia Wong**
**Yong Yoke Lian**

PRODUCTION MANAGER
**Sin Kam Cheong**

## VOLUME EDITORIAL TEAM

EDITORS
**Alysoun Owen**
**Irene Khng**

DESIGNERS
**Tan Seok Lui**
**Felicia Wong**

ILLUSTRATORS
**Anuar bin Abdul Rahim**
**Chai Kah Yune**
**Chu Min Foo**
**Stephen Dew**
**Geoff Denney Associates**
**Stephane Girel**
**Kyaw Han**
**Lee Sin Bee**
**Karen Phillipps**
**Stephen Seymour**
**Sui Chen Choi**
**Tan Hong Yew**
**Yeap Kok Chien**

## CONTRIBUTORS

**Prof. Dr Abdul Latiff Mohamad**
*Universiti Kebangsaan Malaysia*

**Prof. Dr Abdul Samad Hadi**
*Universiti Kebangsaan Malaysia*

**Assoc. Prof. Dr Anizan Isahak**
*Universiti Kebangsaan Malaysia*

**Dr S. Appanah**
*Forest Research Institute Malaysia (FRIM)*

**Assoc. Prof. Dr Asmah Ahmad**
*Universiti Kebangsaan Malaysia*

**Azman Zainal Abidin**
*Universiti Putra Malaysia*

**Prof. Dr Baharuddin Yatim**
*Universiti Kebangsaan Malaysia*

**Assoc. Prof. Dr Chan Ngai Weng**
*Universiti Sains Malaysia*

**Dr Julian Davison**
*Centre of Southeast Asian Studies, University of Hull*

**Rebecca D'Cruz**
*Wetlands International–Asia Pacific*

**Harwant Singh**
*Universiti Malaya Sarawak*

**Assoc. Prof. Dr Hassan Basri**
*Universiti Kebangsaan Malaysia*

**John Howes**
*Wetlands International–Asia Pacific*

**Prof. Dr Ibrahim Komoo**
*Universiti Kebangsaan Malaysia*

**Dr Kadderi Md Desa**
*Universiti Kebangsaan Malaysia*

**Assoc. Prof. Dr Kadir Din**
*Universiti Kebangsaan Malaysia*

**Assoc. Prof. Dr Khairulmaini Osman Salleh**
*Universiti Malaya*

**Assoc. Prof. Dr Khoo Teng Tiong**
*Universiti Malaya*

**Dr Lim Joo Tick**
*Malaysian Meteorological Service*

**Assoc. Prof. Dr Maimon Abdullah**
*Universiti Kebangsaan Malaysia*

**Prof. Dr Muhammad Haji Salleh**
*Universiti Kebangsaan Malaysia*

**Prof. Dr Rakmi Abd Rahman**
*Universiti Kebangsaan Malaysia*

**Dr Ramdzani Abdullah**
*Universiti Putra Malaysia*

**Prof. Dato' Dr Sham Sani**
*Universiti Kebangsaan Malaysia*

**Assoc. Prof. Dr Sharifah Mastura S. Abdullah**
*Universiti Kebangsaan Malaysia*

**Sivananthan Elagupillay**
*Department of Wildlife and National Parks*

**Subramaniam Moten**
*Malaysian Meteorological Service*

**Teh Tiong Sa**
*Universiti Malaya*

**Dr H. D. Tjia**
*Petronas Research and Scientific Services Sdn Bhd*

**Assoc. Prof. Dr Felix Tongkul**
*Universiti Kebangsaan Malaysia*

**Prof. Dr Voon Phin Keong**
*Universiti Malaya*

**Assoc. Prof. Dr Wan Fuad Wan Hassan**
*Universiti Kebangsaan Malaysia*

**Assoc. Prof. Dr Wong Khoon Meng**
*Universiti Malaya*

**Assoc. Prof. Dr Zuriati Zakaria**
*Universiti Kebangsaan Malaysia*

THE ENCYCLOPEDIA OF
# MALAYSIA

Volume 1

# THE ENVIRONMENT

Volume Editor
## Prof. Dato' Dr Sham Sani

**ARCHIPELAGO PRESS**

# Contents

# Introduction

*This volume presents, in a unique way, the physical environment of Malaysia, the impacts made upon it by human interference, and the policy interventions to ensure sustainability. The bias in coverage in favour of the physical environment is intentional; the objective has been to highlight the richness of resources and the unique geological formations so characteristic of the country. However, the biophysical and human environments have not been neglected. The complex nature of the environment and issues relating to it are a product of the interaction between these two elements within a single ecosystem.*

*The short-tailed green magpie (Cissa thalassina) is a scarce resident of the montane forest of Sabah and Sarawak.*

*Paphiopedilum rothschildianum is known as the 'aristocrat of all slipper orchids' and is one of the rarest of Malaysia's 12,500 species of flowering plants. It is endemic to the Kinabalu Park in Sabah.*

## Environmental resources

One of the world's fastest developing nations, Malaysia possesses some of the planet's most unique geological formations, coastal features and river systems. It is also home to one of the world's richest and most varied biophysical resources. Malaysia has been identified as one of 12 'megadiverse' countries. It contains some 185,000 species of fauna and about 12,500 species of flowering plants.

## Development impacts

Following rapid development since the 1970s, there has been a general loss of biological diversity in Malaysia. Extensive logging, the conversion of tropical lowland forests for agriculture, the draining of wetlands, and the diversion and damming of rivers have led to flooding, deterioration in the quality and quantity of water supply, and loss of productive soils and potentially useful biological resources. Such reduction in diversity is particularly noticeable in coastal and marine resources and in lowland rainforests. The speed with which development is taking place in the coastal zone, together with poor planning and design of coastal development projects, has given rise to many problems related to sustaining balanced development. Economic pressures have led to the destruction of mangrove forests to make way for aquaculture, agriculture and tourist resorts, while exploitation of coastal resources in excess of a sustainable level has caused serious depletion in fish catches. In addition, rapid industrial and infrastructural development in the hinterland has contributed to increased organic and inorganic pollution of rivers and coastal waters.

Development in Malaysia has resulted in both good and less attractive environmental effects. Harnessing the sun's energy to power public telephones (top) is a relatively recent advance. Increased urbanization and a more prosperous society have meant more waste by-products. Garbage collectors do the rounds in Muar (bottom).

An impressive sea stack off Sarawak's coast, Bako National Park.

Energy and mineral resources are also being exploited to sustain the current rate of growth and development. Despite the National Mineral Policy of 1992 and the promulgation of the Mineral Development Act 1994, overexploitation of these resources and the environmental degradation that results are major concerns. Apart from depleting resources, development also pollutes the environment. Air and water, in particular, have been seriously affected in recent years. Toxic and hazardous wastes together with municipal solid wastes are also fast becoming problems that need to be addressed.

## Environmental management response

In the early years after Independence (1957), development priorities were considered paramount, with environmental concerns far less important. In many of Malaysia's early development programmes, little or no consideration was given to environmental aspects. Initial

environment-related legislation was not designed specifically to address environmental problems, but rather concentrated on promoting good housekeeping practices in specific sectors that followed the prevailing government policy. By the 1970s, it had become obvious that existing legislation was unable to cope with pollution produced by modern industries. Consequently, in 1974 the Environmental Quality Act (EQA) was passed and a year later a Division (now Department) of Environment (DOE) was created to administer the Act. Since its introduction, the EQA has been amended twice (in 1985 and 1996), each time with additional provisions which are more strict in terms of control, penalties and coverage of jurisdiction. Not all aspects of the environment are adequately covered by the EQA 1974, notably forestry, water resources, mining, wildlife and fisheries. There are currently more than 40 environment-related pieces of legislation on the Malaysian statute books, which are governed variously by federal and state bodies.

## A single ecosystem

This volume presents the extent of Malaysia's diversity, encompassing both the biophysical and human environments and their interactions. While there tends to be an emphasis on nature and on the physical aspects of the environment in the presentation, the biophysical and human environments should not be seen as separate entities. The complex nature of the environment should be seen as the product of interactions between these two elements within a single ecosystem. The environment provides a canvas against which man, and hence culture, can exist and evolve. Formerly degraded areas have been revitalized through innovations in technology and areas that were once developed and later abandoned are now being resettled. These and other issues are captured in this volume.

Posters now and then.
*Top:* The Malaysian Timber Council encourages contemporary Malaysians to go out and capture the wonders of their natural environment on film in an environmental awareness-raising campaign.

*Bottom:* The British introduced the main arteries of communication to Malaysia (Malaya as it was then), including the railway system.

The book is divided into three main segments: the physical environment; man's interactions with, and impact on, the environment; and policy responses to ensure sustainable development. The attempt has been to present the subjects covered as products of ongoing processes. The volume drives home the point that earlier generations created what we see today and our choices and decisions, recorded on the land, are creating tomorrow's environment. The volume begins with the physical environment and highlights Malaysia's geography—its land and people and the major physical features, including weather and climate. The part on physical features refers to the geology and geomorphological processes of the region, but concentrates on the specific physical features unique to Malaysia. The latter include the Titiwangsa Range, Mount Kinabalu, the karst morphology of Langkawi, the Mulu Caves, the peatswamps of Sarawak and the wonders of the tropical rainforest. The Asian monsoon system and the El Niño effect are highlights under weather and climate.

The second segment concerns man's interaction with the physical environment presented earlier. An account of the early impacts of man on his natural world is followed by the colonial and post-Independence onslaughts and the attendant consequences for the forest ecosystem, wildlife, biodiversity, land use and settlement patterns, water and air quality, municipal and hazardous wastes and agrochemicals.

Feeding off the land and using natural resources to create shelter and saleable products remain the way of life for some indigenous people in Malaysia.

The third and final part of the book addresses policy options. This includes coverage of the national environment policy and environmental management, environmental education and awareness, and global dimensions of environmental management.

Consistent with the other volumes in the series, this volume of *The Encyclopedia of Malaysia* is arranged in chapters which consist of a series of double-page spreads, each written by a specialist in the field. Spreads may be read in sequence as part of the overall subject, or as individual discussions of a particular topic. The seas, plants and animals of Malaysia are purposely given brief treatment here as each of them has its own special volume.

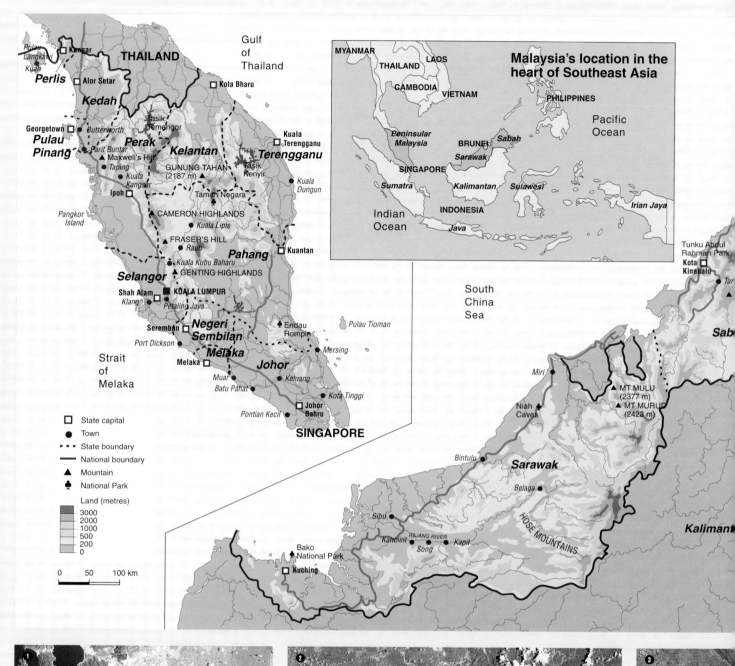

Gulf
of
Thailand

THAILAND

**Perlis**
Kangar
Kuah
Pulau
Langkawi

**Kedah**
Alor Setar

Kota Bharu

Georgetown    Butterworth
**Pulau**     Parit Buntar
**Pinang**    ▲ Maxwell's Hill   Tasik
              Taping          Temengor
              Kuala
**Perak**     Kangsar
Ipoh          **Kelantan**   GUNUNG TAHAN   Tasik
              (2187 m) ▲      Kenyir
              Taman Negara

Pangkor
Island
              CAMERON HIGHLANDS
              Kuala Lipis
              ● FRASER'S HILL
              ● Raub        **Pahang**

              Kuala Kubu Baharu
**Selangor**  GENTING HIGHLANDS
Shah Alam     ■ KUALA LUMPUR
Klang         Petaling Jaya
              **Negeri**
Seremban      **Sembilan**    ● Endau
Port Dickson                   Rompin

              **Melaka**      Mersing
Melaka        Muar          **Johor**
Strait        Batu Pahat    Keluang
of                          Kota Tinggi
Melaka        Pontian Kecil  Johor
                            Bahru

□ State capital      **SINGAPORE**
● Town
··· State boundary
— National boundary
▲ Mountain
♣ National Park

Land (metres)
  3000
  2000
  1000
  500
  200
  0

0    50    100 km

Kuala
Terengganu

**Terengganu**

Kuala
Dungun

Kuantan

Pulau Tioman

South
China
Sea

Malaysia's location in the
heart of Southeast Asia

MYANMAR
THAILAND    LAOS
CAMBODIA    VIETNAM

Peninsular
Malaysia    BRUNEI    Sabah
            Sarawak
SINGAPORE
Sumatra     Kalimantan   Sulawesi
INDONESIA
Indian      Java
Ocean

PHILIPPINES

Pacific
Ocean

Irian Jaya

Tunku Abdul
Rahman Park
Kota
Kinabalu    Tar

**Sab**

Miri        MT MULU
            (2377 m)
Niah        MT MURUD
Caves       (2423 m)

Bintulu     **Sarawak**
            Belaga

Sibu        HOSE MOUNTAINS
Kanowit  RAJANG RIVER  Kapit   **Kalimant**
    Song
Bako
National Park

□ Kuching

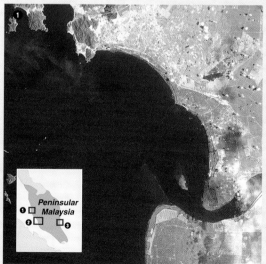

Peninsular
Malaysia
❶ □
❷ □      □ ❸

Puhang

In the Bagan Datok area of Perak, just north of Selangor, the
landscape is slightly hilly (shown in brown) and surrounded by
mangroves (in red).

The commercial agricultural and urban areas of the Klang–Langat River basin have increased
dramatically in area over the last 20 years. The central built-up area (shown in grey), is Kuala
Lumpur and the predominant crop oil palm (in orange).

# INTRODUCING MALAYSIA'S ENVIRONMENT

An Orang Asli house built in a mangrove on Pulau Ketam, off the Selangor coast of Peninsular Malaysia.

Malaysia covers an area of approximately 330 000 square kilometres that almost straddles the equator. The Peninsula accounts for 40 per cent of the total land area with the eastern states of Sabah and Sarawak representing, respectively, areas of 23 and 37 per cent of the country. By the late 1990s, the land supported an estimated population of nearly 21 million and experienced an average annual growth rate of 2.3 per cent. The three largest ethnic groups that make up the population are the Bumiputera (the indigenous people, including Malays), Chinese and Indians. They came to Malaysia in progressive waves of migration, in the first instance to find a better life away from economic privation in their home countries.

The Bumiputera still live to a large extent off the land, and although more Malaysians are moving from rural settlements to towns and cities, where work in the industrial and service sectors is to be found, nearly half of the country's population still maintains a rural existence. The indigenous groups in Sabah and Sarawak, and to a lesser extent in the Peninsula, include those who follow near-nomadic existences and hunt and gather all they need directly from their forest environments. The diverse cultural mix of peoples have adapted to, and likewise transformed, the equally diverse physical landscape of the country. The mountainous terrain of Sabah and Sarawak has meant these states have remained sparsely populated compared to the Peninsula, where vast areas of lowland and richly fertile coastal plains attracted settlers.

To make way for paddy fields and wide expanses of rubber, and later oil palm, once forested land has been felled. At the start of the 20th century, four-fifths of Malaysia was covered by tropical rainforest. Aggressive development, shifting cultivation, mining and commercial logging over the century have significantly reduced the total forested area, so that by the mid-1990s it was one half of its original cover. However, if tree crops such as rubber and oil palm are taken into consideration, then the total area of the country covered by trees remains an impressive 75 per cent of the total land area.

In the post-Independence era (after 1957) and especially during the 1970s, 1980s and 1990s, not only the pristine forests were felled to give way to development, other aspects of the environment also manifested signs of distress. With increased industrialization and urban growth, new forms of 'modern' pollution were introduced affecting the quality of the country's air and water and which in turn affected Malaysia's land and people.

Where the Pahang River meets the coast at Pekan, agricultural settlements (shown in pink) dot forested areas (in green).

# Malaysia's location

*Malaysia is positioned at the centre of Southeast Asia amid a mass of islands and peninsulas between the Indian and Pacific Oceans. It lies entirely within the equatorial region which is characterized by a hot, wet and humid climate and lush tropical rainforests. Much of Malaysia is mountainous and sparsely inhabited, particularly in the eastern states of Sabah and Sarawak. Lower plains, which can be exploited for agriculture and settlement, have been important in the economic development of the country.*

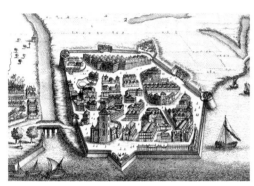

From the 15th century, Melaka was a busy port because of Malaysia's proximity to other parts of Asia and thus to the commodities, such as spices, which were valued by European merchants.

## Position

Malaysia is 329 758 square kilometres in area. It stretches roughly between latitudes (or south to north) 1 and 7 degrees north of the equator and lies between longitudes (or west to east) 100 and 119 degrees east. It consists of two major landmasses, Peninsular Malaysia (previously called West Malaysia) and the north Bornean territories of Sabah and Sarawak, previously referred to as East Malaysia, which face each other across the South China Sea. This location is central to Southeast Asia or that of the geopolitical region known as ASEAN (Association of Southeast Asian Nations). It is located within the major shipping and air routes of the Asia–Pacific and the Trans–Occidental regions and the course of Malaysian history has been

## Mapping Malaysia

LEFT: The 2nd-century astronomer Claudius Ptolemy referred to Malaysia in his *Geographia* as 'Aurea Chersonesus', or the Golden Chersonese. That was how it was chronicled on early maps, such as this from Ruscelli's edition of the *Geographia* (c. 1574). Note the geographically inaccurate coastline.

ABOVE: The superimposition of the Ptolemaic coastline of mainland Southeast Asia (in red) with that of a modern map.

LEFT: Maps prepared by, and for, the Portuguese and Dutch merchant-venturers focused on the west coast of the Peninsula. A thriving port and trading post was maintained at Melaka (Malacca), giving the Europeans access to other riches in Southeast Asia. On maps such as this by John Speed (1676), Melaka was accorded a greater prominence than it geographically deserved, but which reflected its economic importance at that time.

## Geographical greats

Between them, the two parts of Malaysia present a diverse range of landscapes and habitats which are attributable to the country's geographical position. The interior landscape of Sabah and Sarawak is rugged and forested; the coasts of the Peninsula are lapped on both sides by the sea and are dotted with offshore islands.

ABOVE: Southeast Asia's highest mountain, Mount Kinabalu, is 4093 metres high and located in Sabah.

RIGHT: The world's largest flower, *Rafflesia*, is found in the Kinabalu Park.

determined by this strategic position at one of the world's major crossroads. This position and other geographical circumstances have made the country a natural meeting place throughout history for traders from the East and West and for those with political ambitions who have sought a strategic foothold in Southeast Asia.

## Topography

Peninsular Malaysia extends as a long finger of land from the southeast corner of the Asian continent, stretching down from the Thai border to Singapore in the south. It forms part of the Peninsula of Kra, which is the southernmost part of the mainland continent of Asia. The area of the Peninsula is 131 598 square kilometres, approximately the size of England or the state of New York and at its greatest width, between Dindings in Perak and Tanjung Penunjok in Terengganu, it measures 322 kilometres across. The land is dominated by undulating hills and mountain ranges that run north to south.

Modern Borneo consists of the two Malaysian states, the independent Sultanate of Brunei and Indonesian Kalimantan to the south. Between them Sabah and Sarawak, the Malaysian part, offer some stunning geological formations. These include the highest peak and longest cave systems in Southeast Asia and the magnificent rainforests which support a multifarious display of species, including the world's largest flower. The two states developed independently and have retained their own distinct cultural identities.

Sabah is very mountainous, and is dominated by the Crocker Range which disrupts the plains on the west coast cutting them off from the interior. Eastwards the plains are more continuous and some, such as the Kinabatangan, are important agricultural

*ABOVE*: **The largest lake is Tasik Kenyir in Terengganu, which is being developed for its ecotourist potential.**

*ABOVE RIGHT*: **The Rajang, Malaysia's longest river, winds its way to the coast of Sarawak through jungle, swamps and mangroves for over 560 kilometres.**

*RIGHT*: **Malaysia has over 270 islands off the mainland shores. The shallow waters round some of these are renowned for the rich coral and other marine life they support.**

*ABOVE*: **The Gunung Mulu National Park in Sarawak is home to the longest cave system in Asia, the Clearwater Cave, which is 100 kilometres long. The Sarawak Chamber, in the same location, is the largest in the world at 600 metres long, 415 metres wide and with a roof span of 300 metres.**

lands. The island of Labuan (once part of Sabah) lies just 8 kilometres off the western coast. This was declared a Federal Territory on 16 April 1984 and given the status of an International Offshore Financial Centre, or tax haven, in November 1989.

Sarawak is approximately twice the size of Sabah and has a more regular landscape, with rugged terrain in the east which graduates westwards into foothill country and low-lying plains along the western coast. The coastal plains are regularly flooded and the mangrove-fringed coast and extensive swamps make access to the mountainous interior difficult.

### Equatorial influences

With a position just 137 kilometres north of the equator, Malaysia enjoys a uniformly high temperature. The Peninsula is the meeting place of the north and south monsoons which account for the heavy rainfall it receives and for the hot, humid climate. The constant high temperature, humidity and abundant rainfall produce an extraordinary dense and varied natural vegetation. Over half the country is covered by tropical rainforest, ranging from mangrove forests along the muddy coasts to lowland dry forests and mossy forests in the highlands. These are home to some rare and endemic species of flora and fauna.

**Dressing to suit the Malaysian climate means donning loose-fitting clothes of light-coloured fabrics.**

The condition of constant warmth and heavy rainfall means that the landscape is affected by predominantly chemical weathering processes, whereby rocks are decomposed as a result of chemical changes. This is in contrast to parts of the world where frosts and marked extremes in temperature are encountered, and where physical or mechanical weathering typically occur. In Malaysia, therefore, weathering is fairly uniform across the country.

The hot and humid climate has also influenced the way the local people dress. There is a traditional preference for loose, lightly coloured cotton garments. Such clothes help the population stay comfortable and avoid the enervating effect of the equatorial climate.

### Natural wonders

Malaysia has long held a fascination for visitors from overseas. After early traders from the Middle East and India, and later Europe, scientists and adventurers came in search of natural riches. The dramatic features of a tropical environment provoked wonder in the Europeans who visited, particularly those who reached hitherto uncharted territory. Botanists and zoologists have visited in their investigating droves to experience the rich diversity of its plant and animal life at first hand.

William T. Hornaday's travels in Borneo and throughout Asia are recorded in his book, *The Experiences of a Hunter and Naturalist in the Malay Peninsula and Borneo*, first published in 1885.

*Rich in both vegetable [agricultural] and mineral products, teeming with animal life, and filled with both social and scientific problems, Borneo is a most inviting field, interesting alike to the naturalist, the anthropologist, and the student of political economy. . . .*
*Nothing could be more arduous and full of risk of life and limb than overland travel in the interior of Borneo, where the traveller is confronted by dense, dark forests and rugged mountains from the beginning to the end of his journey. The interior is practically an uninhabited wilderness.*

**Handcoloured wood engraving of travels in Borneo from Edward Charton's *Le Tour Du Monde* [The World Tour] published in Paris in 1863.**

*11*

# Land and people

*Malaysia's people are a rich tapestry of different races and religious groupings. Because of its pivotal position on the trade routes between East and West, Malaysia has historically seen a diverse influx of traders and settlers. In addition to Europeans, Indians and Chinese arrived to swell the ranks of the indigenous inhabitants. Groups of the Orang Asli, or 'first people', still roam distinct parts of the country, but rural communities have been reduced at the expense of growing industrialization.*

Living with, and off, the land. Despite the growing size of Malaysia's cities, the population is still fairly equally divided between rural and urban dwellers.

The Malays are traditionally a rural and coastal people. On the east coast of Peninsular Malaysia, a significant part of the population makes its living from the sea (above). Inhabitants of the fertile plains below Mount Kinabalu cultivate vegetables (below).

Negritos of the Bateq community who live in Taman Negara.

### Melting pot of peoples

Malaysians can be broadly categorized into two groups—those who have cultural affinities indigenous to the region, and those who are linked culturally elsewhere. The indigenous people comprise the Bumiputera and Orang Asli while the immigrant groups are known as non-Bumiputera. Descendants of early Orang Asli tribes (Negritos, Senoi and Proto-Malays) still inhabit areas of the Peninsula, but form only a tiny minority of the total population. From the second half of the 19th century, the influx of Indians and Chinese, looking for an escape from poverty, war and revolution in their homelands, was dramatic. The ranks of the indigenous Malay and Malay-related population were swelled, so that today the country's population stands at nearly 21 million.

### The oldest inhabitants: The Negritos

The purest people racially are the Negrito tribes, who are akin to similar peoples in the Andaman Islands, the Philippines, New Guinea and parts of Indonesia. They are found in the northern and eastern part of the Peninsula. They are characterized by some anthropologists as 'Pygmies' as they are relatively small, about one and a half metres or less, although muscular and well-proportioned. Their evolutionary history is somewhat uncertain, but a possible explanation is that they may be survivors of a Palaeo-Melanesian race that once passed through Southeast Asia on its way to present-day Melanesia, some 25,000 years ago. Their language has an affinity with the Austroasiatic language family (different from that of Malay, which is an Austronesian language), which is spoken mostly amongst the peoples of mainland Southeast Asia, including the Khmer and Vietnamese.

The Negritos are true nomads who live in the foothills of the Main (Titiwangsa) Range which extends down the centre of the Peninsula. They roam the rainforest engaging in hunting and gathering activities, practising little or no cultivation. Unencumbered by material possessions because of their mobile lifestyle, they construct simple dwellings of lean-to structures made of palm thatch and are a self-sufficient people, reliant on their own resources and mutual assistance.

Since the Negritos have a strong affinity with their physical environment, their attitudes and ritual practices have been shaped by the natural world. Their social organization is simple, with kinship ties established equally through both parents. Marriage among the Negritos is an informal arrangement, which brings neither financial gain nor social prestige. Marriage between members of an immediate family is not acceptable.

The Negritos are a friendly and peaceful people. Although some groups have now settled down to more conventional living in government schemes, they still return to the forests to gather jungle products, such as rattan, bamboo and medicinal plants which are traded for cash.

### Malays and Proto-Malays

Some of the Malays are believed to have originally come from Yunnan in China. The Malay Peninsula was one of the routes by which these prehistoric peoples travelled south from the heart of Asia, driving the nomadic aborigines away from the coastal areas. The Malays of the east coast of the Peninsula, and in Sabah and Sarawak, tend to be the most long established and predate the colonial era by hundreds of years. The more recent settlers are those who came from Sumatra during the 19th and 20th centuries to work on Malaysia's agricultural plantations. For practical purposes, other ethnic groups, including the Javanese, Banjarese, Boyanese, Bugis and Minangkabau, have been regarded as Malays. The Bajau of Sabah also fall into this category. The bond of Islam and common cultural traits, such as racial descent and similar language, encouraged quick assimilation of these groups into the Bumiputera Malay community.

Malay-related or non-Malay Bumiputera comprise ethnic groups found in Sabah and Sarawak. In Sabah, the Kadazan (Dusun) are the largest ethnic grouping, with the Murut, Kelabit and Kedayan representing significant minorities. The Iban (Sea Dayak) form the largest non-Malay

# Distribution of population

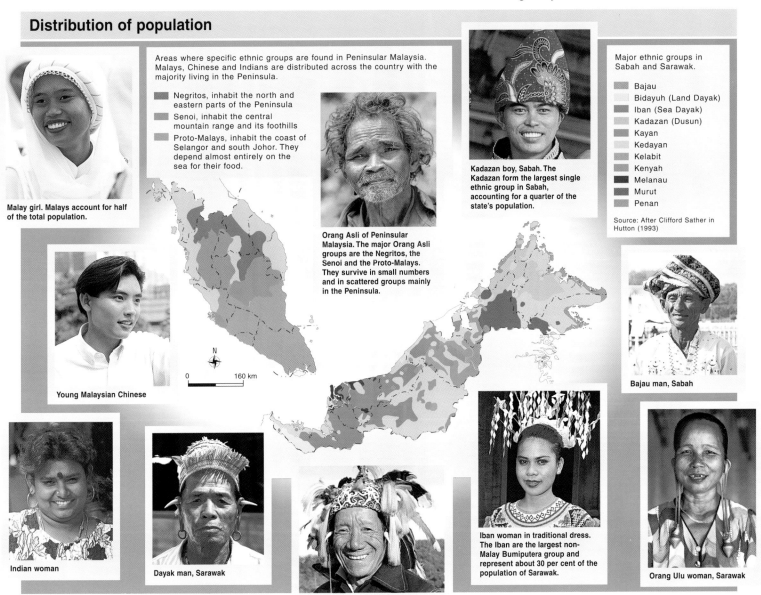

Areas where specific ethnic groups are found in Peninsular Malaysia. Malays, Chinese and Indians are distributed across the country with the majority living in the Peninsula.

- Negritos, inhabit the north and eastern parts of the Peninsula
- Senoi, inhabit the central mountain range and its foothills
- Proto-Malays, inhabit the coast of Selangor and south Johor. They depend almost entirely on the sea for their food.

**Malay girl. Malays account for half of the total population.**

**Orang Asli of Peninsular Malaysia.** The major Orang Asli groups are the Negritos, the Senoi and the Proto-Malays. They survive in small numbers and in scattered groups mainly in the Peninsula.

**Kadazan boy, Sabah.** The Kadazan form the largest single ethnic group in Sabah, accounting for a quarter of the state's population.

Major ethnic groups in Sabah and Sarawak.

- Bajau
- Bidayuh (Land Dayak)
- Iban (Sea Dayak)
- Kadazan (Dusun)
- Kayan
- Kedayan
- Kelabit
- Kenyah
- Melanau
- Murut
- Penan

Source: After Clifford Sather in Hutton (1993)

**Young Malaysian Chinese**

0   160 km

N

**Bajau man, Sabah**

**Indian woman**

**Dayak man, Sarawak**

**Kelabit man, Sarawak**

**Iban woman in traditional dress.** The Iban are the largest non-Malay Bumiputera group and represent about 30 per cent of the population of Sarawak.

**Orang Ulu woman, Sarawak**

Bumiputera, as well as the largest ethnic group in Sarawak. The others are the Bidayuh (Land Dayak), Melanau, Kenyah, Kayan and Bisayah. These groups are of the same basic stock as those who migrated into the country during the early period, but have acquired their present identities or characteristics as a result of separation and refusion.

The Malays are traditionally a rural people and they still represent the majority of the agriculturally dependent population. They are mainly paddy planters, rubber smallholders and, on the east coast, many are fishermen. Aware of their economic position, more Malays are now participating in the trade and industry of the country. This was made possible through the New Economic Policy formulated in 1970 to eradicate poverty and restructure society.

## Other races

The non-Bumiputera groups primarily comprise the Chinese and the Indians, with much smaller communities of Arabs, Sinhalese, Thais, Eurasians and Europeans. The Chinese arrived in Malaysia at a very early date, but it was not until 1786, when British influence was established, that there was large-scale Chinese immigration. These Chinese were brought in to develop the tin deposits of the Malay States. A majority of them came from southern China, with the Cantonese and Hokkien forming the largest dialect groups. Characterized by industriousness and thrift, the Chinese community has played a major role in Malaysia's economic development, and has large stakes in the tin mining and natural rubber industries, in retail and wholesale trading, as well as in small farming.

The presence of the Indians in Malaysia can be traced back to the 5th century CE, when traders from the Coromandel Coast arrived in the Peninsula in large numbers to barter and trade. This was followed by mass migration of Indians early in the 19th century for indentured labour. Most of them came from southern India to work as tappers in the expanding European rubber plantations. The majority have settled permanently and become Malaysian citizens. They play an important part in the administrative, social, economic and political life of the country.

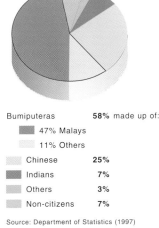

**MALAYSIA'S POPULATION AT A GLANCE**

| Bumiputeras | 58% made up of: |
| --- | --- |
| 47% Malays | |
| 11% Others | |
| Chinese | 25% |
| Indians | 7% |
| Others | 3% |
| Non-citizens | 7% |

Source: Department of Statistics (1997)

Water, as rain, in rivers and in seas, has played a major role in shaping the Malaysian landscape.

Iron-stained and weathered sandstone rock found in Sarawak's Bako National Park.

Craggy formations of calcium deposits in a limestone cave at Kek Lok Tong, Ipoh.

Malaysia is celebrated for its swathes of rich, sandy beaches.

Over half of all Malaysia's land area is covered by forest, that ranges from lowland types, such as mangroves, peatswamps, and lowland rainforest, to montane and subalpine varieties.

# THE PHYSICAL GEOGRAPHY OF MALAYSIA

Malaysia is well endowed with a diverse range of environmental resources. Although the forested land in the late 20th century stands at only 59 per cent of its original, it nevertheless remains one of the best preserved in the world. Being the oldest and most complex tropical rainforest ecosystem, it has become the focus of international attention and a strong pull for both tourists and researchers.

Malaysia is renowned for the wealth of its species, many of which are endemic, such as *Rhododendron wrayi* that grows in the Cameron Highlands.

Malaysia's geology is likewise of renown. The land and sea are not only rich in mineral resources but also offer some diverse and spectacular topographical formations.

Malaysia is mountainous. In Peninsular Malaysia, the Main Range or Banjaran Titiwangsa divides the western from the eastern parts like a rugged spine, as it runs from the Thai border southwards to Negeri Sembilan. In Sabah, the Crocker Range, averaging between 450 and 900 metres in height, separates the narrow lowland of the northwest coast from the interior. Mount Kinabalu, the highest mountain in Malaysia and in Southeast Asia, is located in the Crocker Range. Sarawak boasts the mighty Rajang River and the subterranean calcium carbonate formations—stalactites and stalagmites—of the Mulu Caves. Limestone also characterizes the geography of the Langkawi Islands and the vertical-sided hills of Pahang, Kedah, Perlis and Kelantan. The geological features and their rock and soil foundations are eroded and weathered by the tropical climate and over long periods of geological time are further transformed.

Other significant physical features include Malaysia's shoreline and coasts, river systems and estuaries, islands, mangroves and peatswamps. The coastal wetlands are extremely important for migrant birds, providing them with a sheltered, nutrient-rich base when they arrive from long, exhausting flights. The peatswamp forests at first seem hostile to flora and fauna, but they support a rich selection of wildlife. Extensive mangrove vegetation along the coast helps prevent erosion and simultaneously builds up new land formations by trapping sand and mud sediments. The islands and the sandy beaches of Malaysia are among the best in the world, and the complex offshore coral reefs are among the richest ecosystems on earth.

The undulating hills of the Titiwangsa, or Main, Range typify the country's interior landscape.

# Geological history

*The western part of Peninsular Malaysia was once part of a much larger landmass, a continent called Gondwana. Fragments from this landmass broke off, drifted and, over hundreds of millions of years, assumed their current positions. Malaysia is made up of a series of geological terranes that have affected the nature of the geological activity—mountain building and sedimentation—across the country. These terranes continue to move and the landscape continues to transform itself.*

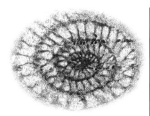

*Fusulinid* sp. (large Foraminifera), a fossil that was found in limestone that dates from the late Carboniferous or early Permian periods of between 320–280 million years ago.

## The formation of Malaysia: The core terrane

Malaysia is composed of several small terranes, or crustal fragments, which evolved at different periods within the country's geological history. The core terrane comprises central and east Peninsular Malaysia, westernmost Sarawak and the Sunda Shelf basement which lies in between. The oldest rocks are about 320 million years old and were formed from sediments deposited under the sea and in inland lakes and river basins. About 250 million years ago, during the Permian and early Triassic, most of the core terrane was below sea level, accumulating thick sediments which, 250–200 million years ago, were subject to magmatic activity.

## Geological principles

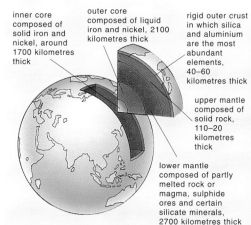

inner core composed of solid iron and nickel, around 1700 kilometres thick

outer core composed of liquid iron and nickel, 2100 kilometres thick

rigid outer crust in which silica and aluminium are the most abundant elements, 40–60 kilometres thick

upper mantle composed of solid rock, 110–20 kilometres thick

lower mantle composed of partly melted rock or magma, sulphide ores and certain silicate minerals, 2700 kilometres thick

### The earth's shells
The earth is like an onion, composed of a series of concentric layers or shells. The uppermost two shells, the crust and upper mantle, together form the lithosphere which is 150 kilometres thick and broken up into moving plates. Scientists have derived details of the composition of the earth's centre by studying meteorites, solid objects that are believed to represent fragments of a disintegrated planet in our solar system. The physical properties, such as thickness of the shells, are interpreted from earthquake waves, gravity and magnetic properties.

### Plate activity (250–200 million years ago)
The earth's surface is made up of eight major and several smaller independently moving plates which converge, diverge or slide laterally against each other. These movements are driven by heat circulation in the earth's lower mantle or by gravitational forces at the plate boundaries and are responsible for earthquakes, volcanic activity, distribution of mineral resources and rock types.

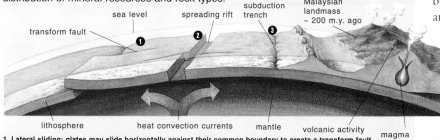

1. Lateral sliding: plates may slide horizontally against their common boundary to create a transform fault.
2. Diverging: plates move apart along a spreading boundary in a process known as rifting.
3. Converging: plates may collide or converge where one plate, usually that composed of denser rock, is forced downwards in a process known as subduction.

## Geological terranes of Malaysia

1. Core region (Sundaland): part of Asia since at least 250 million years ago.
2. Western belt: crustal fragment which joined the core region after breaking from the Gondwana landmass by the early Triassic.
3. Sarawak and Northwest Sabah Basin: formed 90 million years ago.
4. East Sabah: attached itself to Borneo 19 million years ago.

Important sutures—lines where terranes are attached to each other—of the crustal fragments are the Kinabalu suture zone, the Lupar suture and the Bentong suture.

Granite magma from within the earth forced up ridges at the crust to create Malaysia's earliest mountains. The Peninsula landscape of the Jurassic and Cretaceous was dominated by large lakes that formed between the mountain ridges.

Similarly in western Sarawak, by the start of the Cenozoic 67 million years ago, the core terrane had stabilized geologically, displaying no destructive earthquakes or explosive volcanism and mountains had been eroded to become a vast lowland. Large and small depressions on this plain continued to subside for some time and hosted shallow lakes, some of which accumulated plant material that evolved into coal and some into petroleum. A huge lake, now defined by Cenozoic deposits covering a region 500 kilometres long, 220 kilometres wide and more than 10 kilometres deep and known as the Malay Basin, existed on the shelf. Since the later part of the Miocene, the shelf area has become inundated by sea. Later, during at least one of the Quaternary glacial periods, the shelf temporarily became land where huge rivers, now drowned, drained into the South China Sea (see 'Sundaland').

### The other terranes
Fossil evidence and the presence of pebbly mudstone in rock strata dating from the upper Palaeozoic suggest that the Western belt was once attached to an extensive landmass that held together the

Close-up of *Plesioptypmatis*, a marine fossil of a snail found in the southern Madai Hill in Sabah and dating from about 169–70 million years ago or the late Jurassic to late Cretaceous periods.

modern-day continents of Africa, South America, Australia and Antarctica—a huge area known as Gondwanaland. The Malaysian slice broke off and drifted north to become attached to the rest of the peninsula 240 million years ago. The Main Range resulted when magmatic intrusion of the granitic rock took place along the eastern margin of the Gondwana fragment.

## The origins of Malaysia's landmass

Millions of years ago the two parts of Malaysia, what today we know as the Peninsula and Northern Borneo, were in very different positions to those they are in today. In geological history, the earth's plates shifted, broke up and joined many times, causing land to become submerged and new oceans to form. At colliding boundaries mountain ranges and volcanoes developed. In this way Pangea, the supercontinent that existed some 200 million years ago, broke apart, its fragments progressively dispersing across the globe to become the continents that exist today. The maps indicate how, over millions of years, the two parts of Malaysia came to assume their current positions.

1. Before the end of the Palaeozoic, the supercontinent Pangea once existed as a huge landmass, that embraced what we now distinguish as the Americas, Africa, Asia and Europe.

2. When suboceanic forces first divided up the supercontinent Pangea, two large continents were produced. The two continental fragments, Laurasia to the north and Gondwanaland to the south, were separated by the huge Tethys Ocean. Malaysia was part of the southern portion.

Source: After Whitmore (1990)

3. During the Mesozoic, Gondwanaland split into several plates, namely South America, Africa and a landmass consisting of India, Antarctica, Australia and New Guinea. The western belt of Peninsular Malaysia broke off from the Australia–Antarctic landmass and drifted north to become attached to the Asian continent.

4. Africa and then India drifted north to close the Tethys Ocean. Further east, the continental plate comprising Antarctica, Australia and New Guinea moved north and broke into two, leaving Antarctica behind.

5. During the late Cenozoic, the Australia–New Guinea plate collided with the southeastern extremity of Laurasia, resulting in the formation of the Malay Archipelago. East Sabah probably originated from eastern Asia and started to drift south through the opening of the South China Sea basin and docked with greater Borneo in the Miocene.

About 90 million years ago, during the Cretaceous and Palaeogene, central and north Sarawak and western Sabah evolved after a period of subduction provoked by north–south opening of the South China Sea basin. After a period of strong mountain building, large basins developed where thick coastal and marine deposits accumulated, including petroleum-bearing sediments which account for the presence of oilfields off the coast today. The 80-kilometre-wide Kinabalu suture zone is believed to be a relic of a once wide ocean basin that became closed through plate collision. Rocks forming the basin floor were compressed as the East Sabah terrane approached and fused with the rest of Borneo. The East Sabah terrane may be a plate fragment that once was at the continental margin of Asia, possibly in the area near Hong Kong.

## Formation and re-formation

Sabah and Sarawak continue to be active geologically. In Sabah and most of Sarawak, upward movement of the earth's crust as recent as a few thousand years ago is indicated by raised shorelines. Studies have shown that in the last 2 million years some parts of Sabah were raised almost 2 kilometres and more recently the coasts near Miri and Kota Kinabalu show evidence of ongoing land uplift at a rate of a few millimetres each year. The collision of the East Sabah terrane with Borneo (described above) is, among other things, evident from the widespread occurrence of diverse and chaotic assemblages within and near its line of attachment, the Kinabalu suture zone. The granitic body that constitutes Mount Kinabalu and now crowns Borneo rose up from the suture zone only 9–4 million years ago. Its exposure at more than 4 kilometres above sea level permits geologists to estimate that, since its inception, the granite mass has risen 1–2 millimetres each year and is probably still rising.

Millions of years from now the land will again have transformed itself through further geological activities. For example, geologists predict that in the very distant future the Australian continent will fuse with Eurasia, squashing and largely obliterating the Indonesian and Philippine archipelagoes, as well as Malaysia, in the process.

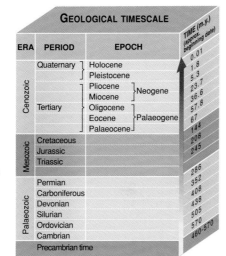

| | GEOLOGICAL TIMESCALE | | TIME (m.y.) (approx. beginning date) |
|---|---|---|---|
| ERA | PERIOD | EPOCH | |
| Cenozoic | Quaternary | Holocene | 0.01 |
| | | Pleistocene | 1.8 |
| | Tertiary | Pliocene } Neogene | 5.3 |
| | | Miocene | 23.7 |
| | | Oligocene } Palaeogene | 36.6 |
| | | Eocene | 57.8 |
| | | Palaeocene | 67 |
| Mesozoic | Cretaceous | | 144 |
| | Jurassic | | 208 |
| | Triassic | | 245 |
| Palaeozoic | Permian | | 286 |
| | Carboniferous | | 352 |
| | Devonian | | 408 |
| | Silurian | | 438 |
| | Ordovician | | 505 |
| | Cambrian | | 570 |
| | Precambrian time | | 460–570 |

## Formation of mountains and hills

Two parallel mountain chains were pushed up during early Jurassic times. The younger western arc became the Titiwangsa Range.

Limestone in Peninsular Malaysia was deposited beneath the seas that covered the area in late Triassic times. Limestone hills in Ipoh are shown above.

The granite peaks that stand up on the islands off Peninsular Malaysia's eastern coast, such as Tioman, were formed by crustal uplift about 200 million years ago.

# Sundaland

*The stable continental shelf known as Sundaland extends southwards from Southeast Asia across an area of 1 800 000 square kilometres. It is mostly covered by shallow seas, but Borneo (Sabah and Sarawak) is an eroded metamorphic part of the shelf that rises up above sea level. The whole area, whose existence was first recorded in 1845, was once above water. The changing geology of the area is thought to have significantly contributed to flora and fauna distribution in this region.*

The distinctive jagged peaks of Mount Kinabalu are due to the effects of ice, snow and glaciers that existed during the last glacial period 20,000 years ago, when the earth's temperature was just 4 °C cooler than it is today.

Water, water everywhere. The shores of the island of Pangkor in the Sunda basin off the west coast of the Malay Peninsula, lapped by the waters of the Strait of Melaka.

## Locating the Sunda region

Sundaland generally refers to a geographical region which includes the Sunda Shelf (sometimes called the Sunda Platform) and its continental rim. The Sunda Shelf comprises the wide and relatively shallow continental shelf of the southern part of the South China Sea between the Malay Peninsula and Borneo, and also the Java Sea between Java and Borneo.

Global climate change is by no means a new phenomenon. During the Pleistocene period (one and a half million to 10,000 years ago), the earth went through several phases of cooling followed by warming. During the cooling down phase, referred to as a glacial period or Ice Age, polar icecaps expanded. Ice extended across land and sea and a considerable amount of water was locked in the icecaps, thus prompting a lowering of the sea level across the earth's surface. On the Sunda Shelf, the extent of sea level decline is variously given, but is thought to be somewhere between 70 and 180 metres. The seas are shallow enough that it is possible to scuba dive, at a depth of no more than 40 metres, from present-day Peninsular Malaysia to Sumatra and on to Borneo and Java, before encountering a deep trench around Bali and Lombok. As the sea level dropped,

the Sunda Shelf dried and an extensive landmass was created as Sumatra, the Malay Peninsula, Borneo and Java effectively merged. This landmass is known as Sundaland.

During the Pleistocene period, the relative positions of the various landmasses bordering the Sunda Shelf were the same as they are today. However, the size of Sundaland has varied. Fluctuations depended on the severity of glacial phases and on the intervening interglacial periods of warming. During the latter, the shelf was drowned as water in the polar icecaps melted. Present-day Sundaland is extensively flooded so that only its higher areas rise above sea level, and the Malay Peninsula is separate from Borneo as well as Sumatra. The extensive erosion and flattening of the shelf are seen in the similar shallow depths of the seas in the area, namely the South China Sea, Strait of Melaka and Java Sea which extend across it.

## Exposing the shelf: Climatic changes

When the Sunda Shelf was exposed during glacial periods, rivers from the present landmasses extended their courses and flowed into the Sunda Shelf, including the Strait of Melaka. Two large river systems existed, one below the South China Sea flowing into the ocean off the Philippines, and the other parallel to the Strait of Melaka and

## The extent of Sundaland

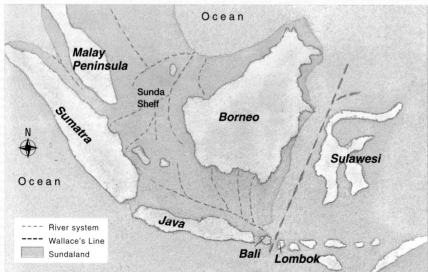
Extent of Sundaland during the last glacial period showing the river systems that developed on the Sunda Shelf and in the Melaka Strait.

## The Sunda Craton
Sundaland is divided into two geological regions. An older stable core, the Sunda Craton, is surrounded by a younger, relatively unstable area. A craton is part of the earth's crust that has not been significantly deformed for many millions of years and is thus described as stable. The Sunda Craton has a complex geological evolution which commenced at least 550 million years ago. The Malay Peninsula, which lies within the craton, can be divided into three geological belts which extend north to Thailand and south to Bangka and Belitung. These belts are noted for their mineral deposits of gold and tin.

discharging into the Andaman Sea. A river delta developed off the west of Langkawi for the latter.

Another important consequence of the exposure of the Sunda Shelf was the change in climate and the consequential differences in vegetation from those prevalent today. During the glacial period, there was a slight drop in temperature of between 2 and 6 °C. A snow line existed at a lower altitude and Sabah's Mount Kinabalu would have been glaciated and covered with snow. In addition, parts of Malaysia which today receive the least amount of annual rainfall, such as areas of eastern Negeri Sembilan and the northern regions, would probably have experienced three extra dry months in addition to the current two. A more seasonal climate with longer dry periods would have resulted in open, seasonal forest or even grassland and not the tropical rainforest that now covers the area.

## Animal magic

Changes in sea level result in changes to landscape and in the biogeography of plants and animals. As the Sunda Shelf dried, animals were able to migrate from Asia, via the Malay Peninsula, to other parts of Sundaland. The animals in the Sundaland area have much in common except for some notable species. The small number of elephants in Borneo has been attributed to some sea remaining, even in dry periods, between the Malay Peninsula and Borneo, and soft ground on the dried-up sea floor being unable to support the weight of the elephants, thus restricting their movement across the exposed shelf. The surface sea temperature during the last glacial period was about 2 °C lower than at present, and some animals would have swum short distances between islands.

During Sundaland's exposed periods, wildlife and groups of plants would have been dispersed in homogenized patterns. However, for many animals their dispersal appeared to halt at Wallace's Line (see box) between Bali and Lombok.

An artist's impression of Indonesia's Krakatau eruption in 1883 that led to tidal waves off Malaysia's coast.

## Subduction and volcanic activity

The western and southern rim of Sundaland is bordered by deep submarine trenches on the ocean side. These trenches are believed by many geologists to be locations where the ocean floor, somewhat like a rigid plate, is moving beneath the current ocean bed at a rate of 5–7 centimetres a year. As rocks deep below the islands readjust to compensate for this subduction process, conspicuous geological activity is unleashed. Earthquakes ensue, the affects of which are sometimes felt on the west coast of

### Wallace's Line

*In the Malay Archipelago we have, I believe . . . indications of a vast continent, with a peculiar fauna and flora, having been gradually and irregularly broken up; . . . At the same time Asia appears to have been extending its limits in a south-east direction, first in an unbroken mass, then separated into islands as we now see it, and almost coming into actual contact with the scattered fragments of the great southern land.*

So wrote the Victorian zoologist Alfred Russel Wallace in *The Malay Archipelago* in 1869. This seminal study catalogues the naturalist's observations of the basic distinctions between creatures and plants found on either side of what came to be universally accepted as Wallace's Line.

On travels through Borneo and Indonesia, Wallace was surprised to discover that Borneo and Sulawesi, although separated by no distinct geographical or climatic factors, displayed such different species. He suggested that Borneo had once been part of an Asian landmass and that Sulawesi, along with New Guinea, had once been connected to a Pacific–Australian continent. He drew a boundary between Borneo and Bali separating Asian from Australian faunas. After more research, Wallace concluded that the line should be drawn further east of his initial assessment, and this effectively followed the contours of Sundaland.

Other zoologists came to similar conclusions, proposing other zoogeographic lines. Where Wallace's lines delimit the eastern boundary of Asian flora, Lydekker's Line, for example, marks the western limit of strictly Australian flora and fauna.

**Wallace's and other lines separating Asian from Australian faunas in the Malay Archipelago**

1. Huxley (1868)
2. Wallace (1863–80)
3. Wallace (1910)
4. Weber (1904)
5. Lydekker (1896)
6. Weber (1894)

Wallace was the first to record the Rajah Brooke's birdwing (*Troides (Trogonoptera) brookiana*).

Peninsular Malaysia. Earthquake activity is far less of a risk on the east coast, because of its distance from the subduction zone. Except for a small area in east Sabah, Malaysia is not itself prone to earthquakes.

Subduction, too, is responsible for the development of volcanoes parallel to the trenches (or subduction zone). Although Malaysia is not subject to violent geological hazards, the proximity to an active subduction zone means that side effects are felt. Present-day Sundaland is free from volcanic action, but residues of old seismic activity exist in the form of large volumes of volcanic ash, some of which was deposited by an eruption 30,000 years ago. Volcanic activities in the Philippines can also deposit ash in Sabah and Sarawak, as they did, for example, after the Pinatubo eruption in June 1991. Tidal waves off Malaysia's coast in 1883 were attributed to the eruption of Krakatau in Indonesia.

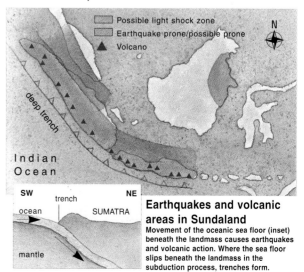

Possible light shock zone
Earthquake prone/possible prone
▲ Volcano

**Earthquakes and volcanic areas in Sundaland**
Movement of the oceanic sea floor (inset) beneath the landmass causes earthquakes and volcanic action. Where the sea floor slips beneath the landmass in the subduction process, trenches form.

# Geology

*Differences in rock associations, their geological ages and structural aspects divide Malaysia into a number of geological domains, each having evolved, in part, separately from the neighbouring regions. Rocks are continually subject to the earth's geological processes that over time create new landforms. Malaysia displays a broad range of rock types, from the sands and silts of the coastal plains to the granite of the Main Range and limestone outcrops of the Langkawi Islands.*

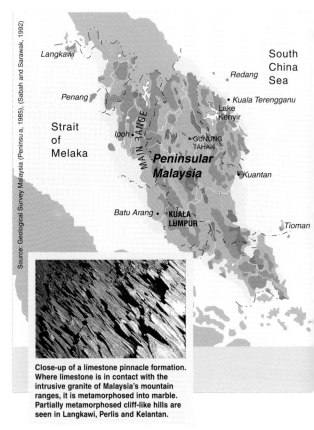

## The rock cycle

All three rock types are interrelated. Each type is eventually transformed into another type through phases of heating, cooling, erosion and deposition.

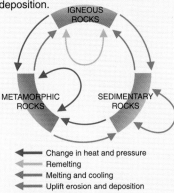

← Change in heat and pressure
← Remelting
← Melting and cooling
← Uplift erosion and deposition

**IGNEOUS** rocks form as magma inside the earth moves to the upper mantle and crust and solidifies. **METAMORPHIC** rocks form in the earth's crust when extreme pressure and heat transforms, or metamorphoses, minerals in older rocks.

**SEDIMENTARY** rocks are formed at the earth's surface from weathered parts of other rocks, such as rock fragments, clay particles, dissolved chemicals and remains of living organisms, that become compacted over hundreds of thousands of years.

Source: After Coch and Ludman (1991)

## Malaysia's oldest rocks

Geologists group rocks into units according to their type, age and environment of deposition. Formation is the most common unit used and each formation is given a geographical name. The Macincang nearshore sediments in Langkawi, and at two other places on the mainland, have been documented as the oldest known geological formations in Peninsular Malaysia. They date from the Middle Cambrian to Lower Ordovician, 525–480 million years ago (see geological timescale, 'Geological history'). Several small outcrops of deformed metamorphosed sandstone and siltstone beneath the gently folded Macincang beds at Teluk Datai, Langkawi, may include even older rocks of the Precambrian era. These would also represent the oldest rocks in Malaysia.

## The geology of the Peninsula

The Northwest and Western geological domains of the Peninsula (see box below) contain Upper Carboniferous–Lower Permian pebbly mudstone, small pebbles to large boulders of varied rock types set in a clayey groundmass. In this particular case, the pebbles and boulders are believed to have separated from melting icebergs onto the sea floor where clay was accumulating at that time. Cool water fossil fauna have been identified in other sediments of the same age.

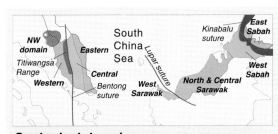

## Geological domains

Peninsular Malaysia's four domains are almost entirely built up of pre-Tertiary rocks. West Sarawak has pre-Tertiary basement rocks and is separated by the Lupar Valley from the rest of the state which consists of Upper Cretaceous and younger marine and continental (deposited on land) sediments and volcanic rocks. The Kinabalu suture zone is composed of Cretaceous–Palaeogene oceanic crust.

Source: Geological Survey Malaysia (Peninsula, 1985), (Sabah and Sarawak, 1992)

**Close-up of a limestone pinnacle formation. Where limestone is in contact with the intrusive granite of Malaysia's mountain ranges, it is metamorphosed into marble. Partially metamorphosed cliff-like hills are seen in Langkawi, Perlis and Kelantan.**

The Central domain is marked by Jurassic–Cretaceous sediments deposited in rivers, lakes and deltas. Such sediments are collectively known as continental (land) deposits. Older rock formations were laid down mainly in shallow to deep marine environments. The changed depositional environment resulted from strong earth movements. Most outcropping formations in the Eastern domain are Carboniferous (352–285 million years ago) in the north, or Permian (286–245 million years) in the south, while late Palaeozoic granitic rocks are most common among the igneous rocks. Two large metamorphic areas are the Triassic Taku schists (or metamorphosed clay) and the Cretaceous Setong migmatite (a mixture of igneous and metamorphic rocks) in the northern part of the Peninsula. Sedimentation after the middle Triassic was mainly continental, and older formations were almost entirely of marine origin. Eocene and other Tertiary sediments also originated in lakes and in river flood plains. The lakes were probably shallow mountain basins where abundant vegetation resulted in the formation of brown coal and coal, such as at Batu Arang in Selangor.

After emplacement of the Titiwangsa granitic masses, the Peninsula achieved geological stability. There are no records of strong earthquakes. Large reservoirs, such as Tasik Kenyir, have been known to trigger weak earthquakes. Impounded water may penetrate existing cracks in surrounding rocks and thus produce minor movements along those cracks. Post-Titiwangsa volcanism has only produced alkali-rich basaltic lavas, such as the early Tertiary Segamat lava flows and basalt flows near Kuantan in Pahang, which are younger than 2 million years old. Alkali

## Distribution of main rock types

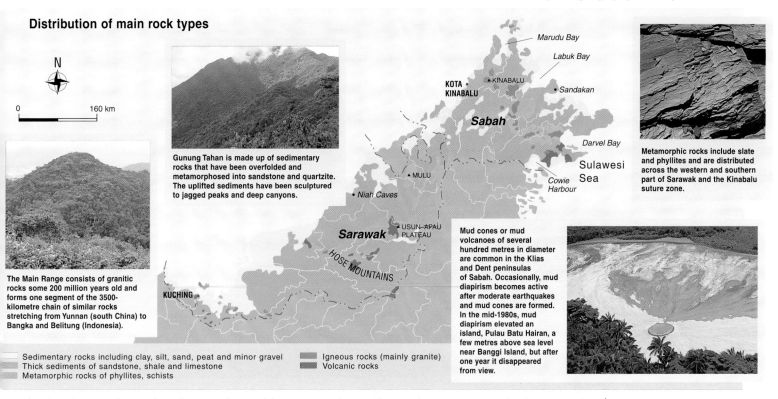

N

0     160 km

Gunung Tahan is made up of sedimentary rocks that have been overfolded and metamorphosed into sandstone and quartzite. The uplifted sediments have been sculptured to jagged peaks and deep canyons.

Metamorphic rocks include slate and phyllites and are distributed across the western and southern part of Sarawak and the Kinabalu suture zone.

The Main Range consists of granitic rocks some 200 million years old and forms one segment of the 3500-kilometre chain of similar rocks stretching from Yunnan (south China) to Bangka and Belitung (Indonesia).

Mud cones or mud volcanoes of several hundred metres in diameter are common in the Klias and Dent peninsulas of Sabah. Occasionally, mud diapirism becomes active after moderate earthquakes and mud cones are formed. In the mid-1980s, mud diapirism elevated an island, Pulau Batu Hairan, a few metres above sea level near Banggi Island, but after one year it disappeared from view.

Marudu Bay
Labuk Bay
KOTA KINABALU
▲ KINABALU
Sandakan
*Sabah*
Darvel Bay
Sulawesi Sea
Cowie Harbour
▲ MULU
• Niah Caves
*Sarawak*
USUN–APAU PLATEAU
HOSE MOUNTAINS
KUCHING •

| | |
|---|---|
| ░ Sedimentary rocks including clay, silt, sand, peat and minor gravel | ▓ Igneous rocks (mainly granite) |
| ▒ Thick sediments of sandstone, shale and limestone | ▓ Volcanic rocks |
| ▓ Metamorphic rocks of phyllites, schists | |

basalt is known, from other places in the world, to be associated with stable crustal conditions.

## The geology of Sarawak and Sabah

Where Sarawak borders the South China Sea, wide, swampy coastal plains exist. In the Lupar and Baram deltas, the coastal plains are up to 75 kilometres wide. Towards the interior, the topography becomes hilly. In west Sarawak, an undulating landscape is studded with steep hills of Mesozoic and Palaeozoic limestone and chert. Further towards Kalimantan, the mountain ranges are formed of Palaeozoic rocks and there are large basins of the same age. The latter are massive, composed of sandstone, and collectively known as the Plateau Sandstone formation. Limestone complexes are typified by rugged, steep-sided hills and mountains, such as the limestone formations of the Niah Caves, Gunung Melinau and the Mulu Caves. In central Sarawak, Palaeogene lavas form mountain ranges. The Usun–Apau and Linau–Balui plateaus rise up as 1-kilometre-high lava elevations of the Neogene and Quaternary, and the dissected lava plateaus of the Hose and Nieuwenhuis mountains are each around 2 kilometres in height.

A very irregular shoreline marks Sabah's outline and also those of its islands. Indentations are created by the deep bays of Marudu, Labuk, Sandakan, Darvel and Cowie Harbour. Resistant sedimentary rocks that form strike ridges, for example, on Gaya Island,

and crystalline rocks, on Banggi, Balambangan and Timbun Mata islands, are responsible for stretches of rugged, cliffed shoreline. In Cowie Harbour and Labuk Bay, rapid sedimentation has led to the irregular coast.

The West Sabah domain is geologically similar to, but slightly younger than, the Central and North Sarawak domain. The Kinabalu suture zone, up to 80 kilometres wide, embraces all known outcrops of ultrabasic rocks (igneous rocks that solidify from low silica magma), spilite (a sodium-rich basalt formed under water) and chert (silica-rich sediment, often deposited in seas) in Sabah. Most mid-Tertiary chaotic rock assemblages also lie in this zone. The chaotic deposits resulted from widespread slumping when the East Sabah terrane docked with greater Borneo (see 'Geological history').

## The geological evolution of Taman Negara

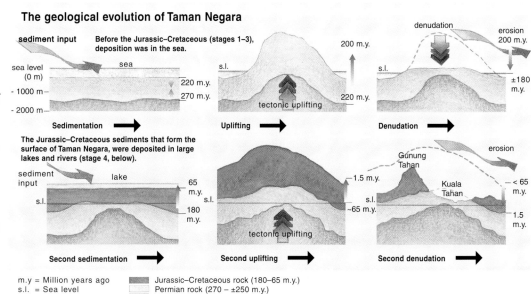

sediment input

Before the Jurassic–Cretaceous (stages 1–3), deposition was in the sea.

sea level (0 m)
sea
– 1000 m
– 2000 m

220 m.y.
270 m.y.

**Sedimentation** →

The Jurassic–Cretaceous sediments that form the surface of Taman Negara, were deposited in large lakes and rivers (stage 4, below).

sediment input
lake
s.l.

65 m.y.
180 m.y.

**Second sedimentation** →

s.l.
tectonic uplifting

220 m.y.

**Uplifting** →

s.l.
tectonic uplifting

–1.5 m.y.
~65 m.y.

**Second uplifting** →

200 m.y.
denudation
erosion 200 m.y.
s.l.
±180 m.y.

**Denudation** →

Gunung Tahan
Kuala Tahan
erosion
s.l.
< 65 m.y.
1.5 m.y.

**Second denudation** →

m.y. = Million years ago
s.l. = Sea level

▓ Jurassic–Cretaceous rock (180–65 m.y.)
░ Permian rock (270 – ±250 m.y.)
▒ Pre-Permian rock (> 270 m.y.)

# Mineral resources

*Minerals have contributed to Malaysia's economic development from the early years of the 20th century. Of the metallic minerals, tin, gold, copper and iron were and still are important, with tin and its associated pewter industry being the single most significant and lucrative resource. Some of the mineral deposits are now exhausted, and although traditional mining still takes place, non-metallic minerals, such as oil and gas, clay, coal, limestone and silica sand, have eclipsed metallic types in economic importance.*

A platform in a Malaysian oilfield, offshore from Miri, Sarawak.

Gravel pumping constitutes the most prevalent method for mining Malaysia's tin. Great open pits are formed in the ground and tin-bearing gravel is pumped up into a sluice box or *palong* where heavier tin is trapped and over which lighter materials are carried away in a constant flow of water.

## Why minerals occur

The parts of the earth's crust are organized into compounds that we refer to as minerals. A mineral is a naturally occurring, inorganic substance, usually with a definite chemical composition and an atomic structure. Vast numbers of mineral varieties exist, together with a great number of their combinations in rocks. A favourable geological environment accounts for the rich variety of mineral deposits in Malaysia. The wide distribution of tin deposits is due to the prominence of certain tin-bearing granitic intrusions to which they are related. For a deposit to exist, some process, or combination of geological processes, must bring about a localized enrichment of the mineral.

Deposits can form when hot, aqueous solutions flow through fractures and spaces in crustal rocks, when there is a concentration of magma in igneous rocks or of precipitation from lake or sea water in sedimentary rocks, or where concentrated weathering of a parent rock takes place. For example, 95 per cent of Malaysia's tin deposits occur in alluvial plains or as eluvial deposits on hills which

have been weathered and carried by rivers and deposited from the Pleistocene epoch. All of Malaysia's coal deposits have been associated with Tertiary rocks believed to be of Miocene or younger age. Gold is mainly found in quartz veins. Copper is related to Miocene adamellite intrusions, and bauxite developed from the weathering of volcanic, sedimentary and granitic rocks.

## Fossil fuels

Coal, oil and gas are together known as fossil fuels and are not, strictly speaking, minerals because they are of organic origin. Peat is formed from slowly decomposing vegetation. Accumulated sediments overlay and compress the peat to form a soft brown coal known as lignite. As the sediments increase in depth and exert more heat and pressure, the lignite eventually is transformed into bituminous and hard anthracite coals. Oil and gas are usually formed from the organic matter that was deposited in marine sediments. Under heat and pressure the matter experiences complex chemical transformations to turn it to oil and gas.

There are a few low-grade lignite coal deposits in the Peninsula found in rocks of the Miocene epoch. The largest, in Batu Arang, Selangor, is now worked out, but significant reserves are located in the sedimentary rocks in Sarawak's Silantek coalfield. Other fields include those at Balingian, Merit–Pila and Bintulu, all in Sarawak. The coal in Sabah, in the Meliau and Melibu basins, is good quality bituminous, low-sulphur coal in seams of more than 5 metres thick and there are reserves of several million tonnes.

### MAIN MINERAL RESOURCES IN MALAYSIA

| MINERAL | OUTPUT STATISTICS | END USE |
|---|---|---|
| **Metallic minerals** | | |
| Tin (Sn) | Mining throughout 20th century; 85 000 tonnes in 1940, 73 800 in 1970 from 1,083 mines; 6 656 in 1996 from 39 mines | cans, pewter ware, plumbing and gun metal |
| Gold (Au) | 143 kg in 1980, 274 kg in 1986, 873 kg in 1993 | jewellery |
| Copper (Cu) | Total production to 1994 of 992 000 tonnes; 40 tonnes gold and 252 silver as by-products | electrical and telephone wires; alloys: brass and bronze |
| Iron (Fe) | First exploited 1921, peaked in 1963 with 7.2 mill. tonnes; 10 mill. tonnes reserve 1996 | building industry; steel bridges; motor parts |
| Aluminium (Al) | Mined as bauxite, almost exhausted; 68 824 tonnes in 1993, 83 431 half-year 1996 | electrical cables, aircraft body parts; cans |
| **Non-metallic minerals** | | |
| Coal | First mined 1915; max. output 781 509 tonnes in 1940; main reserves over 800 mill. tonnes in Sabah and Sarawak | fuel |
| Clay | Reserves of 738 mill. tonnes | ball clay used in local ceramics industry: tiles, tableware, porcelain |
| Silica sand | Reserves of 46 mill. tonnes on beaches of Terengganu | glassware, window panes |
| Oil and gas | First oil well off Miri in 1910; industry developed from 1970s | fuel |

### How coal is made

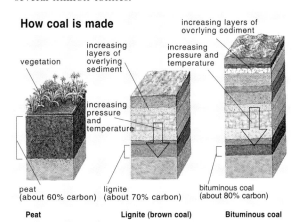

peat (about 60% carbon)  lignite (about 70% carbon)  bituminous coal (about 80% carbon)

**Peat**   **Lignite (brown coal)**   **Bituminous coal**

## Mineral distribution

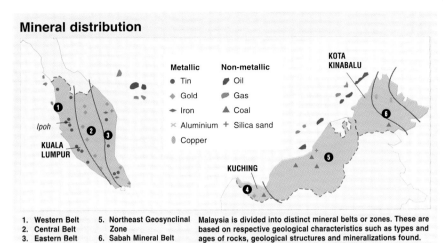

| Metallic | Non-metallic |
|----------|--------------|
| ● Tin | 🖋 Oil |
| ◆ Gold | 🔥 Gas |
| ← Iron | ▲ Coal |
| ✕ Aluminium | + Silica sand |
| 🗘 Copper | |

1. Western Belt
2. Central Belt
3. Eastern Belt
4. Western Sarawak Zone
5. Northeast Geosynclinal Zone
6. Sabah Mineral Belt

Malaysia is divided into distinct mineral belts or zones. These are based on respective geological characteristics such as types and ages of rocks, geological structures and mineralizations found. The mineral belts of Peninsular Malaysia were first proposed by the British geologist Scrivenor in his book, *The Geology of the Malayan Ore-deposits*, published in 1928.

## The world's leading tin producer

Tin from the Malay Peninsula has been mined for centuries. The Malay Sultanate of Melaka employed tin ingots as its currency and the colonizing Dutch built ports at strategic river mouths in order to monopolize Malaysia's trade in tin. It was not, however, until world demand for tin, in particular for the canning industry, increased in the 19th century that the industry really developed. Tin mining dominated Malaysia's economy for the first half of the 20th century and Malaysia was the world's greatest tin exporter, producing more than a third of the world's total production. The collapse of the world tin markets in 1985 led to the decline in Malaysia's tin-mining industry.

Rich tin deposits are found in the Kinta Valley in Perak and around Kuala Lumpur in Selangor. Smaller tin fields are found scattered in the Western and Eastern Tin Belts. Kuala Lumpur and Ipoh, now two major cities and important commercial centres, were developed from tin-mining towns. Mining for tin is by one of three methods—gravel pumping, dredging, or opencast—and involves extracting the tin mineral, cassiterite, from the sand and gravel. Malaysia once had the world's largest dry opencast mine at Sungai Besi, near Kuala Lumpur, but this is now no longer worked.

## Other metallic minerals

With the decline of tin mining, some former operators are looking to gold as a more lucrative mineral resource. Significant gold reserves are found in the Central and Eastern Belts of the Peninsula. In 1993, 873 kilograms of gold were produced. Active centres in the Central Belt stretch from Sokor through to Pulai in Kelantan, Selinsing, Tui, Penjom and Raub in Pahang, to the Kuala Pilah area in Negeri Sembilan. Gold has recently been discovered in the Eastern Belt, with gold rushes reported in Kuala Terengganu and Mersing. Recent exploration by Canadian and Australian companies identified new ore bodies in the Central Belt, and when prospecting for gold in central Pahang they discovered a mineralized shear zone with an estimated resource of 2.98 million tonnes of gold ore. The country's reserves of copper and bauxite are expected to be exhausted before the end of the 20th century, as is the case with the small deposits of iron.

## Future resources

Malaysia's mining sector contributes around 10 per cent to the total Gross Domestic Product (1996). Peninsular Malaysia has been renowned for its tin, but its exploitation of its petroleum and natural gas reserves has only recently come to fruition. Although the reserves off the coasts of Sarawak, Sabah and Terengganu have been in existence as long as the metallic resources, they did not contribute to the country's economic development until the 1970s.

With the exception of gold, the present decline in world demand for metals is forcing the existing Malaysian mines out of operation. However, the future is still bright for non-metallic minerals, especially for clay, whose requirement as a building material is ever increasing. Ball clay is also used in the manufacture of local ceramics.

### CHANGES IN THE ECONOMIC BALANCE OF MALAYSIA'S MINERALS

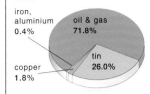

1980 Mining and quarrying 10.08% of GDP

iron, aluminium 0.4%
oil & gas 71.8%
tin 26.0%
copper 1.8%

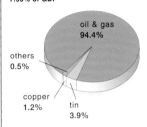

1993 Mining and quarrying 7.95% of GDP

oil & gas 94.4%
others 0.5%
copper 1.2%
tin 3.9%

Note: Mining and quarrying include oil and gas

## Malaysia's pewter industry: A by-product of tin mining

Perhaps the most well-known by-product of Malaysia's tin industry is pewter ware. Pewter is a silvery grey tin which is alloyed with a small percentage of other metals to give it strength. Malaysian pewter contains 97 per cent Straits tin and a total of 3 per cent copper and antimony. Being malleable and bearing a silvery shine, the alloy can be cast and hammered into various beautiful forms.

Pewter drinking containers have a long history. The Romans drank from pewter vessels as this improved the quality of their wine. Pewter ware has come a long way since then and is used not only to fashion cups and joss-stick holders, but to produce elegant objects and gifts. There are a number of pewter manufacturers in Malaysia, the oldest and most famous being Royal Selangor Pewter. The company was started in 1885 by a certain Yong Koon who came to Malaysia from Swatow in China. The company claims to be the world's largest pewter manufacturer and produces over a thousand different tableware and gift items for distribution to more than 20 countries around the world.

1. Pewter is made manually by melting the tin, copper and antimony at 230 ºC then pouring the molten metal into a steel mould or cast.

2. The cast shape is, once cooled and solid, polished and engraved.

3. To give it the desired silvery shine, the pewter is buffed with a 'stone leaf' from a local plant (*Tetvacera scandens*) and then given a final felt polish.

# Soils

*Malaysia's varied landscape presents an equally rich cross section of soils, which in turn support specific vegetation types. Soils—clay, peat, limestone or granite derived—are affected by regional climate, altitude and parent rock, amongst other factors, and are differentiated by their texture and colour. Certain soils are more fertile than others and are exploited for agricultural use; others are important ingredients for specific manufacturing industries.*

Settlements develop where there is water and relatively fertile land, such as alluvial soils. A Penan settlement on highly weathered upland soil in Bareo, Sarawak.

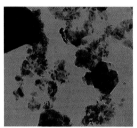

Rounded and hexagonal plates of kaolinite, the most common mineral found in Malaysian soils, as seen under a transmission electron microscope and magnified several thousand times.

## The basis of life

Soil is made up of decomposed rocks. It is on soil that we build our houses and factories and grow our food. The relationship between Malaysia's creatures and plants much depends on the existence of particular soil types. Thus, appropriate use of soils is paramount to successfully maintaining the country's fragile ecosystems.

Soil is formed when an exposed and eroded surface is colonized by simple organisms, such as mosses and lichens. These create a more hospitable environment for other vegetation to take root. The organic material decomposes to become part of the nutrient-rich infant soil and over time more organisms are added. The development of a particular soil depends on a number of factors, including land height, parent material composition and climate. It is therefore not surprising to find that in a particular area the soil on the hilltop is different from that found at its lower reaches although both may have originally developed from the same parent material. Steep slopes are more susceptible to erosion and soils tend to be thinner than on gentle slopes where good drainage and aeration ensure uninterrupted weathering and translocation of dissolved material further downslope.

## Soil composition

Soils are made up of mineral grains derived from the weathered particles of the parent rock, organic material, air and water. The relative proportions of the mineral grains of sand, silt and clay dictate important properties of the soil—such as texture and colour. A limestone-derived soil, for instance, has a highly clayey texture, whereas granite gives rise to sandy clay soils. The reddish brown soil colours that predominate are caused by iron oxides. Intense weathering has also resulted in iron-rich accumulations as found extensively in Melaka, Selangor, Pahang and Kedah. These hard concretions may prove problematic to plant life, denying them water and root-anchoring locations. Flat and enclosed basins suffer from impeded drainage and thus a lower rate of weathering than sloped land.

## Soil types and corresponding vegetation in Malaysia

### 1. Marine clay
Waterlogging is common and the heavy clay texture may accumulate sulphur compounds and have a high salt content. Only mangrove trees that have evolved special 'breathing' roots are able to grow in the anaerobic, swampy conditions.

### 2. Peat
These contain fibrous organic components derived from decomposing woody matter and can be several metres in depth. Generally chemically poor (acidic) and badly drained, they support peatswamp trees and palms which have adapted to the harsh conditions.

### 3. Alluvial
Formed from sediments transported by rivers from higher ground, these vary in texture, ranging from adequately drained sandy loams on raised areas to organic clay on flood plains, such as

## How soil is made

**Climate**
The hot, humid Malaysian climate helps produce highly weathered soils. Heavy precipitation erodes upland soils to lower areas.

**Topography and drainage**
Steep slopes are more susceptible to erosion. Soils tend to be thinner than those on more moderate slopes where good drainage, and thus aeration, ensures uninterrupted weathering and translocation of dissolved material further downslope.

**Time**
Landscapes are weathered and soils developed over thousands of years.

**Vegetation**
Roots spreading underground help disintegrate and distribute soil. Organic matter added to the soil enhances chemical and physical processes.

**Organisms in the soil**
Microorganisms and bacteria break down dead vegetation and enrich it with nutrients. The creation of underground passages by insects and earthworms helps break up and homogenize soil matter.

**Parent rock**
The colour, texture and mineral content of soil depend on the composition of the supporting rock.

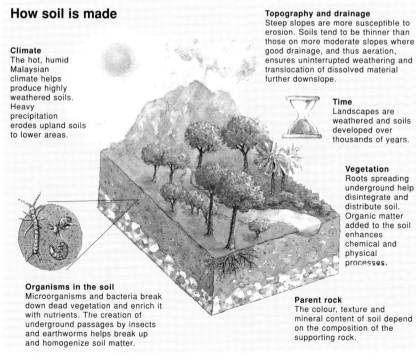

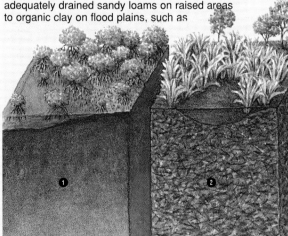

## Manufacturing uses

Along the Malaysian coast, sea water transports and deposits silt and clays in sheltered areas protected from the eroding winds and waves. Together with soils found along river estuaries, marine clay soils are some of the most fertile in Malaysia because of the minerals from which they are composed. Some coastal alluvial soils, high in clay, whitish and plastic, and known as ball clay, are used for making clay-based products such as sanitary wares and tiles. Lower quality clay soils may be used to manufacture bricks, roof tiles, pipes and pottery.

On the east coast of the Peninsula, soils locally known as *bris* soils, develop on sandy ridges which are interspersed with swales. On the freely draining ridges casuarina trees and coconuts abound; wetland species persist in the poorly drained swales. Crops grown on these coastal soils suffer from water and nutrient stress. White sands are found in localized pockets of Malaysia's coastal lands. In places, the sand is mined for silica which is used in the manufacture of glass.

A *periok* from Kelantan made from terracotta clay found by streams and river banks.

## Agriculture

Soils on moderately sloping hills are typically low in silt and high in clay because of intense weathering. Exposure to sun and rain causes leaching and a lack of soil nutrients to support plant life. Only hardier tree crops, such as oil palm and rubber, are grown on such terrain, often with artificial fertilizer support. In the northern states of the Peninsula, paddy is cultivated on clayey alluvials; fruit trees and vegetables are farmed and in the east coast states tobacco is grown. However, tobacco is being discouraged in favour of the rozelle plant, from which a hibiscus-flavoured drink is made. Oil palm grows best on marine clay soils because of its highly fertile nature.

Only human intervention renders nutrient-rich, acidic peat soils suitable for agriculture. Peatland is farmed for pineapples, some vegetables and oil palm. Although peat may pose a problem to the root anchoring of oil palm trees, they are successfully cultivated along the Peninsula's west coast. Peat soils in the Peninsula and in Sabah can reach depths of 10 metres, and in Sarawak can be up to 17 metres.

### Soils and crops
Different crops require different soils in order to prosper.

1. Hectares of oil palm, cultivated on estates across Malaysia, are grown on a variety of soils, but give best yields on fertile marine clays.
2. Rubber is among the crops best suited to the clayey soils of sloping hills.
3. Paddy is cultivated on alluvial soils.

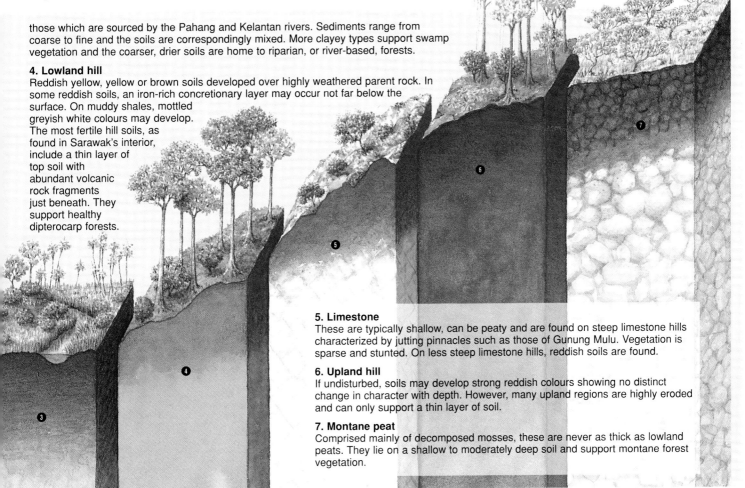

those which are sourced by the Pahang and Kelantan rivers. Sediments range from coarse to fine and the soils are correspondingly mixed. More clayey types support swamp vegetation and the coarser, drier soils are home to riparian, or river-based, forests.

**4. Lowland hill**
Reddish yellow, yellow or brown soils developed over highly weathered parent rock. In some reddish soils, an iron-rich concretionary layer may occur not far below the surface. On muddy shales, mottled greyish white colours may develop. The most fertile hill soils, as found in Sarawak's interior, include a thin layer of top soil with abundant volcanic rock fragments just beneath. They support healthy dipterocarp forests.

**5. Limestone**
These are typically shallow, can be peaty and are found on steep limestone hills characterized by jutting pinnacles such as those of Gunung Mulu. Vegetation is sparse and stunted. On less steep limestone hills, reddish soils are found.

**6. Upland hill**
If undisturbed, soils may develop strong reddish colours showing no distinct change in character with depth. However, many upland regions are highly eroded and can only support a thin layer of soil.

**7. Montane peat**
Comprised mainly of decomposed mosses, these are never as thick as lowland peats. They lie on a shallow to moderately deep soil and support montane forest vegetation.

# Soil erosion

*Soil erosion is a common natural occurrence in Malaysia because of the particular topography, soils and corresponding vegetation that predominate and the extensive rainfall that the country experiences. However, due to rapid land use developments, accelerated soil erosion is becoming a serious problem. Various forms of erosion control have been proposed to develop the land in ways that are sensitive to its geography.*

Highly weathered material being eroded on a hillside near Kampung Sungai Penchala, Kuala Lumpur.

## Erosion risk

Land in Peninsular Malaysia falls into one of five soil erosion categories ranging from low- to very high-risk areas. Highland slopes are all over 20 degrees in gradient, which is considered very steep. They include the Titiwangsa Range. In very high-risk areas, an average of 150 tonnes per hectare of soil is lost per year.

Annual soil loss in tonnes per hectare (hectares/year)

- Low risk (less than 10 tonnes)
- Moderate risk (10–50 tonnes)
- Moderately high risk (50–100 tonnes)
- High risk (100–150 tonnes)
- Very high risk (above 150 tonnes)

Source: After the *New Straits Times* (27 August 1996)

The slopes between Simpang Pulai and Poslin, on the way to the Cameron Highlands, show the classic high-risk features: a steep, high slope devoid of vegetation, prone to heavy erosion.

## The Malaysian situation

Erosion is becoming a major problem in Malaysia affecting people's livelihood and safety, their settlements and agriculture. As land is developed for new purposes, natural forest cover is often replaced by new townships and agriculture. Highways are constructed and mass tourist resorts introduced. Poor planning and disorganized construction work during land clearing provoke conditions that accelerate soil erosion.

When erosion occurs in hilly terrain, for example, the fertile top soil that is needed for the growth of vegetation is depleted. Studies have shown that Malaysia is losing this soil at an alarming rate. This inevitably affects the communities who are dependent on the growth of natural vegetation to maintain their traditional way of life. The Orang Asli who inhabit the foothills of the Titiwangsa Range, for example, rely on the forest materials for their food, housing, medicines and tools.

## Influencing factors

During erosion, soil particles are loosened by rainfall or flowing water and transported away from their original location. The critical factors that influence this process are climate, soil, topography and vegetation cover. In Malaysia, climate and topography are particularly influential.

Malaysia's rainfall is frequent, intense and abundant. This makes the environment susceptible to erosion, particularly in areas where soil is exposed on bare steep slopes. Extremes in temperature lead to weathering and, in the tropics, this often leads to the subsequent formation of a deep layer of soil. If there is little vegetation on the soil, erosion is rife.

The composition of the soil, that is, its mix of organic matter, silt, sand and clay, determines the degree of erodibility. Loose granular soils, for example, absorb and retain water and reduce runoff as well as surface erosion.

The topography of a terrain, such as the inclination and length of the slope, its form and elevation, also influence soil erosion in Malaysia. Almost all the high-erosion risk areas are hilly terrains where the gradient of the slope is greater than 20 degrees. A long, continuous and steep slope, for example, allows runoff to build up

## The relative erosion impacts of different land use

Development projects bring about substantial soil loss. In Sabah, for instance, as much as 55 000 tonnes per square kilometre a year are lost through land clearing, logging track activities and road and infrastructure development. Construction sites on granite rock type are equally responsible for massive annual depletion of up to 40 000–50 000 tonnes per square kilometre. The planting of commercial crops, such as oil palm in Pahang, to replace natural forest also contributes substantially to loss of soil. Shifting cultivation and traditional agricultural land uses, however, are responsible for only limited destruction which can be considered natural soil erosion.

| EROSION RATES BY LAND USE AND ROCK TYPE | |
| --- | --- |
| LAND USE TYPE | RATE OF EROSION (tonne/hectare/yr) |
| Undisturbed lowland rainforest | 0.19–3.12 |
| Selective logging, lowland forest | 0.2–16.5 |
| Selective logging, steepland forest | 11.2–28.5 |
| Shifting cultivation | 0.18–0.34 |
| Logging roads | 10–550 |
| Temperate vegetables, highlands | 2–10.5 |
| Traditional pepper cultivation | 80–85 |
| Conversion of forest to oil palm | 2.2–2.5 |
| Construction site | 400–500 |
| Streams affected by construction activity | 12–100 |

Source: Department of Environment Malaysia (1996)

Major causes of erosion include (from left) granite work sites, logging roads and pepper cultivation.

## The impact of soil erosion on rivers

Soil erosion causes sedimentation in rivers, leading to serious environmental problems which often build up imperceptibly over time.

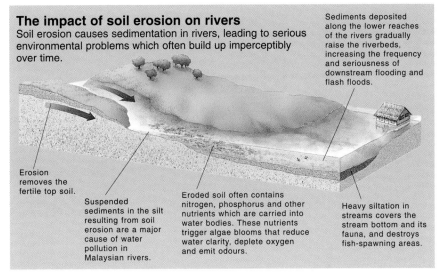

Erosion removes the fertile top soil.

Suspended sediments in the silt resulting from soil erosion are a major cause of water pollution in Malaysian rivers.

Eroded soil often contains nitrogen, phosphorus and other nutrients which are carried into water bodies. These nutrients trigger algae blooms that reduce water clarity, deplete oxygen and emit odours.

Sediments deposited along the lower reaches of the rivers gradually raise the riverbeds, increasing the frequency and seriousness of downstream flooding and flash floods.

Heavy siltation in streams covers the stream bottom and its fauna, and destroys fish-spawning areas.

**Erosion control**
Forms of erosion control include using fibromat (top) or other, leguminous, crop cover (bottom).

momentum and erode the top soil. Vegetation cover, on the other hand, shields soil surface from the impact of falling rain. It slows the velocity of runoff, holds soil particles in place and maintains the soil's capacity to absorb water. Serious cases of soil erosion across Malaysia have occurred where extensive areas of forests and vegetation have been cleared for development.

## River siltation

An increasingly serious result of loss of top soil is reservoir and river siltation. Most of the eroded soil enters the river systems as suspended sediments.

### Types of erosion

1. Rill erosion begins when surface runoff creates tiny, shallow and well-defined channels in the soil surface called rills.
2. Gully erosion develops when runoff cuts rills deeper and wider or when the flow from several rills come together to form a larger and wider channel.
3. Sheet erosion is the most widespread type. It refers to the uniform removal of a thin layer of soil from a particular land area by surface runoff.

The level of sediment in the major rivers of the Peninsula, particularly those that drain through the main land development areas, has increased dramatically. Silt from earthworks and the clearing of vegetation are the chief sources of pollution. River siltation reduces the quality of water in rivers, often transforming natural rivers to urban rivers. In 1995, out of the 116 rivers monitored by the Department of Environment only 32 were found to be free of pollution.

Excessive deposits and accumulation of sediments in rivers and reservoirs reduce their storage capacity, making the area vulnerable to downstream flooding and flash floods. Corrective sediment removal using dredges is a costly activity.

Uncontrolled soil erosion leads to landslides which have destroyed homes and lives. The Pos Dipang mudslide in Perak in August 1996, for example, occurred when heavy rain released a torrent of mud and water on an Orang Asli settlement and buried the village.

## Some basic principles of erosion and sediment control

1. Earthwork development is tailored to the natural contours of the area so that little grading is necessary and the risk of erosion is reduced. Road alignment is made along the contours of the terrain and building platforms are located on the flattest land. Disruption of the land surface is kept to a minimum.

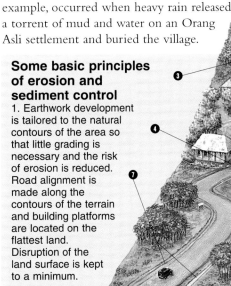

2. Existing vegetation is retained as much as possible; very little erosion occurs in soil covered by vegetation. This includes selective vegetation clearing and the preservation of buffer zones and riparian strips to hold back erosion. Wherever possible, the clearing of vegetation should be carried out a comfortable distance from any buildings.

3. The length and steepness of slopes are minimized.

4. Biodegradable materials, such as mulch, coconut leaves, cow grass, vetiver grass and oil palm fibre, are used in controlling erosion. They cover the land like a protective carpet and, because they are natural fibres, will eventually decompose into the soil.

5. Surface runoff is diverted away from denuded areas into a runoff pool.

6. Fibromat or other vegetation cover is used to cover exposed soil. Hydroseeding together with fibromat may be carried out at slope areas.

7. Drainage channels help to control concentrated or increased runoff.

# Tropical weathering

*Malaysia's landscape provides an environment conducive to prolonged chemical weathering because of its high moisture content, extremes in temperature and the absence of a significant glacial history. Rocks in the tropics normally show extensive transformation by the weathering process. Rocks are turned to thick soils which are rich in oxides and hydroxides of iron and aluminium.*

## Common weathering processes

| | |
|---|---|
| Solution | Minerals and rocks are dissolved by water. |
| Leaching | Solution weathering where minerals and cements are dissolved by water and the dissolved materials washed away. |
| Oxidation | A reaction with oxygen in air and water to form oxides. The characteristic red of highly weathered materials is normally formed by the oxidation of ferrous iron into ferric iron. |
| Hydration | Water combines with other substances and the hydrolysis of a mineral occurs when cations (metal ions) are removed from mineral structures. |
| Carbonation | The action of carbon dioxide ($CO_2$) in air and water with minerals and rocks, or solution of carbonate rocks by weak acid (e.g. $H_2CO_3$) resulting from the combination of $CO_2$ and water. |

## Weathering processes

Weathering is a natural process responsible for softening the earth's surface. The most important agent of weathering is water. In the wet tropics, weathering brings about the formation of soils and aluminium ore, the accumulation of clays and the release of elements to the environment. During weathering the breakdown of minerals—the main constituents of a rock—pave the way for other processes to follow. Together with erosion and uplifting, weathering modifies continental surfaces and maintains the geochemical equilibrium of soils and oceans.

Weathering processes soften a rock and allow plant roots to penetrate into deeper layers, or horizons, of the soil, making essential nutrients available for absorption by the roots.

Transformation of an igneous rock that has been exposed to tropical weathering. The rock before (far left) and after weathering.

Weathering involves chemical, physical and, in some cases, biological processes, but chemical weathering is most dominant in the tropics. Generally, the chemical weathering of rocks involves many stages. The initial stage is *in situ* decomposition of rock into earth materials. At this stage, identification of the weathered rock is still possible. Significant clay formation occurs at the intermediate stage where the decomposition of primary minerals or rock constituents takes place very rapidly. Severe earth displacement, such as landslides, can occur when significant quantities of clays accumulate as a result of weathering. The final stage is the accumulation of reddish materials, predominantly oxides and hydroxides of iron and aluminium. Laterite (iron-rich) and gibbsite (aluminium-rich) are the common products at the final stage of tropical weathering.

Chemical composition, atomic arrangements and temperature during the formation of minerals explain why each type of mineral is different. In a fresh rock, interlocking texture holds the minerals together making the rock strong. However, some minerals are susceptible to faster alteration during chemical weathering and the interlocking texture gradually breaks down, leading to the formation of new minerals. Olivine, for instance, weathers faster than quartz. The atomic arrangement of existing minerals alters, leading to the formation of new ones such as clay minerals.

## Rock weathering and soil formation

Initial physical weathering opens up pathways for water to percolate into, and react with, the mineral constituents of rocks. Water will attack the mineral boundaries first, and then the cleavages and defects in the mineral lattice. This physical action, or weathering, distorts the original texture and weakens the whole rock.

When the rock is still fresh, the boundaries of the minerals interlock with each other. Upon exposure to atmospheric elements, such as rain or

### Interpreting weathered rocks

The intensity of the colours in weathered rocks and soils can provide a clue to the time elapsed since weathering began and to the degree or intensity of the weathering. This sequence shows the textural changes that befall a granite rock as a result of weathering.

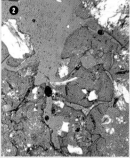

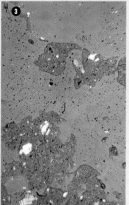

1. A fresh rock under a microscope shows the mineral constituents taken from a road cut along the Karak Highway. Each mineral gives a different appearance under the microscope. Quartz is pale yellow, feldspar is shown by the cross-hatching bands and mica is in greenish and bright yellow layers.

2. Most of the minerals in the granite dissolve during weathering and clays and iron oxides develop in their place. Traces of mica (bright yellow) can still be seen.

3. Total soil development.

sunshine, the minerals expand as the temperature increases and shrink at night when the temperature drops. They expand and shrink at different rates in each heating–cooling cycle. As a result, each mineral glides along their weak lines, their boundaries, or, in the case of some minerals, in their cleavages, muscovite for example. Primary minerals are continuously being weakened, disintegrated and transformed into secondary minerals such as clays.

## The consequences of weathering

Weathering in Malaysia's tropical environment determines the nature of materials that cover the earth's surface in the region. It has important implications in engineering works, water quality agricultural practices and the evaluation of the economic potential of earth materials.

During weathering some constituent elements are released to the environment. These elements enter drinking water, ponds and soils, and determine the quality of water received by humans and aquatic life and the availability and toxicity of natural nutrients for plant growth. Some trace elements, such as selenium and cobalt, are released from the host mineral and are readily available for plant uptake. In certain environments, for example, during the weathering of ultrabasic rock, significant amounts of nickel and chromium are accumulated in the derived soils, resulting in the toxicity of those elements. This can be observed in the stunted growth of some trees in the Ranau and Telupid areas in Sabah.

More severe examples of weathering lead to extensive earth or rock displacements, such as rock falls, landslides and mudflows. Clays accumulate during weathering, presenting a lubricated surface under wet conditions which eventually develops into failure zones. The effects of weathering can also be seen in historical rock monuments, tombstones and other man-made constructions which deteriorate when they are exposed to the weather. In Malaysia, the intense sun and regular heavy rains mean that buildings are prone to such wasting. An understanding of the scientific processes of weathering makes the effective restoration of such monuments possible. Buildings are also effected by plants. Tree roots can infiltrate foundations and mosses and plants grow on urban walls.

### Stages in the weathering of granitic rock

In Peninsular Malaysia, the profuse distribution of granitic rocks that run north to south include the bedrock of the slopes of the Titiwangsa Range. Extensive weathering and erosion have sculptured the mountains into their present form.

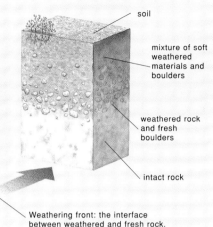

**Initial stage: intact granitic rock with cracks.**

**Intermediate stage: as more chemical reactions take place, the weathering front gets deeper and deeper.**

**Final stage: a top layer of soil is formed with subsequent layers developed at different stages of weathering.**

soil

mixture of soft weathered materials and boulders

weathered rock and fresh boulders

intact rock

Weathering front: the interface between weathered and fresh rock.

Upon exposure to atmospheric elements, such as rain and sunshine, the rock near the surface will weather, notably along the cracks.

**Exposure of weathered surfaces, either by excavation or deforestation, leads to severe erosion as this example at Ipoh shows.**

*RIGHT*: **Exposure to the wind and rain over hundreds of years has taken its toll on historic monuments, such as the Santiago Gate in Melaka.**

*MIDDLE, TOP*: **Weathering can lead to rock displacement, such as this limestone landslide in Perak.**

*MIDDLE, BOTTOM*: **A close-up view of a building's wall showing the powerful effects of wind and rain in a tropical environment.**

*FAR RIGHT*: **The frontage of an old colonial building shows signs of severe tropical weathering and infiltration by plant life.**

# The Titiwangsa Range

*The Titiwangsa Range, also known as the Main Range, is the most prominent and continuous of the mountain ranges of Peninsular Malaysia. Extending the length of the country like a rugged spine, it is important for the rich biological diversity that its peaks support. The lower slopes of the mountains are home to Orang Asli groups, and many of the higher areas, valued for their temperate and tranquil environments, such as the hill stations of Fraser's Hill and the Cameron Highlands, are long-established tourist resorts.*

### Formation of the Titiwangsa Range

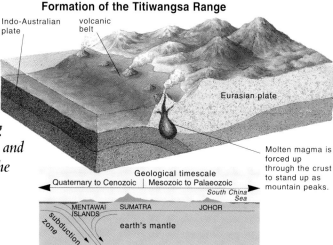

A diagram and a cross section of the earth's crust showing how the Titiwangsa Range would have originated.

## Backbone of the Peninsula

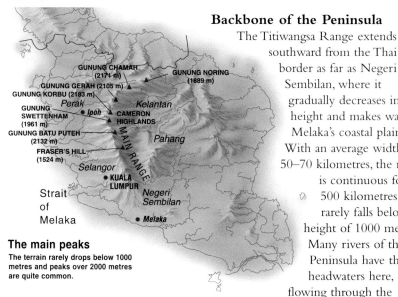

**The main peaks**
The terrain rarely drops below 1000 metres and peaks over 2000 metres are quite common.

The Titiwangsa Range extends southward from the Thai border as far as Negeri Sembilan, where it gradually decreases in height and makes way for Melaka's coastal plain. With an average width of 50–70 kilometres, the range is continuous for 500 kilometres, and rarely falls below a height of 1000 metres. Many rivers of the Peninsula have their headwaters here, flowing through the mountain terrain to drain into the South China Sea or the Strait of Melaka. The landscape is composed mainly of granite, with some areas formed on sedimentary rocks. On its eastern side, the range is flanked by foothills of sedimentary rocks, wide tracts of which have been converted into conglomerates, quartzites and schists by chemical weathering.

## Formation

The Titiwangsa Range resulted from the collision between two tectonic plates. The converging of the oceanic Indo-Australian plate with the continental Eurasian plate forced the heavier oceanic plate below the lighter continental plate. When the descending plate reached a depth of 100 kilometres, the water-rich oceanic crust, and some of the overlying mantle, partially melted. The newly formed magma was less dense than the surrounding mantle rocks and slowly rose up to intrude, or break through, the continental crust above. At the surface it cooled again and crystallized. Over long, long periods of time, such repeated effects created a line of mountainous peaks that have forced themselves through the plate crust, in a process called uplift.

The most recent uplift on the Indo-Australian and Eurasian plate boundaries is associated with the mountain ranges of western

## Profile of the Titiwangsa Range showing how vegetation changes with altitude

1. The characteristic tree of the lowland dipterocarp forest is the *seraya* (*Shorea curtisii*), which occupies the tops of ridges and spurs. The valleys are narrow and steep sided. The floors carry a rich herbaceous vegetation, including gingers and ferns and *Saraca* species. Valuable hardwood trees, such as *terentang* (*Campnosperma auriculata*) and *Pometia pinnata*, commonly grow on the valley sides, whilst on the upper slopes seraya again become dominant, mixed with other dipterocarps such as *Shorea laevis*, *S. multiflora*, *S. faguetiana* and *S. macroptera*. The undergrowth is dominated by stemless *Eugeissona tristis* palms which form thickets up to 6 metres tall.

2. In the upper dipterocarp forest, lowland and hill species of dipterocarp give way to the highland species of which *Shorea platyclados* is the most common. One of the few indigenous conifers in the Peninsula, and also one of the largest upper hill forest trees, is *Agathis alba*. The undergrowth is generally dense and consists of a large number of bamboos, climbers and epiphytes. Towards the higher levels of the forest, the trees decrease markedly in height where most species of the dipterocarps disappear and mountain species become more common.

3. Trees of the oak–laurel forests are members of the families Fagaceae and Lauraceae. In drier areas with poorer soils, the dominant trees may be conifers. Here the trees seldom exceed 24 metres in height. The shrub layer is composed of rattans and stemmed palms, and ferns and epiphytes are also common. The ground surface is usually covered with mosses.

4. Montane ericaceous forest (also called cloud or moss forest) develops best in the cloud belt. In this moist environment, there is an abundance of mosses and epiphytes. The forest itself is dominated by stunted trees that are characteristically twisted and gnarled. Their trunks are typically clothed with lichens, mosses and filmy ferns. A thick accumulation of acid humus soil and peat carpets the forest floor.

**Traditional settlement**
A number of Orang Asli groups, whose livelihood is very much influenced by the mountains, live on the footslopes of the Range.

**Working settlement**
The tea plantations in the Cameron Highlands are still harvested by hand. The workers live in small estate settlements.

## Settlements along the Titiwangsa Range
Certain peaks along the range, namely the Cameron Highlands, the Genting Highlands and Fraser's Hill, have developed into tourist areas. Fraser's Hill is named after Louis James Fraser, a reclusive colonial trader who lived in the hills in the early years of the 20th century. He is said to have run an illegal opium and gambling den from this remote position, but he, and his illicit goings-on, had long departed by the time the area was developed as a hill resort. The station, at a cool height of 1524 metres, is quiet and relatively undeveloped. There are plans to build a new road and some high-rise accommodation more akin to the hotels at the Genting Highlands (1700 metres), which did not start to develop as a popular resort until the 1970s.

The continued success of the region as an important tourist destination depends on maintaining the natural balance of the area, one of the reasons visitors are attracted to the hills in the first place.

**Colonial settlement**
A typical colonial-style bungalow nestling in the temperate and verdant Fraser's Hill.

Sumatra and Java in Indonesia. The Titiwangsa Range forms part of an earlier episode in this form of mountain building, and the granite bedrock of the Titiwangsa Range is derived from such magma crystallization. Being part of a much older and more stable episode of mountain building, the range is not subject to any active uplift today. Processes such as slope weathering and erosion are the more dominant forces at work, sculpturing the mountains into their present forms.

## Ecosystems and environment
While the absolute number of species in mountain environments may be smaller than those found in the lowland forests, the montane tropical forests that dominate the Titiwangsa Range are home to a great wealth of endemic and endangered species and communities. This biological diversity is regarded as one of Malaysia's most valuable resources.

Height
❹ Montane ericaceous — 1500 m
❸ Oak–laurel
1200 m
❷ Upper dipterocarp
750 m
❶ Hill dipterocarp
300 m
Lowland dipterocarp
Floristic zone

Tree fern in dipterocarp forest, Genting Highlands.

Montane forests are characterized by stunted trees and shrubby vegetation.

Deep inside the dipterocarp rainforest, the floor is rich with gingers and ferns, climbers and epiphytes.

*31*

# The mountains of Sabah and Sarawak

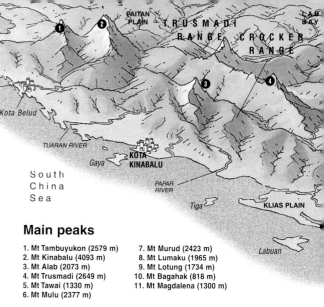

*The mountains of Sabah and Sarawak dominate the terrain of their respective states. Although not high by Himalayan standards, there are several peaks that exceed 2000 metres. Mount Kinabalu, the highest mountain, rises up much higher than any peak on Peninsular Malaysia. The rugged mountain ranges not only provide watersheds, but have also helped shape the settlement patterns and cultural life of the local people.*

Mud volcanoes are found throughout Sabah and Sarawak. They are expressions of the continued geological compression exerted on the island of Borneo.

One of the world's rarest pitcher plants, *Nepenthes trusmadiensis,* is found exclusively on one of the summit ridges of Mount Trusmadi. Other species abound on the mountain slopes.

## Main peaks

| | |
|---|---|
| 1. Mt Tambuyukon (2579 m) | 7. Mt Murud (2423 m) |
| 2. Mt Kinabalu (4093 m) | 8. Mt Lumaku (1965 m) |
| 3. Mt Alab (2073 m) | 9. Mt Lotung (1734 m) |
| 4. Mt Trusmadi (2649 m) | 10. Mt Bagahak (818 m) |
| 5. Mt Tawai (1330 m) | 11. Mt Magdalena (1300 m) |
| 6. Mt Mulu (2377 m) | |

## Sabah: Morphological features

About 60 per cent of the total land area of Sabah is mountainous. Such terrain is mostly located in the western and central part and displays morphological features developed through years of denudation processes. The high mountain ranges (more than 1000 metres) of the west gradually give way to lower ranges in the east. Mount Kinabalu rises majestically from the Crocker Range, Sabah's most prominent mountain region, which is more than 40 kilometres wide and stretches over 200 kilometres in length through western Sabah. Along this range, several peaks such as Mount Lumaku to the south, and Mounts Alab, Kinabalu and Tambuyukon to the north, form the major watershed area in the state. Further north, the Crocker Range swings eastward and gradually disappears into the Labuk Plain. On the Crocker Range's eastern side, a series of discontinuous ranges also run north to south, namely the Witti Range, and the Trusmadi and Meliau ranges. Except for Mount Trusmadi, which rises up to more than 2000 metres, the rest of the mountains are not as prominent as those in the towering Crocker Range.

## Sarawak: Morphological features

The mountains of Sarawak rise up steeply to average altitudes of 1200 metres, with some in the northeastern part reaching 1800 metres, forming a belt of rugged hill country that runs northeast to southwest then swings west, in the interior, along the entire length of the state. The hills decline as they get further from the mountains, dropping and merging into the alluvial plains near the coast.

The Tama Abu Range (Kelabit Highlands), where Sarawak's highest peak, Mount Murud, is located, forms the southern continuation of the Crocker Range in Sabah. This north–south oriented range gradually swings east–west as it stretches further south into the Iran and Nieuwenhuis mountain ranges which are located along the Kalimantan–Sarawak border. In central Sarawak, where the Dulit Range is found, a tight bending of the mountain ranges occur. Here the linear ranges are interspersed with large plateaus, the main ones being Usun–Apau, Batu Laga and Merurong. Near the border with Brunei, a prominent limestone ridge, known as Mount Mulu, rises up.

## Mountain formation

The mountain ranges of Sabah and Sarawak, together with those in Kalimantan, were formed by a series of collisions between the island of Borneo and the surrounding areas during the past 40 million years. Shortening of Borneo's earth crust due to continued compression in this region resulted in the gradual uplift of the mountain ranges above sea

### On the roof of Malaysia

Malaysia's five highest mountains are located in Sabah and Sarawak. The top three are in Sabah. (1) **Mount Kinabalu** at 4093 metres dominates the geology and culture, as well as the horizon, of Sabah, standing almost 1450 metres higher than its nearest competitor. The summit has expanses of bare igneous rock which were glacially eroded one million years ago. The Trusmadi Range in Sabah rises above the Sunsuron–Tambunan Plain. **Mount Trusmadi** (2), 2649 metres, is the highest peak in the Range. Mount Tambuyukon, with an altitude of 2579 metres, is situated within Sabah's Kinabalu Park.

Located next to the Indonesian border, **Mount Murud** (3) at 2423 metres is Sarawak's highest point and Malaysia's fourth highest mountain. **Mount Mulu** (4), 2377 metres, is a sandstone mountain within the Gunung Mulu National Park.

Map labels (illustration):

LOKAN PLAIN ⑤ | MAITLAND RANGE | KINABATANGAN PLAIN | BRASSEY RANGE | ⑩ | Sulawesi Sea
ITTI ANGE | MELIAU BASIN | ⑨ | TAMA ABU RANGE | ⑪ | Tawau
MALIGAN RANGE | ⑦ | ⑥ | ⑧ | Kalimantan | IRAN MTS | NIEUWENHUIS MTS
Brunei | USUN–APAU PLATEAU | BATU LAGA PLATEAU
BARAM RIVER | MERURONG PLATEAU | HOSE MTS
Miri | DULIT RANGE
Bintulu | LUMUT RANGE
KEMENA RIVER
TATAUR RIVER
BALINGIAN RIVER
MUKAH RIVER | Sibu
RAJANG RIVER

level. Today, active mud volcanoes, like those on Pulau Tiga (Sabah) and in the Gunung Mulu National Park (Sarawak), provide an outlet for this compressive energy.

The mountains of Sabah consist largely of highly folded sedimentary rocks previously deposited as shallow to deep sea sediments. The deformed sedimentary rocks are intruded by several bodies of igneous rocks which form prominent mountains. Mount Kinabalu is formed from granitic rocks, whereas Mounts Tambuyukon and Tawai have rocks of ultrabasic origin. In eastern Sabah, Mount Magdalena and Mount Bagahak were once active volcanic sites.

The mountains of Sarawak are composed predominantly of highly folded sedimentary rocks deposited during the Tertiary period, similar in character to those in Sabah. Several bodies of igneous rocks intrude the folded belt; the most prominent ones are located near the Usun–Apau and Batu Laga plateaus in central Sarawak.

## Benefits from the mountains

Apart from providing the main watersheds of the major rivers of Sabah and Sarawak, the mountainous areas support complex and diverse ecosystems. Plant species and other living organisms, as old as the mountains themselves, have evolved. The hill forest, dominated by dipterocarp trees, some of which measure 60 metres in height, is a rich source of timber, but this resource is fast disappearing because of unsustainable felling.

A variety of moss forest exists on many peaks, such as Mount Mulu,

owing to permanently damp conditions.

Interspersed are edaphic heath forests called *kerangas*, which are supported by leached sandy soils. A high floral species diversity abounds in the area, which forms part of the Malesian phytogeographic region. *Rafflesia*, the world's largest flower, is found deep in the Crocker and Trusmadi ranges and in the Kelabit Highlands.

Map legend:

| | |
|---|---|
| ■ | Above 2000 m |
| ▤ | 1000–2000 m |
| ▨ | 100–1000 m |
| □ | Below 100 m |

KINABALU — Sulu Sea
Kota Kinabalu — TAMBUYUKON
Labuan — TRUSMADI — Sandakan
Sabah
South China Sea
BRUNEI
MULU & API — MURUD
DULIT
Sarawak — N
SANTUBONG
Sibu
Kuching
0 — 500 km

The orientation of the illustration above is as if approaching from the South China Sea, and as indicated by the black arrow.

## Mountain living

At the foot and edge of the mountains, where major rivers carve through rugged terrain and forested areas, the hill peoples of Sabah and Sarawak maintain their traditional ways of life. The mountainous areas act as natural barriers between different ethnic groups who have developed their own distinct languages and culture. Mount Santubong rises up behind a settlement near Kuching (right). A Kadazan (Dusun) woman from the fertile Tambunan valley below Mount Kinabalu carries a *wakid* full of bamboo on her back (left).

33

# Mount Kinabalu

*The highest peak in Southeast Asia, Kinabalu, rises majestically to 4093 metres above sea level. Geologically, it is a young mountain whose summit of bare rocks, clefts and pinnacles has been created by erosion and glacial activity. The mountain is home to Sabah's Kadazan people and the inspiration for numerous legends.*

The varied forces of glaciation and erosion have created a fascinating land surface on the stark, imposing summit of Mount Kinabalu.

Rock surface smoothed out by glacial flow.

A cloud zone daily envelops Mount Kinabalu, increasing moisture on the vegetation known as fog-stripping.

## Morphological features

Mount Kinabalu is made up of igneous rock, which is relatively hard compared to sedimentary rock. It overlooks the rest of the folded mountains in Sabah's Crocker Range, towering above Mount Trusmadi (2649 metres) and Mount Tambuyukon (2579 metres) which lie to the south and north respectively and which rank as the second and third highest mountains in Malaysia. Its base, at about 1500 metres above sea level, roughly where the Kinabalu Park Headquarters is located, covers an area of approximately 250 square kilometres. From this altitude, the mountain rises up steeply, especially on its western side. It is comparatively gentle on the southeastern side towards the towns of Kundasang and Ranau.

At a height of about 3000 metres, the cone-shaped Kinabalu massif juts upwards forming a jagged outline punctuated by several prominent peaks, such as those of Low, St John, King Edward, King George, Victoria, and the colourfully named Ugly Sisters' and Donkey's Ears peaks. Years of scouring by running water, ice sheets and rock boulders have transformed the surface of the bare igneous rock, which exhibits unique erosional features characterized by linear grooves and deep gorges. Low's Gully, one of the deepest gorges in the region (1500 metres), divides the mountain in

## Major peaks of Mount Kinabalu

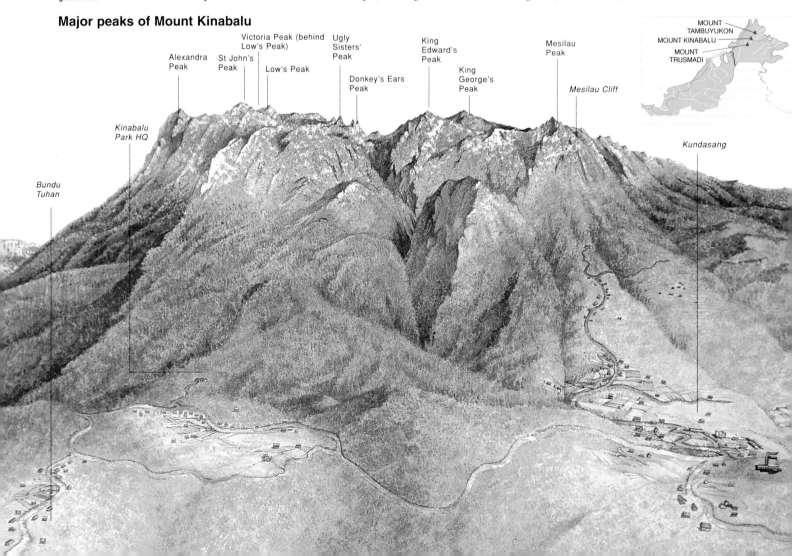

Alexandra Peak

St John's Peak

Victoria Peak (behind Low's Peak)

Low's Peak

Ugly Sisters' Peak

Donkey's Ears Peak

King Edward's Peak

King George's Peak

Mesilau Peak

Mesilau Cliff

Kinabalu Park HQ

Bundu Tuhan

Kundasang

MOUNT TAMBUYUKON
MOUNT KINABALU
MOUNT TRUSMADI

two—the Kinabalu West and the Kinabalu East. Waterfalls, more than 100 metres in height, and narrow, V-shaped valleys have developed on the flank of the mountain. Over time, boulders and gravels have accumulated along the valley floors.

### Formation of the mountain

Mount Kinabalu is considered one of the youngest mountains in the world. Its formation began some 40–50 million years ago when the island of Borneo was submerged beneath the sea. Thick marine sediments accumulated on an oceanic floor consisting of basic and ultrabasic rocks in the area that is now Kinabalu. Over a period of time, these alternating layers of sand and mud were transformed into sedimentary rocks by pressure and temperature.

About 15–20 million years ago, the sedimentary rocks, together with the ultrabasic rocks, were folded, faulted and subsequently uplifted to form a series of mountain ranges, now known collectively as the Crocker Range, which stretch for over 200 kilometres the length of Sabah.

Continued compression in this region resulted in the development of a huge ball of molten rock or magma under the folded mountain. About 9 million years ago, the molten rock intruded into the overlying sedimentary rocks. As it cooled and hardened, a mound called a pluton was formed and remained deep beneath the earth's surface until just over a million years ago when it was forced upwards along a major fault zone, through the Crocker Range. Erosion of the overlying sedimentary rocks finally revealed the Kinabalu massif, together with

### Aki Nabalu

Mount Kinabalu's name remains a mystery although several opinions have been put forward about its origin. The most popular view is that the word derives from the Kadazan (Dusun) term *Aki Nabalu*, meaning 'the revered place of the dead'. Local communities believe that their spirits dwell on the mountain top. Among the bare rocks of the summit grows a moss which early Kadazan guides believed provided food for the spirits of their ancestors. In the past, these guides would often perform religious rites upon reaching the summit. During the ceremony, chickens were slaughtered to appease the spirit of the mountain as well as the ancestral spirits who lived there. Nowadays, a commemorative ceremony is held annually by guides from the Kinabalu Park. Others contest that 'Kinabalu' derives from *Kina* meaning 'China' and *Balu* meaning 'widow'. A Kadazan legend tells the story of a Chinese prince who climbed the mountain in search of a huge pearl guarded by a ferocious dragon. The prince succeeded in slaying the dragon and stealing the pearl. He then married a Kadazan woman, but soon abandoned her and returned to China. Heartbroken, the wife wandered to the mountain to mourn and where she was turned to stone.

parts of the ultrabasic oceanic floor. Glaciation, during the last Ice Age, and erosion further sculptured the summit and deposited a chaotic assemblage of rock fragments known as till.

### Measuring the mountain

Low's Peak is regarded as Kinabalu's highest point. Since it was measured in 1910, its height of 4101 metres has not been in question. However, 87 years on, in June 1997, a measuring expedition set off, equipped with sophisticated, new satellite technology called the Global Positioning System. The accuracy of GPS revealed that the supposed highest peak had dropped 8 metres. The adjacent Victoria's Peak is now thought to be higher. The news was beamed across the globe that Kinabalu has a new (lower) height of 4093.372 metres.

### The geological evolution of Mount Kinabalu

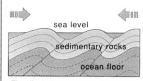

The Kinabalu area was subjected to the process of folding, faulting and uplifting 15–20 million years ago.

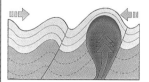

Magma intrusion took place about 9–12 million years ago.

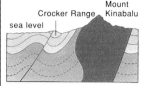

Just over a million years ago, glaciation and erosion over time exposed the Kinabalu massif that we see today.

Rice fields in the plains below Mount Kinabalu.

Kadazan picking tea on the slopes of Kinabalu.

### The Kadazan (Dusun) on Mount Kinabalu

The Kadazan people, Sabah's largest indigenous community, live on the lower slopes of Mount Kinabalu. They traditionally practise rotational agriculture where secondary forest is cleared to make way for rice, along with tapioca, sweet potatoes, sugar cane and tobacco. More recently, temperate climate vegetables, such as cabbage, lettuce and asparagus, have flourished in the cooler, higher areas around Bundu Tuhan and Kundasang. The change from natural vegetative cover to more formal vegetable plots, and the uncontrolled use of chemical pesticides, have affected the volume and the quality of the rivers in the vicinity.

Many Kadazan work as rangers and guides for the Kinabalu Park. Since 1975, the mining of copper, gold and silver in the Mamut area, located on the southeastern flank of Mount Kinabalu, has provided employment for local communities. The mining activity has had detrimental environmental effects by causing a deterioration in the quality of the rivers. Some of these rivers generate hydropower on a small scale for local communities.

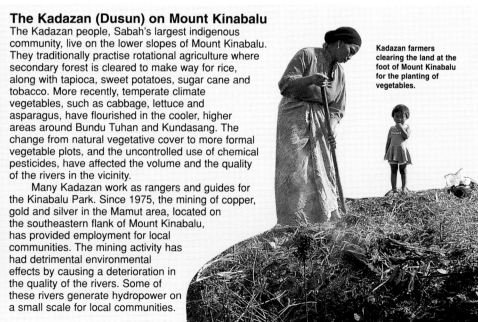

Kadazan farmers clearing the land at the foot of Mount Kinabalu for the planting of vegetables.

# Mount Kinabalu: A unique mountain ecosystem

*Mount Kinabalu is a protected area within the 753-square-kilometre Kinabalu Park. From the lowland forest to the mountain peaks, the Park is home to a unique array of vegetation and habitat types that together harbour a huge diversity of plant and animal species, some of which are rare or endemic to the area. This makes Kinabalu one of the most important biological sites in Asia.*

Slipper orchid (*Paphiopedilum sp.*), found on ultramafic rock on Mount Kinabalu.

There are nine species of pitcher plants (*Nepenthes spp.*) on Mount Kinabalu. The unique and strangely shaped *N. lowii* is shown.

There arc 24 species of rhododendron found on Mount Kinabalu, of which five are endemic. *Rhododendron stenophyllum* (*angustifolium*) grows on the mountain.

## The environment

The Kinabalu massif, on which the Kinabalu Park is sited, is an important water catchment area and the source of numerous streams and rivers. These streams dissect the rugged landscape, providing special habitats for plants and animals, and at the same time help to maintain the characteristic hydrological balance of the areas they drain into.

Mount Kinabalu supports a myriad of site conditions and habitats, from gentle to steep slopes, and from sheltered valleys to exposed ridges, as well as a wide variety of soil cover, ranging from bare rock and mosaics of soil derived from ultramafic rocks (rocks low in silica and rich in iron and magnesian minerals), and from sandstones, which form the main surface of Kinabalu, to the granitic summit. Distinct communities, dominated by the trees *Tristaniopsis elliptica*, *Leptospermum flavescens*, *L. recurvum*, *Gymnostoma sumatranum* or in combination with other species, are dispersed over the ultramafic substrates. In addition, grassland-type (graminoid) communities, dominated by sedges, also occur on Marai Parai and the Tambuyukon summit and a range of alpine scrub communities are present on the top of the mountain.

## Plant diversity and speciation

The total plant diversity of Kinabalu is staggering. It includes some 4,500 vascular plant species,

Low's buttercup (*Ranunculus lowii*) is only found at high altitudes.

possibly as much as 10 per cent of the plant life of Malesia—the floristic region comprising Sumatra, Peninsular Malaysia, Borneo, the Philippines, Java, Sulawesi, Maluku and New Guinea. Many of these plants are extremely rare and poorly documented; about a quarter have been scientifically collected only once.

What makes Kinabalu one of the most important biological sites in Asia?

The reasons are many, but the answers can be found in the extreme physiography of the mountain. Over the millennia, its sharp, high ridges have created effective barriers to seed and plant dispersal; geologically the area is very diverse, leading to a wide range of vegetation communities; and the harsh and changing climate demands rapid evolution and adaptation. Together these have led to the isolation of plant populations and the evolution of new species and forms.

Another 'evolutionary mechanism' at work on Kinabalu has been competition between similar plants for the same resources (light, moisture and nutrients). This ultimately will lead to competing species either becoming segregated into different areas or zones, or weaker species displaced to other sites or becoming extinct. On mountains like Kinabalu, this usually means that two closely related species will be found at different altitudes. For instance, the bamboo *Racemobambos hepburnii* occurs

### Flora and fauna of Kinabalu's floristic zones

Mount Kinabalu has been categorized into four broad floristic zones which correspond, to a certain degree, to the climatic zones. Their boundaries represent critical altitudes where plant composition changes and plant species typical of one zone are replaced by those of another, and where distinct substrate and climatic characteristics develop. The different habitats are home to correspondingly distinct animal species.

### Lower montane
1. Binturong (*Arctictis binturong*)
2. Leopard cat (*Prionailurus (Felis) bengalensis*)
3. Atlas moth (*Attacus atlas*)
4. Ginger (*Hornstedtia incana*)
5. Clouded leopard (*Neofelis nebulosa*)
6. Kinabalu tree frog (*Rhacophorus baluensis*)
7. Trilobite beetle (*Duliticola paradoxa*)
8. Maiden's veil fungus (*Dictyophora duplicata*)
9. Rothschild's slipper orchid (*Paphiopedilum rothschildianum*)
10. Kinabalu orchid (*Bulbophyllum lobii*)
11. Hose's civet (*Hemigalus hosei*)
12. Bornean gibbon (*Hylobates muelleri*)
13. Short-tailed magpie (*Cissa thalassina*)
14. Birds' nest fern (*Asplenium nidus*)

### KINABALU'S WEALTH OF PLANT GROUPS

| PLANT GROUP | TOTAL FOR BORNEO (no. species) | REPRESENTATION ON KINABALU (%) |
|---|---|---|
| Mosses | 650 | c. 55 |
| Ferns and fern allies | 800 | 60–75 |
| Orchids | 2,000 | 40–50 |
| Palms | 290 | c.20 |
| Rhododendrons | 50 | c.50 |
| Dipterocarp trees | 268 | c.15 |

between 1100 and 2200 metres whilst the endemic *R. gibbsiae* is restricted to 2000–3000 metres. Diverse genera on Kinabalu, such as *Ficus* (the fig genus, 98 species), the orchids *Bulbophyllum* (88 species) and *Dendrobium* (62 species), and the *kelat* or *ubah* genus *Syzygium* (at least 66 species), may also have followed such evolutionary paths.

The endangered Kinabalu serpent eagle (*Spilornis kinabaluensis*) soars above Malaysia's highest peaks.

### Animal life

Kinabalu's fauna is as diverse as its flora although much less immediately visible. More than half of Sabah and Sarawak's total bird species fly around the Park, of which 262 are resident and 23 endemic to Borneo. The many rare birds include the endangered Kinabalu serpent eagle, sighted only in northwest Borneo's higher mountains. Other resident birds include the Kinabalu friendly warbler, Whitehead's trogon, Whitehead's broadbill and the red-breasted partridge. Among 112 moth species

The nocturnal slow loris (*Nycticebus coucang*) occurs to an altitude of 1300 metres.

### Subalpine
1. *Rhododendron buxifolium*
2. Mountain schima (*Schima brevifolia*)
3. Pitcher plant (*Nepenthes villosa*)
4. Summit rat (*Rattus baluensis*)
5. Low's buttercup (*Ranunculus lowii*)
6. Moth (*Hypocometa titanis*)
7. Heath rhododendron (*R. ericoides*)
8. Bornean mountain ground squirrel (*Dremomys everetti*)
9. Mountain blackbird (*Turdus poliocephalus*)

Elevation: summit
Climatic zone: polar; mean daily temperature dips to around 6–8 °C and on rare occasions there are freezing ground temperatures.

Elevation: 2800–3400 metres
Climatic zone: temperate
Floristic zone: subalpine

Elevation: 2350–2800 metres
Climatic zone: temperate
Floristic zone: upper montane

Elevation: 1200–2350 metres
Climatic zone: temperate
Floristic zone: lower montane

Elevation: Below 1200 metres
Climatic zone: tropical; mean daily temperature 28 °C
Floristic zone: lowlands

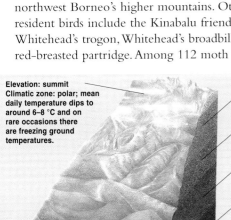

Tropical lowland forest, including that on the lower slopes of Mount Kinabalu, is dominated by the tree family Dipterocarpaceae.

Mount Kinabalu is the only locality in Malaysia which has altitudes high enough to support alpine flora and fauna.

### Upper montane
1. Kinabalu friendly warbler (*Bradypterus accentor*)
2. Fern (*Blechnum vestitum*)
3. Orchid (*Dendrochilum* sp.)
4. Long-tailed mountain rat (*Niviventer rapit*)
5. Sun bear (*Helarctos malayanus*)
6. Pitcher plant (*Nepenthes rajah*)
7. Pitcher plant (*Nepenthes lowii*)
8. Ferret-badger (*Melogale personata*)
9. Whitehead's trogon (*Harpactes whiteheadi*)
10. Trees draped with lichens, mosses and bamboos

documented here, more than 50 per cent of those occurring from about 2500 metres to the summit zone are endemic, as are a third of the lower montane species. The probable effects of isolation or past climatic changes on the evolution of new forms are reflected, for example, by related pairs of moth species, such as *Agylla bisecta*, which is endemic to Kinabalu, and *A. divisa,* found from Borneo to the Himalayas, and *Hypocometa titanis,* endemic to Kinabalu and *H. leptomita,* also seen in Sarawak. Many other insects, including beetles, are similarly diverse.

Among vertebrate forms, the 40 fish species documented for the Kinabalu area do not appear to occur above 1580 metres. Some 75 species of frogs and toads of mostly lowland forest or lower montane forms are also known. More than half of the 22 mainly montane mammal species are endemic to Borneo, including the black and Kinabalu shrews, known to exist exclusively on the mountain. Other inhabitants include Whitehead's pygmy squirrel, Kinabalu rat, civet, mousedeer, porcupine, pangolin, ferret-badger, slow loris, western tarsier, long-tailed and pig-tailed macaque, and Bornean gibbon. Even the orang utan of the Kinabalu area, known only in the northern and eastern parts, may be ecologically distinct from those in east Sabah.

# Limestone and karst morphology

*Only 0.3 per cent of the land area in Malaysia is covered by limestone, but the dramatic landscape that the rock gives rise to guarantees it a noteworthy place in the geology and geomorphology of the country. Limestone hills in Malaysia are mainly of the tower karst type and are characterized by sheer cliffs. Striking karst forms include those of the Langkawi Islands and the underground phenomena found in the caves of Mulu.*

## The development of tropical tower karst topography

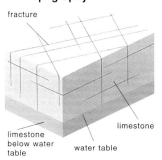

A thick limestone deposit forms a plateau. Rain and ground water seep into the fractures of the brittle rock, dissolving the limestone and widening fractures into fissures and caves.

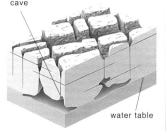

Caves develop along the line of the water table and fractures. They increase in size as further weathering takes place and as their roofs and walls collapse.

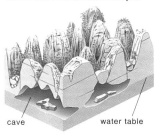

When the water table remains deep, the landscape eventually becomes rugged, consisting of limestone towers.

Limestone karst hills are a major feature of Kuala Perlis.

## Limestone locations

The most extensive limestone areas in Peninsular Malaysia can be found in the Gua Musang region of Kelantan, the Kinta Valley of Perak, and in Perlis and north Kedah. Craggy limestone hills also occur in the more isolated mountain ranges of the Mulu and Niah Caves, both located in Sarawak, and the Gomantong Caves in Sabah. Limestone is composed of calcium carbonate that readily dissolves in slightly acid rain water or in river water. This gives rise to the remarkable features that are characteristic of Malaysia's limestone hills and formations.

## Creation of a karst landscape

In vast limestone terrains, a distinct landscape, known as karst, is carved out by river and ground water. Named after the formations along the Dalmatian coast of the former Yugoslavia, karst is now applied to the topography of any limestone area which displays specific characteristics. Although most common in limestone areas, karst also occurs in areas where other soluble earth material is present, such as on rock salt in arid environments.

## Underground features

A karst landscape is unique in that it is at least partially drained by underground streams. When river or ground water percolates through cracks and fissures in limestone, it slowly dissolves the rock and enlarges the openings. As ground water continues to drip downward and eat away at the rock, vertical caves develop above the water table (the level up to which the ground is permanently saturated). At the

The limestone topography of the Langkawi Islands includes drowned karst forms.

## The main limestone areas

water table itself, caves may develop and extend horizontally. The principal underground features of karst are caves or caverns and their connecting tunnels. Subterranean rivers contribute to the formation of these caverns. As cave formation proceeds very slowly and water table conditions change seasonally or over a short time, caves commonly acquire complex shapes. Some of the most extensive and fascinating in Malaysia are found in the Gunung Mulu National Park in Sarawak which contains over 100 kilometres of mapped and explored caves in the Clearwater system (see 'Caves and cave systems').

During cave creation, exquisite deposits of calcium carbonate, found for example in the Wind and Lang Caves of Mulu, form as depositional features. River and ground water in limestone terrains are usually saturated with calcium bicarbonate, which is formed by the chemical reaction between carbonic acid in rainwater and the calcium carbonate in the rock. When the saturated water cools or evaporates within the cave, it leaves behind residues of the

Looking up at a swallow hole from inside Deer Cave.

## The origin of limestone

Limestone is made up of at least 80 per cent calcium carbonate. Limestone is typically hard, grey and crystalline. It contains many fossils and the skeletons and parts of many single-cell marine animals and plants. These organic materials indicate that the limestone was formed on a bed of a warm, clear sea. Thick layers of carbonate accumulations include coral reefs. Corals grow abundantly in a tropical marine environment where annual temperatures remain fairly constant, the water depth is relatively shallow (about 20 metres) and the water is clear enough for sunlight to penetrate. A rigid sea bottom allows the reef to grow.

Limestone layers may also form through the accumulation of mollusc shells. Fossil organic limestone provides geologists with important information about deposition that has occurred in seas over millions of years. Substantial limestone accumulations may also result from inorganic sources, for example, from the evaporation of sea water in arid climates and from water droplets from hot springs.

## Cave swiftlets and their nests

Malaysian caves, such as the Niah and the Gomantong Caves, are often associated with their resident swiftlets. For a few hundred years, men have undertaken the hazardous task of gathering 'white gold'—the nests of swiftlets. These edible nests are made into bird's nest soup, a Chinese culinary delicacy.

The nests are made out of long, thin strings of glutinous saliva that the swiftlets weave against the surface of the rock. There are two main types of birds' nests—white and black. The white nest of pure saliva is built by the *Aerodramus fuciphagus* and is considered of superior quality because it does not contain the twigs and leaves woven in the black nests. The black nest of *A. maximus* includes the bird's feathers. The rare red nest is a great delicacy. It is believed to be tinted by the blood of the exhausted swiftlets who strain to weave a second nest when their first has been lost. A more prosaic explanation is that the red nest has been tainted by iron oxide found in the limestone.

The harvesting of the nests is almost an art. The nests in Sabah's Gomantong Caves are harvested twice in a season. The first batch are gathered as soon as the swiftlets build their nests and before the eggs are laid. The birds will then rebuild their nests and these will be left undisturbed for the birds to lay their eggs and raise their young. Once the fledglings leave, the nests are removed for a second time.

Bird nest collection is a lucrative business. The harvesting of them is strictly controlled by Malaysia's wildlife departments to protect the swiftlet species.

*RIGHT* : The nest gatherers climb rattan ladders and use long bamboo poles to reach the nests, which are often tucked in inaccessible niches high up in the caves. This often means traversing vast voids on a skeleton structure with only a torch for light.

*ABOVE*: When a nest is discerned in the dark, it is scraped off the wall of the cave. The nests are glued to the rock surface by the bird's saliva.

calcium carbonate. Over a long period of time, these deposits develop into flowstones or banded travertines (calcium carbonate crystals deposited in transparent layers), stalactites, stalagmites and other forms of carbonate precipitation in caves, which are collectively known as speleothems.

A drip curtain of calcium carbonate hanging down inside Lang Cave, Mulu, Sarawak.

## A karst topography

Above the ground, karst landscape is dramatic. Rivers may suddenly disappear into steeply slanting fissures and shafts in the limestone, known as swallow holes or sinkholes, to become underground drainage systems. Karst is distinguished by extremely rugged topography.

In Malaysia, limestone masses have evolved into large hills, with steep to practically vertical walls called tower karsts or mogotes. A shallow water table results in a karst topography of conical hills (in Malay aptly compared to inverted half coconut shells or *tempurung*). The hill tops are relics of a limestone surface, which prior to weathering and dissolution, was once extensive. Mogotes predominate in Malaysia, although a few conical karst hills can be seen in the Kisap area of Pulau Langkawi. The Langkawi Islands also consist of partially drowned karst forms.

A house built into a limestone hill, Perak. Human settlement on limestone is limited and dispersed because of the poor natural resources, especially the lack of water and good soil.

# The karst morphology of Langkawi

*The eastern flanks of the Langkawi Islands present an outstanding example of karst morphology. Two kinds of limestone, differing in composition and age and separated by thrust faulting, distinguish the unique landscape. The topography in this region is characterized by a mix of continuous limestone ridges and isolated hills.*

An aerial view of the Langkawi Island group.

### A living landscape

Langkawi is a group of up to 104 islands (some sources give only 99, see 'Islands of Malaysia') 30 kilometres off Peninsular Malaysia's northwest coast. It is composed predominantly of limestone which is in a state of active chemical solution because of the abundant rainfall that the island group receives. The rugged karst topography is marked by abrupt and irregular slopes, cliffs and bare exposed outcrops. Pinnacles of rock abound. Areas with a chaotic mass of hollows and pits— sinkholes and swallow holes—reveal that the limestone in the region is actively being weathered by rain and sea water in a process called solutioning. Such holes can range from 2 to 100 metres in depth and from 100 to 1000 metres across. Valleys, locally called *wang*, are deep and dry bottomed and are usually surrounded by high cliffs. They are formed as a result of advanced solutioning and the collapse of underground caves.

The hills and numerous islands which distinguish Langkawi are the result of partial submergence of mogotes (vertical-sided limestone hills) and karst. The presence of hundreds of these partially submerged mogotes, each one with steep cliffs and rugged peaks, creates a unique landscape called island karst.

### The geology of limestone

The most spectacular karst morphology in Malaysia is found in the limestone formations of the

### Geological formations

**The caves of Langkawi**
Millions of years ago, the sea level and the ground water level at Langkawi were much higher than they are today. The fossils of large colonies of sea shells that have been found in the limestone caves high above the present sea level testify to this. Gua Langsiar and Gua Cerita are fossil caves found 10–80 metres above sea level. They are no longer active but indicate where the sea level once was. Many smaller caves, such as Gua Pasir Dagang, however, are still in the process of formation. More than 20 caves have been found, some of which are still waiting to be explored, and there are believed to be many more which have yet to be discovered.

On the islands of Langkawi, caves are formed through the consistent wave action of sea water. Such chemical solutioning starts where underground cracks meet the sea level. Fluctuations of the water table slowly enlarge the fissures into corridors and galleries. As these enlarge, their roofs collapse producing even greater chambers.

Gua Langsiar, a fossil cave, now stands more than 80 metres above sea level.

## Pulau Langkawi and surrounding islands

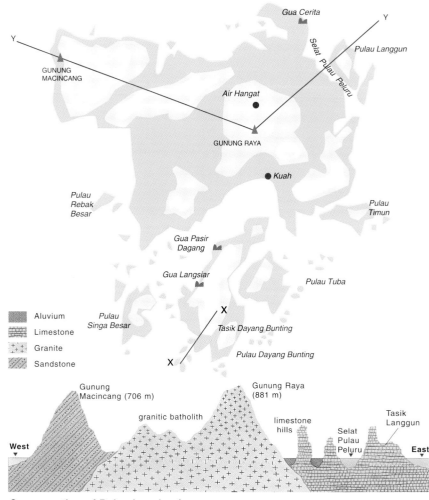

### Cross section of Pulau Langkawi
The geological cross section of Pulau Langkawi from west to east (Y–Y) presents three kinds of rock formation. Macincang Range, the oldest sandstone formation on the island, and the Setul limestone formation were intruded by Gunung Raya, a granitic batholith. (For cross-section of X–X see next page.)

Langkawi Islands which exhibit two types of limestone. Limestone formed between the Ordovician to Devonian geological ages (see 'Geological history' for the geological timescale) is called Setul formation and has a thickness of more than 1500 metres. The rock is composed of hard, brittle, dark-coloured and thick-bedded crystalline limestone and contains numerous fossils. It stretches from the eastern seaboard of Pulau Langkawi to Pulau Timun, Pulau Dayang Bunting and Pulau Tuba.

Limestone formed during the Permian to Triassic ages is called Chuping formation. It is confined to Pulau Dayang Bunting and some small areas on Pulau Langkawi itself. This formation consists of uniform deposits of massive white crystalline limestone, which have started to metamorphize into marble. The Setul formation has distinct microfeatures called stylolites, which are curious structural features impressed upon the limestone, and which are caused by high compression during its formation. Stylolites composed of harder material, such as quartz, are more visible along the coast because they are more resistant to weathering.

Various other microfeatures can be seen on barren, exposed karstic hills. These are products of solution by rain drops and appear in the form of rills, pillars, depressions and ridges. They are collectively called karren and they make limestone

*FAR LEFT*: **Rills created by fresh water flowing on the surface of limestone.**

*LEFT*: **The initial formation of sea caves.**

*RIGHT*: **Sea stacks of limestone are shaped by rain and sea water.**

An aerial view of Tasik Dayang Bunting.

Limestone formation below Tasik Dayang Bunting. The southwest–northeast cross section is indicated (by X–X) on the map on the previous page.

Southwest / Northeast

sea / lake / limestone hill

fractures / collapsed underground cavities / highly fractured blocks of limestone

areas almost inaccessible by foot because of the terrain's highly irregular nature.

## Coastal features

The coastal landforms of the Langkawi Islands are different from other coastlines in Malaysia because the geology of the region is susceptible to the unique combination of solutioning and wave action. Some researchers believe that bioerosion (erosion by marine fauna) also contributes to the process.

The continual action of waves crashing on the shore, combined with tidal fluctuation and chemical solutioning, produces an effective and powerful erosive mix. Notches and sea caves are carved out at the base of limestone cliffs. As the notches penetrate deeper into the cliff, the cliff is unable to sustain its own weight and collapses. Such collapse produces vertical and overhang cliffs.

Ferns (*Drynaria bonii*) grow in unexpected microhabitats in limestone on Pulau Langgun.

Fossiliferous limestone of Pulau Anak Tikus.

### The Lake of the Pregnant Maiden

Tasik Dayang Bunting is the largest lake in the Langkawi Islands and takes its name from the land around it which is in the shape of a pregnant woman. It was formed millions of years ago when the roofs of underground limestone caverns of one of the many islands collapsed. Measuring 1 kilometre in length and 0.5 kilometre in width, it is separated from the sea by a thin wall of rock. The lake is surrounded by sharp, high-sided cliffs, thick with forests. This large natural lake holds a mixture of fresh and saline water, a result of sea water infiltration through subterranean cavities.

The lake is shrouded in legend. A celestial princess chose it as her bathing pool and left her dead infant in its waters before she returned to her heavenly home. She blessed the lake, conferring fertility on all childless women who bathe there.

### Limestone flora

Limestone constrains vegetation. Only those plants which can survive on a thin layer of soil are able to successfully take root.

The flowers of the rare *Chinita calipinosa* which is found exclusively on limestone.

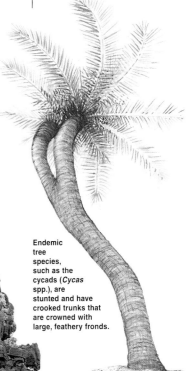

Endemic tree species, such as the cycads (*Cycas* spp.), are stunted and have crooked trunks that are crowned with large, feathery fronds.

# Caves and cave systems: The Mulu Caves

*The caves of Mulu portray a spectacular subterranean world which is still evolving. The relentless activity of underground water in humid tropical areas produces caves and passages renowned for their immense size. At the same time, drops of water drip slowly from cave ceilings to craft some of the most delicate and intricate limestone sculptures.*

ABOVE: The gently undulating hills of Mulu house an active network of caves that are still in the process of being shaped.

RIGHT: Over millions of years the limestone of Gunung Mulu has been eroded by heavy tropical rainfall, resulting in the formation of the razor-sharp Pinnacles.

Gunung Mulu National Park

The Gunung Mulu National Park lies in northeast Sarawak. Its northern boundary forms part of the border with Brunei.

MEDALAM RIVER
GUNUNG BUDA (963 m)
GUNUNG BENARAT (1580 m)
MELINAU RIVER
PINNACLES
GUNUNG API (1750 m)
N
Sarawak Chamber
Wind Cave
Clearwater Cave
GUNUNG MULU (2376 m)
Deer Cave
Garden of Eden
Lang Cave
Limestone hills

## Caves and cave systems in Malaysia

In Malaysia, abundant rainfall (2600 millimetres a year) combined with consistently high temperatures provide ideal conditions for limestone cave formation. In a temperate region, limestone landscape is lowered at a rate of only 10 millimetres every thousand years, but in the tropics this rate increases to more than 300 millimetres per thousand years. Cave formation is therefore more common in the tropics than in temperate regions, and the resulting cave systems correspondingly more complex. The cave passages in Malaysia are also much more vast than in most other parts of the world because the cracks in the parent rock are widely spaced and the rock is very strong. This means that a few large passages, rather than a cluster of small ones, are formed and that the large caverns, such as the Deer Cave, do not collapse as they would in weaker rock.

Rainwater has carbon dioxide within it, which it has

Stalagmites in Lang Cave.

absorbed from the air. When rainwater falls to the ground it becomes a weak carbonic acid and on contact with limestone starts to chemically corrode it. The carbonic acid percolates through cracks and fissures in the limeston formation, slowly dissolving the rock and enlarging any openings that already exist. At the water table, ground water moves laterally towards a natural outlet, such as a river system. At this juncture, solutioning is maximized eventually leading to the creation of caves. Sometimes the water table drops. When this happens, water in the subterranean passageways then seeps down to the new level. Over time, various levels of cave systems are formec such as those found in the Clearwater Cave. As caves gro larger, their roofs become unstable and eventually collaps further enlarging caves and in the process often creating enormous chambers.

Malaysia's high annual rainfall also means that there is huge amount of surface running water. Tropical rivers erode limestone through the geological processes of solution and mechanical attrition. The Melinau, Medalam and Melinau Paku rivers in Sarawak, for example, have carved caves and exceptionally huge passageways in the Mulu Cave system.

## The ultimate cave system

### The longest cave system in Asia

The Clearwater Cave in the Gunung Mulu National Park has the distinction of being the longest cave system in Asia and the tenth longest in the world. It has a mapped length of 100 kilometres. It is believed that connections to other cave systems exist but these have yet to be discovered. The Clearwater River flows through this cave system and is one of the biggest known underground rivers in the world. During periods of high water, 250 cubic metres of water pour through the passage every second. Some caves in the Clearwater Cave system are completely filled with water and can only be explored by highly trained divers. The cave system consists of both fossil and recently formed caves. New cave building is actively taking place, with an estimated 1 kilogram of limestone being dissolved every second.

Clearwater River leading to the mouth of the cave.

### The world's largest underground chamber

The Sarawak Chamber, at 600 metres in length, 415 metres in width and with a roof span of 300 metres, is the largest geological feature of this type in the world It is a colossal void created by the recurrent collapse of a portion of the roof of the Good Luck Cave in the Gunung Api limestone formation. The cave is pitch black, and even with powerful lamps, it is not possible to see the whole cavern from wall to wall or from floor to ceiling. Its area is equivalent to 20 football fields The Sarawak Chamber defies scientific laws, which theoretically claim that limestone is too weak to support a roof span of such proportions. The chamber' uniqueness lies in its sheer size and overwhelming darkness.

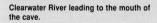

A spectacular evening sight: bats in mass formation flying out of the Deer Cave.

The entrance to the mighty Deer Cave.

## Composition of the Wind and Lang Caves

These caves represent the optimum stage of dripstone formation. Drops of water, which have been flowing continuously over the last few thousand years, have slowly sculptured limestone of incredible beauty. The widest range of exquisitely architectured stalactites, stalagmites, columns and drip curtains are found in this underworld limestone garden.

1. Limestone
2. Drip curtain
3. Stalactite
4. Flow stone
5. Stalagmite
6. Column
7. Cave floor full of guano
8. Cave mouth or entrance

## Cave deposits

In Mulu, abundant amounts of water drip constantly into the caves, creating a great variety of cave features. As water drips through a fracture in the roof of a limestone cave, a small amount of calcium carbonate is left behind because of the partial evaporation of water. A small ring of calcite is then deposited around the fissure, or crack, in the roof which then develops into a tube. As water seeps from adjacent areas and flows down the calcite tube it acquires a cone-like shape. Cave deposits formed through this process are collectively known as dripstone.

There are many varieties of dripstone. Icicle-shaped forms growing down from the ceiling are called stalactites and are pointed. Corresponding deposits of calcium carbonate growing up from the floor are called stalagmites. They are typified by rounded or flat tops which may contain a pool of water. The formation is enlarged at its sides as the water flows over the edge of the pool. Many stalactites and stalagmites eventually merge to form columns. Water dripping from a fissure in the roof can also form thin vertical sheets of calcium carbonate called a drip curtain.

### Sarawak Chamber plan

N

0 ____ 300 km

*ABOVE:* **The Sarawak Chamber is so vast that, for example, 40 Boeing 747 aeroplanes could be parked on its floor.**

### The world's largest underground passage

The Deer Cave lies at the south end of Mulu's limestone chain in the Southern Hills. At the mouth of the cave, water cascades from a limestone roof 120 metres high. The cave passage is 160 metres wide and leads to an opening 750 metres away, which is aptly named the Garden of Eden. This opening marks the start of the extensive underground tunnel which has been worn by dripping water.

Sambar deer frequent the cave, thus its name. While the deer passes through the cave en route to other pastures, about a million bats (predominantly wrinkle-lipped bats, *Tadarida (Chaerephon) plicata*) have made the roof of the passage their permanent home. In the evening the bats routinely fly out in sinuous wave patterns, peppering the sky for hours in their distinctive formation because of the large number of bats involved. Between them they consume many tonnes of insects at night and deposit several tonnes of bat dung or guano on the cave floor each day.

Inside the Lang Cave.

A female sambar deer (*Cervus unicolor*), a frequent visitor to the Deer Cave.

43

# River systems

*Malaysia has an intricate and substantial network of rivers, which, over millions of years, have helped shape the landscape. Since a ready supply of water is essential for life, the river systems have always played a key role in the establishment of human settlements. Along the course of Malaysia's rivers economic, social and cultural needs and activities meet and at times conflict with the ecological aspects of the river and the landscape it runs through.*

## Some typical features of Malaysian rivers

1. Rivers are dammed in their upper and middle courses to develop lakes for hydroelectric power, such as Lakes Temengor and Chenderoh in Perak. Hydroelectric power generation and the supply of water to industrialized centres is important for Malaysia's burgeoning economy and population, but extensive industrialization may bring ecological problems. Soil erosion and siltation can lead to floods downstream. Kuala Lumpur has regular floods as a result of rapid urbanization in the Klang River basin.

2. Rivers do not have an easy journey to the seas from their mountain sources. They bend and twist as they negotiate geological structures along their course, actively eroding, transporting and depositing sediments on their way. River cliffs, cataracts and waterfalls—the results of erosion—are seen along the tributaries of the Perak and Pahang rivers.

3. In Sabah and Sarawak, where logging activities are most evident, logs are transported downstream to sawmills either by boat or as floating rafts.

4. The traditional use of rivers for fishing and agriculture on the alluvial flood plains has declined in economic importance. Paddy is irrigated by river water.

5. Settlements have always emerged where there is a ready supply of water. Traditional riverine kampongs were well-established along the Perak, Kelantan and Muar rivers even before Melaka emerged as an important port in the 16th century.

6. Deltas form at river mouths where deposits of sands, silts and clays build up. The Klang Delta was once home to a rich ecosystem, but its flora and fauna are diminishing due to excessive land excavation and erosion.

7. Large settlements support commercial and tourist activities, such as offshore aquaculture, container ports, hotels and pleasure cruises. Sibu, in the lower Rajang, Sarawak, once a small town, is now a bustling centre.

8. Small riverine islands and sand bars are conspicuous along the river channels. They provide habitats for riverine animals, such as terrapins, crocodiles and certain bird species. Upstream activities, such as sand mining, along certain stretches of Malaysia's rivers have disrupted these delicate ecosystems.

A river winds through Sabah's forest as it makes its way to the coast.

An aerial view over Sabah showing a kampong and riverine islands.

In their upper courses, rivers are often dammed to create lakes for hydroelectric power use. The Klang Gate Dam is shown.

A waterfall along Ulu Kelenting River, Perak.

# The Rajang River

*Sarawak's majestic Rajang River flows for 560 kilometres. It is the longest river in Malaysia and irrigates a third of the state of Sarawak, an area of about 40 000 square kilometres. It is an important inland waterway for the people living in the Belaga, Kapit and Song divisions, where the road system is poorly developed, and links the coastal townships with inland settlements and timber camps.*

## Riverine lifestyles along the Rajang

1. The longhouse, such as this just north of Sibu, is the traditional dwelling place for the Rajang inhabitants. Home to a group of families, the houses are made from wood felled from the forests of the interior. The *atap* thatch roofs are gradually being replaced by corrugated iron.

2. An aerial view of the bustling town of Sibu, the Rajang's largest settlement and main port. Situated 60 kilometres upstream from the sea, Sibu's waterfront sports all manner of craft. It is to here that raw materials from the interior, such as logs and gravel, are brought for transshipment and export.

## The course of the Rajang

The Rajang River system, which includes several major tributaries, stretches east to west across central Sarawak. The river and most of its tributaries, in the main, faithfully follow the form of the mountain ridges. The tough, rugged landscape dictates that the course of the river is predominately straight and that it does not meander to any degree until its lower reaches where it fans out across an alluvial plain into a web of smaller rivers.

**Rajang River system**

The Rajang begins in the highlands towards the east, near Sarawak's border with Kalimantan, and flows westward into the South China Sea, draining the Kapit, Sibu and Sarikei divisions of the state.

The river's main tributaries, the Baleh, Balui, Murum and Linau, have their source in the Nieuwenhuis and Iran mountain ranges. Another tributary, the Belaga River, originates in the Dulit Range and Usun–Apau Plateau.

## Geological formation

In their upper courses, the tributaries flow over hard sedimentary formations in narrow valleys, and have relatively steep gradients with many rapids and stretches of turbulent water. Some of the well-known rapids, like the Pelagus, Mikad, Bungan, Tibang, Bakun, Murum and Sekatong, occur when rivers cut through more resistant sedimentary strata. In its upper and middle course, between Belaga and Song, the Rajang flows through a narrow valley. Below Song, the valley broadens and alluvial plains are more well developed. In its lower reaches, below Sibu, the river meanders sluggishly through alluvium and peatswamps and is tidal for considerable distances from its mouth. Together with other tributaries, a large delta complex of about 4000 square kilometres has developed here. The development of the present river system is not known precisely, but the depth of peat deposits, which are as much as 15 metres in the Rajang Delta, suggest that it must have existed for the last 5,000 years. The average rate of peat production is 1 metre every 300 years.

*Top:* An aerial view of the Rajang Delta as it enters the alluvial plain after winding 560 kilometres through Sarawak.

*Bottom:* The river cuts through peatswamp forest en route from Bakun.

*Right:* A family in the upper Rajang along the Belaga River, near Bakun.

## River settlements

The changing course of the Rajang tributaries and the accumulation of muddy sediments near the river mouth discourage the development of a deep water seaport. Further inland, however, where the course of the Rajang is more established, the towns of Sarikei, Bitangor and Sibu have developed. These three towns have been the engine of economic growth for the Sarikei, Sibu and Kapit divisions. The import and export of goods started in the mid–18th century under the auspices of the British ruling dynasty, the Brooke Raj, and continue today. Other smaller towns, like Kanowit, Song, Kapit and Belaga, are located further inland and are important commercial centres for the indigenous population.

Along the banks of the Rajang different ethnic groups have settled. The lower reaches are dominated by the Chinese, Melanau and Malays and the middle and upper reaches by the Iban and Orang Ulu respectively. The Iban and Orang Ulu live in longhouses, which consist of a number of *bilik* (rooms) housing separate families, joined side by side with a common veranda, the whole structure being raised on stilts to about 3 metres above ground level. The longhouses of Long Jawi, along the upper reaches of the Balui River, constitute the furthest major inland settlement.

The Rajang River, like its major tributaries, has a high sediment load due to excessive deforestation by logging, road building and farming activities. Large wooden debris floating in these rivers can be hazardous to small longboats and express boats.

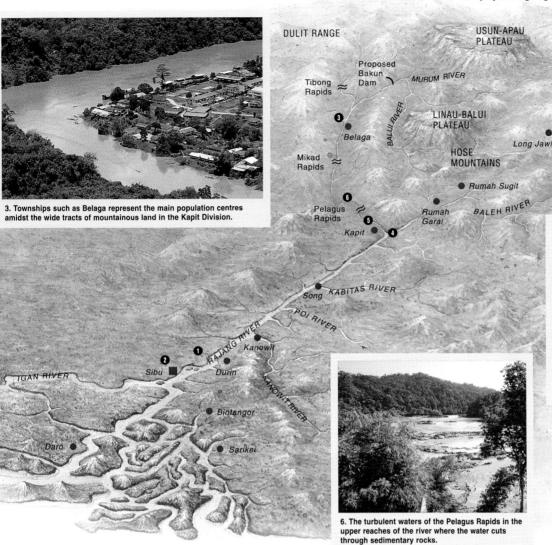

DULIT RANGE

USUN-APAU PLATEAU

Tibong Rapids

Proposed Bakun Dam

MURUM RIVER

**3**

Belaga

Mikad Rapids

BALUI RIVER

LINAU-BALUI PLATEAU

Long Jawi

HOSE MOUNTAINS

Rumah Sugit

**6**

Pelagus Rapids

**5**

Kapit

**4**

Rumah Garai

BALEH RIVER

Song

KABITAS RIVER

POI RIVER

RAJANG RIVER

**2**

**1**

Kanowit

IGAN RIVER

Sibu

Durin

KANOWIT RIVER

Bintangor

Daro

Sarikei

3. Townships such as Belaga represent the main population centres amidst the wide tracts of mountainous land in the Kapit Division.

4. Iban constitute the main ethnic grouping in Sarawak and inhabit longhouses along the Rajang and Baram rivers. The rivers play a vital role in the daily lives of the people as they are used as water supply for cooking and washing.

5. The small town of Kapit on the southeastern bank of the river dates from the days of the White Rajahs. For the upriver people, it is their 'big' city where local products are traded.

6. The turbulent waters of the Pelagus Rapids in the upper reaches of the river where the water cuts through sedimentary rocks.

## Benefits from the Rajang

The Malays, Melanau and Iban who live in the coastal areas utilize the sago and *nipah* palms that grow well in the swampy lower reaches of the river for starch, food and roofing. The mangrove trees that thrive in certain areas are used for firewood and for making charcoal. The fertile alluvial plains near Sibu, Sarikei and Bitangor, formed from fine silts brought down by the river as it erodes along its course, provide farmers with rich land for the cultivation of food crops and fruit trees.

Considerable areas adjacent to the main rivers have been planted with rubber by Chinese and Iban. In the upper reaches, Dayak communities depend on the rivers for fish, water for domestic needs and for transportation to their farms and local towns to sell their agricultural and forest products.

The presence of several rapids with distinctive features has high potential for recreational and tourism-related activities. The Pelagus Rapids, stretching for about 5 kilometres, located a few kilometres above Kapit town, for example, have been developed for such a purpose. The numerous narrow gorges that developed as the rivers cut through hard sedimentary rocks are ideal for the construction of hydroelectric dams. Numerous gravel and sand deposits have been located along the river and are a good source of road-making material and concrete aggregate. Clay from river bank alluvium, suitable for making pottery and bricks, occurs in large quantities in many parts of the lower Rajang. Coal outcrops are found in the Merit–Pila area, just north of Kapit.

## River transport

The Rajang River system has been the main route or communication system for the different ethnic groups that live along its course. Although a number of new logging roads have been constructed in the past few years, the river system remains the main means of communication and a major waterway for the transportation of timber and mineral resources, such as coal and gravel to the towns of Sibu and Sarikei. Although river travel is slow, land and air transport remain too expensive and unreliable for most people in the interior. Small ships ply up to Sibu town, situated about 150 kilometres from the sea, and express boats can reach the interior town of Belaga. Motorized longboats become the prime means of transportation further upriver.

Transport in the wider reaches of the lower Rajang is by river express.

A Shell station near Kapit where commercial boats wait to refuel.

A family set off for home from Kapit in their longboat having sold their produce at the market there and stocked up on supplies.

47

# Lakes and reservoirs

*Malaysia's inland water bodies include natural lakes, which are generally rich in nutrients and aquatic life, and are often shallow. They are associated with picturesque habitats and have been developed as tourist sites. Man-made reservoirs and lakes started to be created in pre-colonial times, and are more numerous. Reservoir water is used for domestic and industrial consumption and the generation of hydroelectric power.*

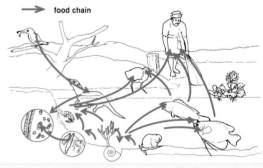

Tasik Temengor is a man-made lake, formed when part of the Perak River was dammed. The bare upper branches emerging from the lake indicate that the water level was once much lower and that a forest occupied the site.

## Lake zones

Large lakes in Malaysia generally have three basic life zones. Smaller lakes typically lack the profundal zone.

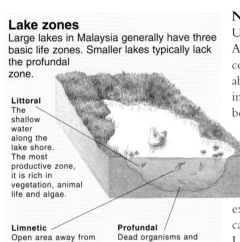

**Littoral**
The shallow water along the lake shore. The most productive zone, it is rich in vegetation, animal life and algae.

**Limnetic**
Open area away from the shore that extends down as far as sunlight penetrates. Its main organisms are microscopic plankton.

**Profundal**
Dead organisms and sediments get deposited here. As it receives minimal light, the habitat tends to be mineral rich and anaerobic (lacking oxygen).

## Natural lakes

Unlike Scandinavia or North America, Malaysia is not a lakeland country. The landscape does not abound with naturally occurring inland water bodies, primarily because the geological history of the country has never been associated with glacial and volcanic activities. Natural lakes develop through many processes, but the main prerequisite for their existence is the ability of a land cavity to collect and retain water. Lakes are generally short-lived phenomena, since they may evaporate or drain and their water level fluctuates for both geological and climatic reasons. Lakes also

follow a natural path, whereby, in time, they silt up, are colonized by plants and eventually dry up.

Peninsular Malaysia has no areas of internal drainage. The only sizable natural lakes, Tasik Bera (6150 hectares), Malaysia's only Ramsar site or 'Wetland of International Importance' (see 'Lowlands and wetlands') and Tasik Chini (less than 1000 hectares), both lie over 50 kilometres from the mouth of the Pahang River. Tasik Loagan Benut (c. 900 hectares), important economically, culturally and for its biodiversity, is Sarawak's largest natural lake. Most of the natural lakes are formed as swamps become inundated with water. Lakes that form this

## The food web in a lake ecosystem

A typical Malaysian lake is home to a rich ecosystem of plants and animals. It is important that such an environment is protected and pollutants kept away, so that the natural balance is maintained. Man, animals, birds, plants and lower life forms are dependent on each other for survival and are linked together by an intricate food chain. The species depicted are all commonly found in Malaysia's freshwater lakes and ponds.

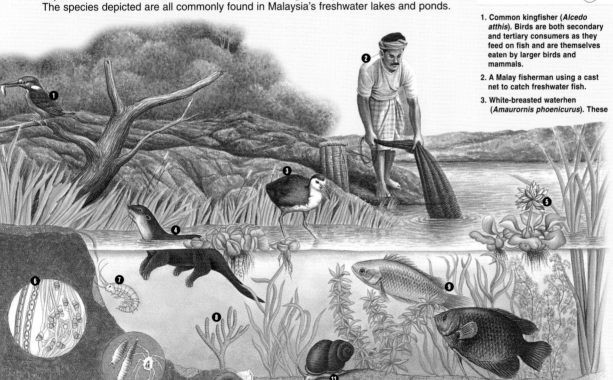

1. **Common kingfisher (*Alcedo atthis*).** Birds are both secondary and tertiary consumers as they feed on fish and are themselves eaten by larger birds and mammals.

2. **A Malay fisherman** using a cast net to catch freshwater fish.

3. **White-breasted waterhen (*Amaurornis phoenicurus*).** These waders are found in agricultural estates, paddy fields, swamps and mining pools.

4. **Oriental small-clawed otter (*Amblonyx cinerea*).** Mammals and rodents live in river banks and prey on fish and birds, as well as some plants.

5. **Freshwater plants** include reeds, fanwort (*Hydrilla*), water hyacinths and floating moss.

6. **Bacteria and fungi** 'feed' on nutrients released from plants and meiofauna, and are decomposers rather than consumers.

7. **Freshwater prawn (*Macrobrachium*).** These secondary consumers are eaten by fish and other animals. They occur in natural waters and are also farmed.

8. **The simplest of green plants,** green algae, are nourishment for fish and molluscs.

9. **Climbing perch (*Anabas testudineus*) (top),** and giant gourami (*Osphronemus goramy*). Fish are at the centre of the food chain. They feed on arthropods, other fish and plants in the water, and are food for man, mammals and birds.

10. **Tiny grubs and worms** make up the meiofauna, or lower animal life, in the lake.

11. **Ramshorn snail (*Indoplanorbis exustus*).** Molluscs are found amid vegetation on the lake bed.

way evolve their own natural ecosystem that provides a habitat for a rich diversity of biological life. The lakes attract migrant species of birds in search of temporary sanctuary during their lengthy flights. Small, shallow lakes are a temporary feature of granite landscapes, especially during periods of heavy northeast monsoon rains, when debris from hillslides may restrict, or dam, a river's course. This is particularly so in the east of the Peninsula, where they are more frequent. Lakes can be both freshwater and saline (salt) habitats. The latter often exist, again as temporary formations, as shallow lagoons when sandbanks restrict a river's journey to the sea. Oxbow lakes form in the flood plains of major rivers, such as the Kinabatangan River, Sabah.

## Reservoirs: Man-made lakes

As Malaysia has few natural reserves of inland water to call upon for water supply, artificial lakes, or reservoirs, have been created. The damming of rivers for water resource development and hydropower generation have led to the formation of a number of man-made lakes. These include the lakes associated with Tasik Temengor and Tasik Chenderoh, both in Perak, and Tasik Kenyir in Terengganu. The latter is Malaysia's largest man-made lake. Tasik Temengor was formed as the upstream areas of the Perak River were dammed, and Tasik Chenderoh created as part of the river in its middle course was similarly channelled. Other man-made reservoirs include the Pedu and Muda reservoirs, which were specifically constructed to provide irrigation to the paddy areas of Kedah. A characteristic of man-made lakes is the many dead trees, whose denuded tops poke out of the water. These have, literally, been drowned as an area is submerged during the damming process.

In addition to man's deliberate intervention, lakes can be formed by indirect human action. Abandoned tin mines in Perak and Selangor provide deep pits in which rain and flood waters collect. Locally called *tasik lombong*, these are very deep and without draining outlets, unlike man-made reservoirs, which are drained by their original source rivers. Like many of the natural lakes, they have been developed for their tourist potential. They also provide an important flood water storage capacity in urban areas.

## Lake destruction

Malaysia's lakes, like the country's rivers and seas, are under threat from both natural and human-induced events. Pollution, whether natural or man-made, may lead to the destruction of individual organisms and thus threaten the complete ecosystem. Other detrimental activities include overfishing and overdevelopment of certain sites. Without active management all natural lakes risk being destroyed. As lakes silt up they are colonized by swamp species and will eventually evolve as dry land forests.

### Tasik Chini and the sunken city

Malaysia's second largest natural lake, Tasik Chini ('Chinese Lake'), nestles in Pahang's tropical landscape. The lake is a major tourist attraction, not least because of the mythical tales that have grown up around its still waters, which from July to January blossom with pink and white lotus flowers. A magical dragon, with fiery red eyes, is said to inhabit its depths. He guards an ancient city of gold which, according to a legend of the Orang Asli, once graced an island in the centre of the lake. The ancient city was home to a beautiful princess, who had fled there to escape marrying the man chosen for her by her father, and now lies submerged. The Orang Asli who live on the lake shores and fish in its waters, point to pottery fragments as evidence of the city's existence.

Lakes are 'closed' ecosystems with complex food webs and a delicate balance (see box on the previous page). Such closed systems are prone to eutrophication, particularly small and shallow lakes. Eutrophication occurs when nutrients in a water body increase. This is usually the result of man's activities, such as agriculture and development, in adjacent areas, whereby nutrients (for example, chemical fertilizers, organic matter and waste), are flushed into the lake. High nutrient content leads to excessive growth of plants such as algae or water hyacinth, which can grow so dense that they prevent light penetration and also absorb most of the oxygen that other aquatic life needs to survive. When the plants die, they decompose and fall to the bottom of the lake. Thus eutrophic lakes are characterized by high nutrients, high plant biomass, low oxygen levels and shallow depths. Most lakes in Malaysia near to human settlements show some signs of eutrophication.

Deep lakes, such as Pergau Dam and Tasik Kenyir are rich in freshwater fish. Most fishing activities are, by netting or hook and line, from boats. Rowing boats, or more commonly small motorized craft, are regular sights on the lakes as fishing by tourists and sport enthusiasts vies with subsistence fishing by locals. In some of the man-made lakes, floating cage aquaculture also takes place. If, however, commercial fishing is not restricted the number of fish may dwindle considerably. From the estimated stocks of 300 tonnes in Tasik Kenyir, 68 tonnes are annually fished. Stipulation of a minimum size of fish allowed to be caught, a quota system, and the restocking of mature fish are possible remedies to the problems.

### Economic use of lakes

Disused pools in old mining sites are often exploited for new economic ends, notably for tourism and farming.

*FROM THE TOP*: At the centre of the Mines Resort near Kuala Lumpur is a huge man-made lake that covers 150 acres. A duck farm in a former mining lake at Chemor. Damming creates reservoirs, such as the Semenyih Dam, which are used for hydroelectric and other industrial purposes.

# Tropical rainforest

*The Malaysian rainforests are some of the oldest forests in the world and the huge diversity of vegetation, flora and fauna that they boast has evolved over millions of years. Many of the wonders of the different forest types are exclusive to Malaysia and are of global importance. The plants, animals, soils and water that interact with each other, and which are mutually dependent for continued survival, represent one of the most complex ecosystems in existence.*

### Distribution of forest vegetation

Peninsular Malaysia

**KUALA LUMPUR**

Strait of Melaka

South China Sea

*Kota Kinabalu*

**Sabah**

*Sarawak*

*Kuching*

■ Forests of peatswamps, freshwater swamps and mangroves
☐ Lowland tropical rainforest including limestone vegetation
■ Montane tropical rainforest

## Evolution of the rainforest

Almost 200 million years ago, when dinosaurs still inhabited the earth and the land was enjoying a warm, moist climate, tropical rainforests started to evolve. Forests covered much of the land, which was all part of the Pangea supercontinent. Fossil evidence reveals that the forest's pioneer plants were non-flowering conifers and fern-like species. Over the ensuing 100 million years, flowering plants developed and became more robust, growing into

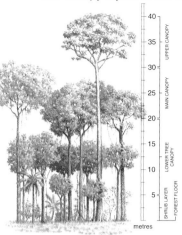

## Why forests are important: The carbon cycle

The carbon cycle illustrates how plants and animals of the rainforest rely on each other for survival. But rainforests are productive environments only if they remain intact. CO₂ is converted to organic matter via photosynthesis. In turn, it is released by living organisms into the atmosphere through respiration.

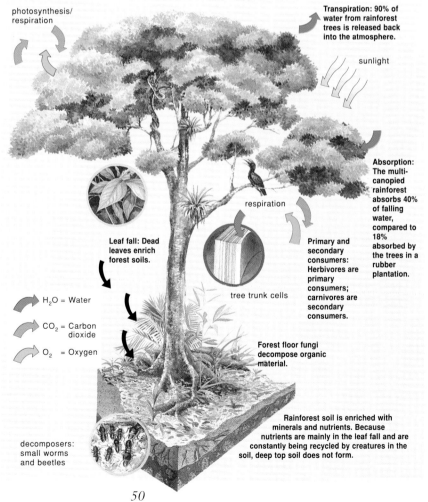

photosynthesis/respiration

Transpiration: 90% of water from rainforest trees is released back into the atmosphere.

sunlight

respiration

Absorption: The multi-canopied rainforest absorbs 40% of falling water, compared to 18% absorbed by the trees in a rubber plantation.

Leaf fall: Dead leaves enrich forest soils.

tree trunk cells

Primary and secondary consumers: Herbivores are primary consumers; carnivores are secondary consumers.

H₂O = Water

CO₂ = Carbon dioxide

O₂ = Oxygen

Forest floor fungi decompose organic material.

Rainforest soil is enriched with minerals and nutrients. Because nutrients are mainly in the leaf fall and are constantly being recycled by creatures in the soil, deep top soil does not form.

decomposers: small worms and beetles

the tree canopies we see in the Malaysian forests today. As the flowers were evolving, Pangea was breaking up and the 'new' continents assuming, over time, their present positions.

Rainforest thrives in Malaysia because of the consistently warm, moist climate. Being located in the tropics and close to the equator, Malaysia receives more sunlight than most other parts of the world. Sun is fundamental to the survival of living things, and in the depths of the rainforest competition for the sun's nurturing rays is stiff. It is this striving for light that dictates the structure of the rainforest and the plants and animals that inhabit its various strata or canopies. The forest floor is the darkest, coolest and dampest part of the forest because sunlight has been progressively filtered out by higher layers, which in turn release moisture to the lower reaches.

## A dynamic and complex ecosystem

The rainforest is Malaysia's richest natural resource. It fulfils many needs and not only enriches, but also sustains the lives of animals, plants and humans. In Malaysia, more than 19 million hectares are under natural forest cover, and at the Rio Earth Summit, in June 1992, Malaysia pledged to maintain half of its land as permanent forest. The forests are largely self-sustaining, requiring only external supplies of water and sunlight. The forests are, in effect, large recycling centres, which support a wealth of mutually dependent organisms (see carbon cycle diagram).

Forests help maintain climatic conditions and are a critical part of the water cycle. Trees not only absorb carbon dioxide and release oxygen so that life forms can breathe, but also filter dust particles and pollutants. In addition, they provide shelter from the harmful effects of the sun's rays and from heavy rains, enrich the soil and prevent erosion, and act as natural reservoirs of water. Forests provide shelter and food for a remarkable diversity of animals and plants and are the source of timber and other forest products, such as paper, medicines, spices, game and rattan. Malaysia's forests thus fulfil a combination of important functions: ecological, biodiverse, economic, scientific and recreational.

# Major rainforest types in Malaysia

## Lowland forests

### Freshwater and mangrove swamps
Land covered by freshwater swamp forest is regularly inundated with mineral-rich fresh water of a fairly high pH, and the water level fluctuates allowing periodic drying of the soil surface. In the Peninsula, they occur in southeast Johor and Pahang, but much of the forest has been lost to development. Freshwater swamp forest is now the rarest forest type in Malaysia. In sheltered coastal areas, stilt-rooted mangrove trees, specially adapted to tidal influence and saline waters, form an even, continuous canopy (shown above).

### Peatswamps
Lowland peatswamp forests were once extensive on both coasts of Peninsular Malaysia and in Sarawak, with highland peat forest, or *kerangas*, prevailing in Sarawak's Kelabit Highlands (above). The upper tree canopy is consistent at 30 metres. In the state of Johor, much of this forest has been cleared to make way for oil palm and pineapple plantations.

### Beach forests
Along Malaysia's lengthy coast, where soils are sandy and there is no mangrove, beach vegetation prevails, such as at Pulau Rumbia, Perak. Typified by thick, mat-like vegetation and thorny grasses, the forest (including casuarina, cashewnut and *simpoh* trees) helps control erosion. Vegetation can stretch 1 kilometre inland, merging well with coconut plantations.

### Lowland dipterocarp
This is the most extensive forest type and is found below 300 metres altitude. Dipterocarp trees predominate. There is a considerable variation of species composition and above ground biomass from area to area, and it is here that the most important commercial timber species are found.

## Montane forests

### Upper montane ericaeous
On Malaysia's few peaks that tower over 1700 metres, trees of the Ericaceae family, such as *Rhododendron* and *Vaccinium*, grow. Branches are gnarled and covered with mosses, liverworts, lichens and other epiphytes, and the forest appears perpetually damp because of the blanket of cloud and mist that envelops it.

### Montane
Above 1220 metres, a two-tiered canopy exists and trees seldom exceed 20 metres in height. Species of the Fagaceae and Lauraceae families predominate in oak–laurel forests, such as on Mount Kinabalu, above.

## Hill forests

### Limestone hills
Craggy limestone hills and outcrops form a striking part of the landscape in many parts of Malaysia—Pulau Langkawi, central Perak, south Kelantan, Selangor, eastern Sabah and around Gunung Mulu National Park in Sarawak.

### Hill dipterocarp
Similar to those of the lowland, but distinguished by *seraya* (*Shorea curtisii*) trees, lower dipterocarp forests grow at altitudes of 300–750 metres. Upper dipterocarp forests rise to 1200 metres and become the target for logging activities once lowland forests have been depleted. A forest at Ulu Langat in Selangor is shown.

## Secondary forests
Where the natural forests have either been logged or cleared during shifting cultivation, secondary forests evolve. In terms of structure, productivity and composition, the secondary differs from the primary forest. Most valuable species of the initial forest have been felled, leaving seedlings to mature into the new forest. Pioneer secondary species, such as *Macaranga*, *Mallotus* get established. Over a long time, secondary forests develop into areas as mature as the original, although with a new composition. Below, a compacted log landing area is ploughed to make way for new dipterocarp seedlings.

# Lowlands and wetlands

*The lowlands of Malaysia constitute vast areas of alluvial and coastal plains that slope very gently down to the coasts. They spread across 3.3 million hectares, or 10 per cent of Malaysia's total land area, and are diverse in character. Lowland flood plains and coastal plains are rich in natural resources, with important habitats like mangroves, peatswamp forests and intertidal mud flats providing a refuge for wildlife.*

A wetland inhabitant uses *nipah* palm leaves to weave *atap* thatch.

## Lowlands

Lowlands in Malaysia are formed mainly by river and coastal processes. The major flood plains in the country, for example, the Kemubu Plain in Kelantan and the Muda Plain in Kedah, are alluvial plains formed by the periodic flooding of the Kelantan and Muda rivers. The coastal plains of Terengganu, Perak and Selangor, on the other hand, are mainly influenced by the processes of marine deposition. These coastal plains consist mainly of marine clay, silts and sands. Two of the most extensive lowlands

of this kind are the deltas of the Kelantan and the Pahang Rompin river systems.

Because the lowlands of Malaysia are rich in natural resources, they attract settlements and have been progressively converted for agricultural, industrial and infrastructural development. However, efforts are being made to preserve lowland habitats, such as wetlands, because they provide many of the resources needed by man, and because they are home to an enormous diversity of wildlife.

## Wetlands

A wetland is literally a place where there is water. In Malaysia, this primarily includes rivers and streams, lakes and ponds, or marshes and swamps. There are over 100 river systems in Malaysia. The largest river is the Rajang in Sarawak, which has a catchment area of 51 000 square kilometres. In the Peninsula, the catchment area for the Pahang River is about half this size. Wetlands also include other natural habitats, such as mangrove forests, freshwater and peatswamp forests, beaches and intertidal mud flats, and even coral reefs and inshore waters. Man-made habitats such as paddy fields, canals and reservoirs can also be classified as wetlands.

Malaysia has a very rich natural heritage in the form of its wetlands, and its people have long been associated with such areas, either directly or indirectly. The loss of wetlands through destruction is a threat to this association. The protection of these wetlands is more than a national concern; their loss would deprive the world

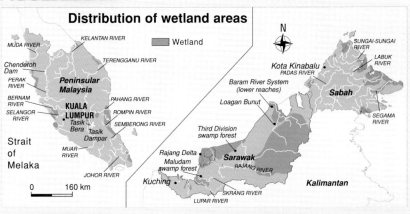

Distribution of wetland areas

MUDA RIVER
KELANTAN RIVER
TERENGGANU RIVER
Chenderoh Dam
PERAK RIVER
Peninsular Malaysia
BERNAM RIVER
SELANGOR RIVER
KUALA LUMPUR
PAHANG RIVER
ROMPIN RIVER
Tasik Bera
SEMBERONG RIVER
Tasik Dampar
Strait of Melaka
MUAR RIVER
JOHOR RIVER

Wetland
N
Kota Kinabalu
PADAS RIVER
SUNGAI-SUNGAI RIVER
LABUK RIVER
Baram River System (lower reaches)
Sabah
Loagan Bunut
SEGAMA RIVER
Third Division swamp forest
Rajang Delta
Maludam swamp forest
Sarawak
RAJANG RIVER
Kuching
SKRANG RIVER
Kalimantan
LUPAR RIVER
0   160 km

## Wetlands defined

The (Ramsar) Convention on Wetlands of International Importance, named after the town in Iran where it was launched in 1971, is the world's oldest environmental treaty. In 1995, Malaysia became the 84th signatory to the Convention and nominated Tasik Bera in Pahang as its first 'Wetland of International Importance' (Ramsar sites).

There are nearly 900 Ramsar sites worldwide, covering more than a total of 670 000 square kilometres. Having signed the Ramsar Convention, Malaysia, like the other 105 member countries, is obliged to promote the wise use and conservation of its wetlands. The Convention defines wetlands as 'Areas of marsh, fen, peatland or water, whether natural or artificial, permanent or temporary, with water that is static, flowing, fresh, brackish or salt, including areas of marine water, the depth of which at low tide does not exceed six metres.'

Malaysia's peatswamp forests are fast disappearing. The largest area of peatswamp forest in the Peninsula, the Southeast Pahang Peatswamp Forest, is also the largest remaining area of peatswamp forest on mainland Asia. Tasik Bera in Pahang, Malaysia's largest natural lake, is a freshwater habitat and swamp forest that has been designated Malaysia's first wetland area of international importance under the Ramsar Convention. The lake and surrounding forest are an outlet for the flood waters of the Pahang River.

## Some wetland varieties

1. Mangrove swamps not only provide protection from coastal storms and erosion, but also yield a multitude of products such as timber, medicines, fish and shellfish. Malaysia is internationally recognized as the global centre for mangrove diversity with over 60 species recorded (this compares with 7–12 in tropical Africa and the Americas).

2. Disused mining pools, that litter the landscape of Selangor and Perak, are significant man-made wetlands. Many have become important wildlife habitats and green spaces on the edges of cities and towns. These pools also serve as reservoirs, which collect flood water in urban areas.

3. Freshwater wetlands, and the wild varieties of rice they support, are maintained as an important gene pool to assist in the development of new fast-growing or pest-resistant varieties. Most of the paddy fields in Malaysia were historically freshwater swamps that have been converted to agricultural lands and are now irrigated. In the Peninsula, most of the rice-growing areas are in the northern states of Perlis, Kedah and Perak with small areas in Selangor.

of some of its richest and most diverse ecosystems. Although only about 6 per cent of the earth's total surface is covered by wetlands, they provide habitats for an estimated 20 per cent of known species.

## The benefits of wetlands

The true worth of wetland habitats is not measurable in ringgit, although wetlands provide many local inhabitants with their livelihood. *Atap* thatch, woven mats and baskets are made from the *nipah* palm that grows extensively in peatswamp and mangrove forests. The sap of the palm is used to produce vinegar, and other indigenous plants are harnessed for medicinal and culinary use. Fishing, the making of charcoal and tannin, and other forest activities are also significant socioeconomic benefits. Even Malaysia's staple food crop, paddy, is a wetland species.

In many wetland areas, water transport is both the most efficient and the most environmentally friendly means of communication. Water is used to transport people and to move goods and cargoes of agricultural and wetland products.

The vegetation, size and water depth of some wetlands—swamps, marshes and flood plains—help slow the flow of water. This means that sediment in water is deposited and toxic elements removed as it enters such wetland areas. In addition, the wetlands assist in flood control by absorbing and storing and then releasing flood water in a controlled way. The tangled webs of mangrove tree roots also help reduce coastal erosion by providing a physical barrier against incoming sea and wind.

## Typical Malaysian wetland types

Malaysia is richly endowed with wetland areas. The diverse types range from swamp forests to lakes and rivers.

1. Man-made lakes, such as reservoirs, are dammed for hydroelectric power, for example, the Temengor Dam reservoir.

2. Highland rivers, including mountain streams and waterfalls occur at the river headwaters.

3. Oxbow lakes, crescent-shaped shallow lakes occupying the abandoned channel of a meandering stream, are common in vast flood plains, like the Kinabatangan River in Sabah.

4. Lowland rivers, such as the Pahang River, meander through the coastal flood plain.

5. Peatswamp forests grow on organically rich, waterlogged soils on the flood plain. In the Peninsula, the largest peatswamp forest is in southeast Pahang.

6. Estuaries, or river mouths, such as Port Klang and Klang Islands at the mouth of the Klang River, are where fresh water and salt water mix.

7. Mangrove forests are typically found along the sheltered west coast of Peninsular Malaysia. The trees are adapted to grow in salt water, and have developed characteristic aerial and stilt roots to survive.

8. Intertidal mud flats, located near the river estuary, are covered at high tide and exposed at low tide.

9. Shallow inshore waters fringe mud flats and coral reefs, where the water depth at low tide is less than 6 metres.

10. Corals, such as those at Pulau Tioman, are created by tiny reef-building organisms and nourished by the nutrients from mangroves.

## The mangrove and coral link

Mangrove leaves fall into the mud and gradually decompose or are eaten by worms, crabs and some fish. In time, their nutrients are released into the water and carried by offshore currents to supply food for coral polyps.

In some cases, the link is more direct: fish that make the coral reefs their home may migrate with the daily tidal cycle into the mangroves to feed. Upon return to their coral habitats they release the mangrove nutrients to the polyps in their faeces.

Some fish migrate into the mangroves to breed. The complex tangle of roots provides a safe nursery for the young fish away from predators. When large enough, the fish make their way back to the coral reefs to feed and mate.

A web of tangled mangrove tree roots.

# Peatswamp forests of Sarawak

*Sarawak is the largest state in Malaysia and has, proportionally, the largest area of wetlands. Swamp forests constitute the largest wetland habitat in the country and the vast majority of these are peatswamp forests. Peatswamps cover more than 2 million hectares, of which about 80 per cent, or 1.2 million hectares, are in Sarawak. These swamps are vitally important because of the endemic plant species and the endangered animals they support, and they are increasingly being regarded as significant freshwater habitats which need protecting.*

## Decline of peatswamp forests in Sarawak

- 1974: 1.6 mill. ha
- 1995/6: 1.2 mill. ha

Peatswamp tree species such as ramin (*Gonystylus bancana*), bintangor (*Calophyllum ferrugineum*), jelutong (*Dyera costulata*), meranti buaya (*Shorea uliginosa*) and *alan* (*Shorea albida*) are all valuable sources of commercial timber.

Due to the high porosity of the soils, peatswamp forests have been converted to paddy fields. However, only in their natural state do the peatswamps act like sponges to absorb excess rain and flood waters, releasing water slowly in the dry season to ensure a continuous supply for local communities.

The 'king of fruits', the durian, was originally cultured from its wild species (*Durio carinatus*), which is found in peatswamp forests.

## What is a peatswamp?

Peatswamp forests occur on low-lying areas where there is permanent waterlogging of the soil, leading to anaerobic conditions. The peat is formed by an accumulation of decaying plant matter—twigs and leaves—in these naturally low oxygen and highly acidic areas. The peat can vary in depth from 1 to over 20 metres. The partially decaying plant material releases tannin and gives the peat water its characteristic tea colour, which has earned it the name 'blackwater swamp'. Peatswamps develop in small river valleys but are most extensive as coastal basins which form around flat estuarine plains and river deltas. The environment of a peatswamp is harsh, with a highly acidic substrate, poor in minerals and subject to periods of varying water levels.

Ten per cent of Sarawak's land is peat forest which has evolved only over the last 4,000 years. In places it is up to 10 metres thick and is extensive on the coastal plains. Although the peat soils are poor in nutrients, they support timber trees such as *alan* (*Shorea albida*) and a wide range of fruit tree species.

## Protecting the forests

Peatswamp forests are an important source of commercial timber. The alan is not only economically significant, but alan forests are also highly aesthetically pleasing and are of scientific significance. The rapid rate of exploitation of alan forests in Sarawak calls for urgent conservation measures to ensure their continued presence in the state. Peatswamp forests were among the first areas to be logged in Sarawak. Mechanical logging started in 1947, and by 1979 almost all peatswamp forests had been licensed for timber extraction. More recently, large areas of forest have been converted to oil palm cultivation and this is set to continue into the 21st century. In a move to protect its remaining areas of peatswamps, the Sarawak Forest Department has initiated a conservation programme which combines protection of the unique wildlife with maintenance of the livelihoods and other needs of the local people in a sustainable manner. The forests function as a water supply, owing to the sponge-like absorbency of their peat soil.

## The peatswamp ecosystem

Sarawak's peatswamps support some of the last remaining viable populations of Malaysia's most threatened species.

### FLORA
1. Wild durian fruit (*Durio carinatus*) on the forest floor
2. Nibong palm (*Oncosperma tigillarium*)
3. Sealing wax palm (*Cyrtostachys lakka*), popular as an ornamental plant
4. Rasau palm (*Pandanus helicopus*)
5. *Alan bunga* (*Shorea albida*), an important timber species endemic to Sarawak's peat forests
6. Red creeping figs (*Ficus* spp.)
7. Fan palm (*Licuala* spp.)
8. Typical stilt roots of a peatswamp tree (*Garcinia bancana*)

### FAUNA
9. Wrinkled hornbill (*Rhyticeros corrugatus*), sacred bird of the Iban
10. Grey-headed fish eagle (*Ichthyophaga ichthyaetus*)
11. Lesser adjutant stork (*Leptoptilos javanicus*)
12. Proboscis monkey (*Nasalis larvatus*), endemic to Borneo
13. Red form of banded leaf monkey (*Presbytis melalophos cruciger*), one of the world's most endangered primates, found only in Sarawak's Maludam swamp forest
14. Water monitor lizard (*Varanus salvator*)
15. Storm's stork (*Ciconia stormi*)
16. Hairy-nosed otter (*Lutra sumatrana*)

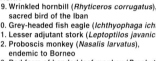

17. Forest gecko (*Gekko stentor*), which lives in tree holes
18. Pikehead fish (*Luciocephalus pulcher*)
19. Dragon fish (*Scleropages formosus*), wild form of the famous *arowana*, found in quiet backwaters of Sarawak's freshwater and peatswamp forests
20. Kissing gouramy (*Helostoma temminckii*)
21. Shoal of *Rasbora* spp. fish (not endangered)
22. False gharial (*Tomistoma schlegelii*), fish-eating crocodile that breeds in the swamps along Sungai Ensengai and is restricted to peatswamps in Southeast Asia

# Mangroves

*Mangroves are one of the major wetland types in Malaysia. Over half the total mangrove forests are located in eastern Sabah. As an ecosystem, the mangrove forest is dynamic and relatively fragile, and thus very sensitive to changes brought about by both natural phenomena, such as strong winds, localized storms and seasonal tidal surges, and human intervention. For this reason, preservation of the country's mangroves has become a national concern.*

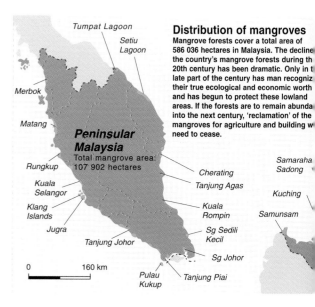

### Distribution of mangroves

Mangrove forests cover a total area of 586 036 hectares in Malaysia. The decline the country's mangrove forests during th 20th century has been dramatic. Only in t late part of the century has man recogniz their true ecological and economic worth and has begun to protect these lowland areas. If the forests are to remain abunda into the next century, 'reclamation' of the mangroves for agriculture and building w need to cease.

Tumpat Lagoon
Setiu Lagoon
Merbok
Matang
**Peninsular Malaysia**
Total mangrove area: 107 902 hectares
Rungkup
Kuala Selangor
Klang Islands
Jugra
Tanjung Johor
Cherating
Tanjung Agas
Kuala Rompin
Sg Sedili Kecil
Sg Johor
Pulau Kukup
Tanjung Piai
Samaraha Sadong
Kuching
Samunsam
0    160 km

Mangrove forests are characterized by tangled webs of stilt-like roots.

## Environmental benefits of mangroves

Mangroves provide shelter from the wind.

Cutting down mangroves means exposure to storms.

Mangroves protect the shoreline.

Felled mangroves can lead to flooding and coastal erosion.

Source: After Davies and Calridge (eds.) (1993), Wetlands International

## A mangrove habitat

Ever since he has been associated with the open seas, through coastal navigation and fishing, man has recognized the importance of mangroves. As a natural belt of more or less homogeneous vegetation, mangroves act as a buffer against storms and erosion for the many coastal villages that line Malaysia's shores. The impact of human activity is clearly felt in the reduction of mangrove areas, which have been steadily and systematically cleared for agriculture, and especially aquaculture and human settlement, since the mid-20th century.

The substrate in the mangrove forest is usually a firm to soft mud. It can also be richly organic, with peat made up largely of accumulated underground mangrove root systems. Muddy substrates release a pungent hydrogen sulphide smell that indicates the anaerobic, or oxygen-free, nature of the waterlogged soil in the mangrove forest. Such conditions provide ideal breeding grounds for mosquitoes. Mangroves have historically been considered 'wastelands', and thus reclaimed for development for urban, industrial and agricultural purposes.

## Flora and fauna

Malaysia is the global centre for mangrove diversity with over 60 tree species recorded. This is an extremely rich collection when compared to tropical Africa and the Americas where only 7–12 species grow. Mangroves are extremely rich in invertebrate animals such as molluscs,

The intertidal mud flats along the coast serve as 'refuelling' sites for migratory shore birds (waders) during the months of October to April. Pulau Bruit in the Rajang Delta is the most important site in Malaysia for such birds, and has been known to support as many as 50,000–80,000 during a single migration season.

crustaceans, worms, crabs, snails and oysters, which live in water as well as in the intertidal zones and serve as a food base for aquatic life as well as for humans. In the otherwise monotonous canopy, many birds are also found. In Kuala Gula, Perak, for example, the mangroves have long been stopover sites for migratory birds from the northern hemisphere. For this reason, the area has been designated a bird sanctuary, managed by the Department of Wildlife and National Parks of Peninsular Malaysia. In the past, many larger

Malaysia's mangroves are important stopover sites for some migrating bird species. Bar-tailed godwits (*Limosa lapponica*), transequatorial migrant shore birds, are shown flying along the East Asian flyway.

animals—snakes, crocodiles, wild pigs, monkeys, even tigers—were found in the mangroves, but, with the advent of human intervention, the number and abundance have been considerably reduced.

## Fisheries

Mangroves supply all kinds of nutrients to marine communities through water movements. They also provide a habitat for some commercially important species, such as prawns and cockles, and support oysters and shellfish that grow in mud.

Currently, mangroves are under constant threat through conversion to other land use, especially agriculture and aquaculture. Mangroves are exploited for forestry, fisheries and agriculture—uses which may be in conflict with each other since the

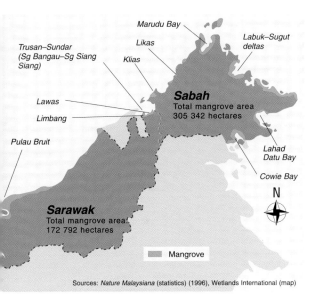

Marudu Bay

Likas

Labuk–Sugut deltas

Trusan–Sundar (Sg Bangau–Sg Siang Siang)

Klias

Lawas

**Sabah**
Total mangrove area
305 342 hectares

Limbang

Pulau Bruit

Lahad Datu Bay

Cowie Bay

N

**Sarawak**
Total mangrove area
172 792 hectares

Mangrove

Sources: *Nature Malaysiana* (statistics) (1996), Wetlands International (map)

## Use and exploitation

Mangroves constitute a minor part of Malaysia's forest resources since they occupy a limited percentage of the total land area, but they provide a diverse number of products. They are the building blocks upon which Malaysia's coastal villages are founded, providing logs and timber for the construction of houses, boats, fishing poles, fish traps and scaffolding. Tannin from the sap of mangrove trees is traditionally used to waterproof fishing nets.

Unsawn poles are the most extracted products. In 1 hectare of productive mangrove forest, a total of 550 poles may be produced. Fuel woods, tannins and dyes, local traditional medicines and poisonous plants are also obtained. Only the Matang Mangrove Forest Reserve in Perak and some mangroves in the Sandakan area still provide substantial timber for charcoal production. The species used are *Rhizophora mucronata*, *R. apiculata* and *Bruguiera gymnorhiza*. About 500 tonnes of fresh wood produce about 100 tonnes of charcoal, to satisfy local consumption only. As a resource, mangroves, if properly managed on a renewable basis, could give a healthy dividend.

Casting a fishing net in the Ibaj River in Terengganu.

Feeding mangrove wood into a charcoal kiln. Charcoal is used as fuel by communities throughout Malaysia.

Mangrove poles piled ready for use in housing construction.

policy that is best for one may be detrimental to another. Forestry may advocate use that degrades the resource, while the agricultural sector would favour conversion and replacement by more valuable resources such as oil palm. In the states of Selangor, Perak, Johor, Sarawak and Sabah, the demand for ponds to cultivate prawns, eels, fish and cockles has taken a heavy toll on the existing mangrove areas.

This sudden shift in land use is due to the great economic returns brought about by aquaculture products. The dire consequences are often irreversible, resulting in the loss of income for the local fishermen, increased coastal flooding and erosion, siltation of rivers and reduced tourism potential. The challenge now lies in the sustained management of mangrove forest to optimize the potential yield of forest products while effectively sustaining the potential values when mangroves are retained in their natural state.

This is well practised in Matang, Perak, where sustainable yield management is employed. Annually, specific tracts of mangroves are harvested to supply cut timber for the charcoal operations in the area. Each tract is harvested only once every 20 years. The Matang Mangrove Forest Reserve has been sustainably managed for timber production since 1902 and supports a thriving fishing industry. It has been hailed as one of the best managed mangrove forests in the world.

### Protecting a unique resource

The preservation and utilization of mangrove forests directly or indirectly for agriculture, fisheries and forestry at both the local and

A woman amasses clams to sell at market. Mangroves and their associated mud flats serve as important breeding, feeding and nursery grounds for commercially valuable fish and prawn species.

industrial levels, are seen as competing influences for the same limited and often sensitive resources. Though mangroves may be simple ecological communities in terms of species diversity, they are exceedingly complex ecosystems to evaluate scientifically. To date, there is a lack of biological information about how to achieve sustainable use of mangrove forests. The best way to preserve the forests is to limit their destruction. Protected mangroves can also be exploited economically as ecotourist sites, which, if appropriately managed, can mean little disruption to the forests and greater public environmental awareness. Such development, like that at Kisap on Langkawi and in the Kuala Selangor Nature Park, if exploited properly, can be compatible with the long-term use of mangroves.

The Malaysian Forestry Department has for a very long time recognized the vital role mangroves play in the welfare of local communities and in the national economy as a whole. Mangroves are now considered vital in coastal wildlife management and vegetation conservation plans.

The skin of the *tumu/berus* (*Bruguiera*) fruit can be applied to stop bleeding, while the juice is used to treat eye conditions.

### The mangrove medicine chest

In Malaysia, cures for illnesses have traditionally been obtained from the roots, leaves and flowers of mangrove species.

Oil extracted from *nyireh* (*Xylocarpus* sp.) fruit can be used as a mosquito repellent, and to treat insect bites and dysentery.

A mouth gargle made from *bakau minyak* (*Rhizophora* sp.) bark is used to soothe sore throats and stomatitis.

Extracts of *tengar* (*Ceriops* sp.) bark reduce malarial fevers.

Smoke from burning *buta buta* (*Excoecaria* sp.) bark is reputed to assist in healing leprosy.

The fruit of the *pong-pong* (*Cerbera* sp.), a mangrove tree commonly planted on Kuala Lumpur's verges, is used as a rat poison. The extracted oil acts as a purgative, provides relief from rheumatic pain, and is said to prevent toothache.

# Shorelines and coasts

*Malaysia's coastline stretches a lengthy 4800 kilometres. The shoreline, wide open to the uncontrollable forces of nature, has been worn and weathered to produce some of Malaysia's most varied and rapidly changing landforms. Waves, tides and winds from the sea, coupled with sediments brought down to the coast by inland rivers, create sandy and pebbly beaches, mud flats and dramatic cliffs.*

Breaking waves are a powerful force that help shape the Malaysian coastline.

## Wind and wave power

The main elements affecting Malaysia's vulnerable coastline are the at-times powerful incoming winds, tides and waves that attack from the sea. Malaysia's equatorial monsoon climate produces seasonal wind patterns or rhythms that have major influences on coastal processes. The four seasons—the northeast monsoon, southwest monsoon and two transitional periods—are dictated by the changing speed and direction of the prevailing winds. Winds create significant waves in shallow, coastal waters. When strong winds blow onshore they generate tall waves which dash heavily and destructively against rocks and shorelines which are thereby eroded. The eroded particles are in turn transported by waves and deposited either onshore, offshore or alongshore to build up new landforms. Waves and their associated tidal movements have substantial long-term affects on the changing profile of beaches and features along Malaysia's coast.

## Coastal features

The amount of sediment on a beach is directly related to the forces to which the coast is exposed and the type of material available at the shore. Coasts which are sheltered from strong incoming winds, and thus unaffected by large waves, are referred to as coasts of low-wave energy. The west coast of Peninsular Malaysia is protected by the island of Sumatra which acts as a buffer zone against the strong winds of the southwest monsoon. Marine processes here are weak, allowing fine sediments, like mud, to accumulate in sheltered inlets, such as lagoons, and other protected foreshore areas. The majority of the western shoreline is composed of muddy beaches where mangrove forest also proliferates. Rapid sedimentation and the relative calm of the Strait of Melaka have created large swathes of alluvial flats along the coast.

Sabah's rugged coastline is characterized by a preponderance of inlets or bays of varying sizes. Sandy and muddy beaches are evenly distributed along the coast, with beaches built up from muddy deposits predominating in the southeastern part. Almost half of Sarawak's shoreline is mud beach intersected by tidal creeks. Access to Sarawak's interior is via large rivers that feed into the sea,

## Muddy and sandy beaches of Peninsular Malaysia

**The west coast**
Muddy beaches are found along 60 per cent of the west coast of Peninsular Malaysia. Large tracts of alluvial flats have accumulated over time. The island of Sumatra shelters the west coast from the full brunt of the southwest monsoon winds.

**The east coast**
Sandy beaches characterize the shores of the east coast and can range in width from a few to a few hundred metres. Waves of the northeast monsoon are active along the east coast which has no protective land barrier between it and the great expanse of the South China Sea.

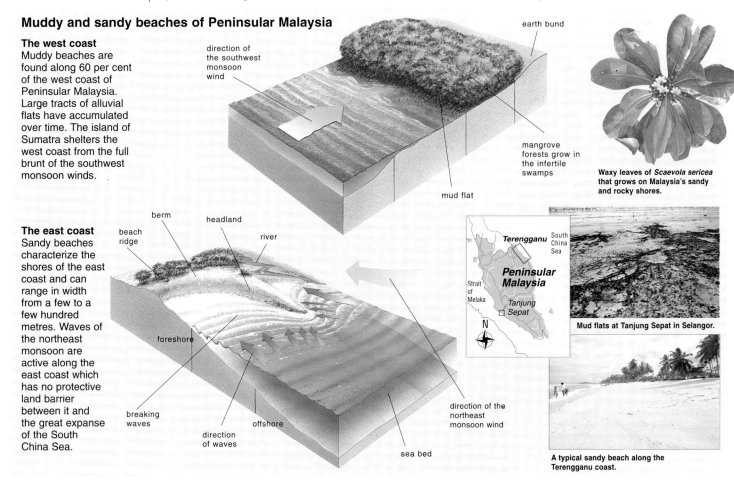

Waxy leaves of *Scaevola sericea* that grows on Malaysia's sandy and rocky shores.

Mud flats at Tanjung Sepat in Selangor.

A typical sandy beach along the Terengganu coast.

A retreating tide reveals a foreshore composed of rock fragments beyond the coast's sandy beach.

but the size of vessel is limited by the sand bars—ridges of sandy sediment—that lie at the mouths of these rivers.

Sandy beaches are found along the exposed east coast of Peninsular Malaysia which experiences seasonal moderate to high-wave energy. Sandy shorelines are also found along parts of Sabah's west coast and along the west coast of the Peninsula, but they are less extensive than on the eastern side.

The east coast of the Peninsula is characterized by strongly developed headland bays. A continuous series of asymmetrically curved bays joining one headland to the next can be found along more than 60 per cent of the coast. Known locally as *permatang*, they are built up from sediments carried down from the major rivers of Terengganu, Dungun, Kemaman, Kuantan and Pahang. They support only very poor vegetation, such as seaside grasses, a few scattered trees and low Cape rhododendron bushes.

Cliff coasts are a rarer shoreline feature in Malaysia than either muddy or sandy deposits. Their associated beaches are rocky and usually not easily accessible. Where they appear off Sabah's north coast, the cliffs stand up as headlands.

## Sand movement in the coastal system

Waves breaking on the shore stir up sandy deposits. The sand grains are then carried by the waves and wind-driven currents and deposited further along

Sheer cliffs on Pulau Berhala off Sabah's eastern coast near Sandakan Bay.

Contrasting shoreline patterns showing (left to right) rocks on a beach at Pulau Gaya, Sabah; sandy ripples at Bako, Sarawak; and mud flats at Langkawi, a typical coastal characteristic of the west coast.

the coast. This movement of material is the most significant process at work on the Malaysian coast and is responsible for the development of a large number of distinctive coastal features, such as sand spits and bars.

The amount of sand being moved depends on the location and source of the material. Generally, the sediment transfer off the west coast of the Peninsula is much less than that on the east coast because of its more sheltered position. At Kundor beach on the coast of Melaka, for example, the amount of sediment carried in the coastal system is less than 35 000 cubic metres per year, while at Kertih beach, on the east coast, it rises to over 250 000 cubic metres a year.

Obstruction of sand movement in the littoral zone caused by human activities, such as the development of new settlements and dredging, can lead to coastal erosion (see 'Coastal erosion'). The Malaysian coastline of the early 21st century may have become irrevocably reshaped as a result of huge land reclamation projects. In the state of Kedah, a large portion of the 148-kilometre coastline has been made available to developers who plan to create a series of artificial islands from sand dredged from the sea. A similar island is planned off the coast of Melaka. Such reclamation projects not only have an impact on local communities and the mangrove forests that line the shore, but also pose geographical risks. If a man-made island is placed too near the coast it may slow down the natural sand dispersal patterns and lead to sediment build-up, causing the island to join the mainland in due course. This is particularly so for muddy shores. The new islands may be unstable and dredging invariably stirs up sediments which may disrupt the aquatic food chain.

Flower of the coastal *Rhodomyrtus tomentorus*.

Cherating beach, a sandy half-heart bay on the east coast of Peninsular Malaysia.

# Islands of Malaysia

*Small islands dot the coastline of Malaysia, some in tightknit clusters, others in solitary form. The exact number of islands is not known, but there are at least 270. Kedah claims to have 110, of which 99 form the Langkawi Island group. Most of the islands are unpopulated, small, remote and support rich marine life. Because of their isolated position, the islands have been fertile ground for tales of magic and mystery.*

Layang-Layang, a sand cay on a coral atoll extended by land reclamation and developed into a resort.

### How islands form

The uniqueness and fragility of islands are influenced by their size, their distance from the Malaysian mainland, their geology, and the way in which they evolved. Islands are formed as a result of dramatic geological upheaval, coral build-up, or by an area of land becoming isolated from the mainland in a period of rising sea level.

### Island types in Malaysia

Malaysia's main island types are known as low and high islands. Some are oceanic and others continental in origin. Oceanic islands rise from the deep ocean floors to appear as high oceanic outcrops or low atolls (circular coral reefs or a string of coral islands surrounding a lagoon). Continental islands are part of a mainland that has become submerged as sea level has risen and they are thus structurally still part of it. Islands are also formed when submerged reefs are lifted above water by tectonic activity, as occurred recently off Kudat, or when a narrow arch connecting land to the mainland collapses, or the narrow neck of a spit erodes away.

Low islands rise just above the high watermark, and are usually small in size and flat. Muddy mangrove islands, such as Kukup, Carey, Ketam and Indah, lie close to the mainland. Sand cays (banks) composed of coral fragments are, in contrast, located far out to sea, for example, Selingan, Bakungan Kecil, Gulisan, Mabul, Omadal and Kalampunian Besar. Sipadan, rich in marine life, is a low oceanic island that rises abruptly from the sea floor. Low islands are unstable and geologically young and are especially vulnerable to erosion and drowning as the sea level rises. Some have been extended by land reclamation schemes or are completely man-made, such as Pulau Melaka, an artificial island off the coast of Melaka.

## Some islands and their geographical features

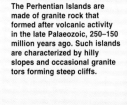

The Perhentian Islands are made of granite rock that formed after volcanic activity in the late Palaeozoic, 250–150 million years ago. Such islands are characterized by hilly slopes and occasional granite tors forming steep cliffs.

Pulau Redang is composed of metasediment rocks and granites. The former were first deposited about 250 million years ago under the sea and uplifted by granite intrusion 60 million years later.

### Langkawi Island group

Rebak Besar, Langkawi, Langguh, Intan Besar, Beras Basah, Timun, Singa Besar, Dayang Bunting, Tuba, Bumbun Besar

Sandstone islands often have very interesting coastal features, such as honeycomb weathering close to shore.

Carey Island is protected from tidal submergence by bunds. It was formerly covered by mangroves and has since been converted firstly to coconut plantations and later to oil palm. The island is being linked to Indah, a former mangrove island now being reclaimed and developed into a new industrial and commercial hub.

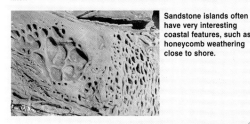

### Carey Island

Ketam, Tengah, Klang, Selat Kering, Indah (formerly Lumut), Pintu Gedong, Che Mat Zin, Carey

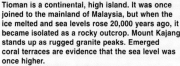

Tioman is a continental, high island. It was once joined to the mainland of Malaysia, but when the ice melted and sea levels rose 20,000 years ago, it became isolated as a rocky outcrop. Mount Kajang stands up as rugged granite peaks. Emerged coral terraces are evidence that the sea level was once higher.

### Perhentian Islands

Perhentian Kechil, Perhentian Besar, Redang, Pinang, Lima, Ling, Kerengga Besar, Bidong Laut

### Tioman group

Cebih, Tulai, Labas, Tioman, Pemanggil, Tinggi, Aur

Langkawi, Perhentian, Penang, Jerejak, Redang, Kapas, Tenggul, Kendi, Aman, Gedung, Kuala Lumpur, Berhala, Tioman, Rawa, Cebih, Labas, Pangkor, Carey, Besar Sibu, Johor Bahru, Besar, Kukup, SINGAPORE, Tinggi, Aur, Peninsular Malaysia, South China Sea, Sarawak

High islands rise high above the sea and are usually large in size and hilly. Most are old in origin and are the remains of hilltops or volcanoes that survived drowning at the end of the Holocene Marine Transgression 20,000–6,000 years ago. During this period the sea is estimated to have risen 120 metres, to about 3 metres above its present level, before gradually receding. Relics of higher seas are commonly preserved on the islands in the form of emerged dead oyster beds and corals. Bodgaya and Boheydulang are remains of a drowned volcanic caldera—a large basin-shaped crater at the top of a volcano—and the nearby Mantabuan is a sand cay, sitting on the rim of another drowned volcano. South of Semporna, Mount Conner on the mainland, and the offshore islands of Sipanggau, Nusa Tengah and Manampilik, are remnants of another crater rim.

Some former islands have become linked to the mainland by tombolos, for example, Cape Rachado, a prominent headland south of Port Dickson, or, as in the case of Bukit Keluang (Terengganu), are the result of coastline build-up. The beginning of this evolutionary process can currently be observed in Rebak where the cusp-like foreland at Pantai Chenang is growing towards the island.

Coastal land reclamation is a common practice on Malaysia's islands. The whole southwest coast of Penang has been reclaimed for the Bayan Lepas Free Trade Zone and more recently the Bayan Bay Marina, and Kuah town on Langkawi is expanding onto land recently won from the sea.

*An artist's impression of the mythical Garuda, associated with the islands of Langkawi.*

## Lands of myth

### Tales from the Water Islands

*The chain of beautiful islets that form an arc to the south of Melaka were formed, legend tells us, from fragments of the storm-ravaged ship of Malaysian hero Nakhoda Ragam. The galley became Pulau Hanyut, the cake tray Pulau Nangka, the water jar Pulau Undan, the incense burner Pulau Serimbun, and the hero's cabin Pulau Besar, the largest of the group. Batu Berhala (Johor) was also formed from the wreck of a ship, with the rocks' highest points representing the rudder and stern of a Chinese junk.*

### The Garuda of Langkawi

*In an attempt to prevent the marriage between a handsome prince, Prince Rum, and a Chinese princess, the Garuda kidnapped the princess and brought her to Langkawi. He attacked and evoked a whirling storm that sank a fleet of Prince Rum's ships and then boasted of his powers to overturn fate. But the prince survived by clinging to a floating plank and returned to China with his bride-to-be. Shamed at his failure, the Garuda fled.*

### The dragon of Tioman

*A thousand years ago, a female dragon on her way to marry a male dragon, dropped her earrings and shawl. Because day was breaking and dragons can only travel at night, she rested. Her feet got entangled with the corals and she became trapped, unable to move again. So there she remained and was transformed into the island we see today.*

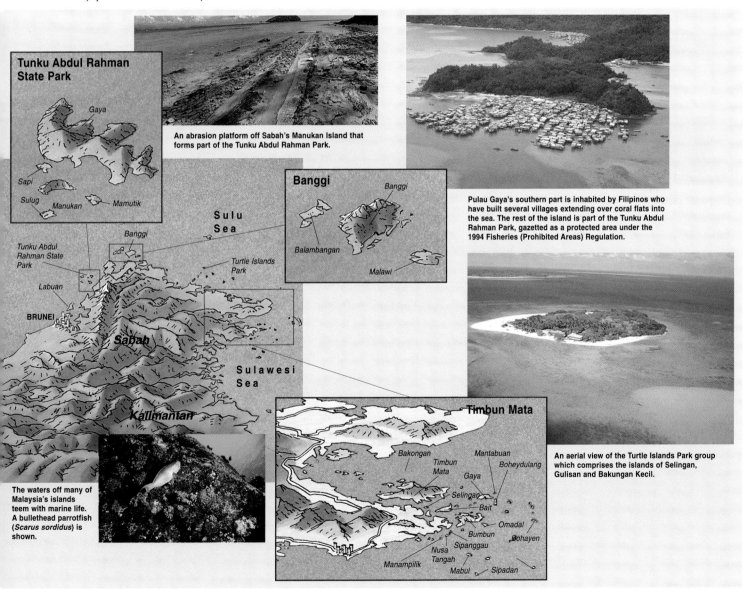

**Tunku Abdul Rahman State Park**

An abrasion platform off Sabah's Manukan Island that forms part of the Tunku Abdul Rahman Park.

**Banggi**

Pulau Gaya's southern part is inhabited by Filipinos who have built several villages extending over coral flats into the sea. The rest of the island is part of the Tunku Abdul Rahman Park, gazetted as a protected area under the 1994 Fisheries (Prohibited Areas) Regulation.

The waters off many of Malaysia's islands teem with marine life. A bullethead parrotfish (*Scarus sordidus*) is shown.

**Timbun Mata**

An aerial view of the Turtle Islands Park group which comprises the islands of Selingan, Gulisan and Bakungan Kecil.

Heavy winds and storms often bring floods in their wake. Above, Kota Bharu lies under flood waters.

*ABOVE:* **Bright sunshine after a light afternoon shower breaks through the clouds over the Danum Valley Conservation Area in Sabah.**

*RIGHT:* **Rain trees help shade the road that runs through Taiping's Lake Gardens from bright rays of the Malaysian sun.**

# WEATHER AND CLIMATE IN MALAYSIA

In Malaysia, where temperatures are generally high and show little variation during the course of the year, it is not possible to differentiate between summer and winter as in temperate regions. Neither is it feasible to divide the year into wet and dry seasons as heavy rainfall may occur anywhere and at any time of the year. Although relatively short, dry spells may be experienced in a particular year, these are not sufficiently long and regular in their occurrence to justify being called 'dry' seasons. Nevertheless, the climate of this region does have a seasonal rhythm which is controlled largely by the synoptic wind system which is dominated by the monsoon. The latter, together with local and regional disturbances and topographical features, determines the general pattern of the wind seasons which, as over most parts of Southeast Asia, are reflected in the rainfall patterns.

Colonialists at the Residency at Larut, near Taiping, in a sketch from *The Graphic*, titled 'At the Residency Larut: A Wet Day'.

The monsoon represents a significant change in wind direction and humidity associated with widespread temperature changes over land and water. The monsoon is caused by a combination of factors: the differential effects of heating and cooling of the Siberian landmasses and the surrounding seas, the northward movement of the Inter-Tropical Convergence Zone (ITCZ) (where the trade winds meet) during the northern summer, and the interference to the atmospheric circulation caused by the Himalayan mountains.

There are four recognizable seasons in Malaysia during the course of a year. The northeast monsoon lasts from November or early December until March and the southwest monsoon from June until September or early October. There are two intermonsoon seasons that operate, respectively, from April to May and from October to November. In Peninsular Malaysia, the northeast monsoon normally brings heavy rain and the southwest monsoon season is relatively dry, especially during June and July. From August until the end of the season, the monthly rainfall at most places shows a steady increase. These characteristics describe the average climatic conditions that are likely to be experienced in any one year in Malaysia. These features do, however, vary from year to year depending on the broader scale circulation of air currents in the atmosphere and currents in the seas. Local-scale effects on the climate include the haze, which brings smog to the region, and the periodic El Niño phenomenon. The latter has been identified as the cause of major climate extremes. In Malaysia, extremely high temperatures and all-time rainfall lows were recorded in 1983 and 1998 coinciding with El Niño events.

Malaysia has high temperatures and ample sunshine the whole year. However, due to varying weather conditions, the actual amount of radiation received varies from day to day, putting a limitation on the industrial application of solar energy, but progress has been made to harness it for domestic purposes and in rural areas.

# Rainfall

*Malaysia has an annual rainfall of around 2600 millimetres, which is above the global average, but considered normal for an equatorial region. From year to year, the total annual rainfall of Malaysia shows considerable fluctuation and within the country there are significant spatial and temporal variations. Rainfall is inextricably linked to the seasonal monsoons, with particular impact on agriculture and fishing.*

Rain drops on a lemon leaf. There are thousands of tonnes of water above our heads. Small droplets are absorbed by larger ones, which become too heavy to float in the air and fall as rain.

## Causes of rainfall in Malaysia

The basic physical process of rainfall is one of recycling. Water from the earth's surface is carried into the atmosphere as water vapour to form clouds, and is later discharged back to the earth as rain drops. Malaysia receives three main types of rainfall—convectional, orographic and cyclonic. Convectional rain, however, is the most prominent.

## Rainfall distribution

The amount of rainfall received by a specific location in Malaysia depends on a number of factors, such as geographical location, the influence of mountains in the vicinity, the surrounding seas, and the monsoons. In Peninsular Malaysia, along coastal north Pahang, for example, the average annual rainfall is 3000 millimetres, whereas along the north coast of Perak, or in

### Distribution of annual rainfall

Annual rainfall (mm)
- >3800
- 3400–3800
- 3000–3400
- 2600–3000
- 2200–2600
- <2200

The total annual rainfall for Malaysia from 1967 to 1995 shows considerable variation. The mean annual rainfall of 2661 mm is shown by the dashed line.

Source: Malaysian Meteorological Service

Perlis, the average annual rainfall is less than 2000 millimetres. The First Division of Sarawak has an average annual rainfall of over 4000 millimetres, the highest in the country, in contrast to the Tawau Residency in Sabah, which in a typical year receives slightly less than half that amount.

## Types of rainfall

### Convectional

This is is associated with late afternoon thunderstorms and showers. Moist air is heated when it comes in contact with the earth's surface. The warm, moist air then rises (convectional lifting). If it rises above the level where condensation takes place, clouds develop. With sufficient moisture and uplifting, clouds can grow to heights exceeding 10 kilometres and are normally called cumulonimbus or thunder clouds. A typical afternoon thunderstorm often develops following a bright, sunny morning. The heavy downpour is accompanied by strong, gusty winds that can cause flash floods and uproot trees, and lasts 1–2 hours.

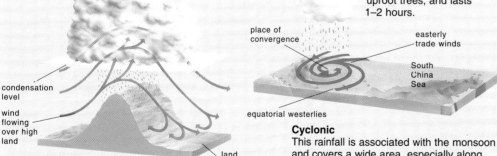

### Orographic

This is associated with mountains. The ranges in Malaysia, most notably the Titiwangsa Range in the Peninsula and those in Sabah and Sarawak, play a significant role in producing rainfall and determining the manner in which it is distributed spatially. This type of rainfall is produced by orographic lifting. Air is raised above the condensation level. It condenses to form clouds and subsequently falls as rain, mainly along the windward side of the mountain.

### Cyclonic

This rainfall is associated with the monsoon and covers a wide area, especially along the Peninsula's east coast and the coastal areas of Sarawak. The easterly and westerly trade winds meet in a cyclonic manner (anticlockwise in the northern hemisphere), forcing moist air to ascend, which then condenses to form rain. During the northeast monsoon, there is heavy and continuous rain lasting two days or more. This monsoon rain is one of the major causes of floods in the country.

## Seasonal variation

In some parts of the country, variations from one month to the next can be very high. In the coastal areas of Kelantan and Terengganu, for example, the average monthly rainfall in November exceeds 600 millimetres, compared to less than 80 millimetres in February.

The higher rainfall over the east coast states of Peninsular Malaysia and the western part of Sarawak is attributed to the northeast monsoon rains, which supply nearly 50 per cent of the annual rainfall total in the three months from November to January. The first heavy monsoonal rains start in Kelantan and Terengganu in November and progressively extend south to Pahang and Johor in December. By late December and January, the monsoon rains shift to Sabah and Sarawak.

The west coast states of the Peninsula, which receive mostly convectional rainfall, have significantly higher amounts of precipitation during the intermonsoon months of April–May and October when the transition from the northeast to the southwest monsoon and vice versa takes place.

During these periods, winds close to the earth's surface are weak and variable, creating conditions favourable for active convective processes which are further aided by the land–sea breeze (see 'The Asian monsoon') and orographic effects. During the later half of the northeast monsoon, from early January to March, Peninsular Malaysia receives relatively little rainfall. During the southwest monsoon season, from June to August, the southern half of the Peninsula and western Sarawak receive less rainfall compared to the other months in the year.

## Diurnal variation

Paralleling regional differences in the monthly rainfall are regional differences in the diurnal (daily) variations across the country. Over the mainland, not far from the coast and where the influence of the monsoon is not great, a higher percentage of rainfall occurs between mid-afternoon and early evening. Rainfall here is partly due to the land–sea breeze effect. Where this is insignificant, for example, at Temerloh located in the centre of the country, the rain falls much later, around late afternoon and lasts into the early part of the night.

Over hilly areas, such as the Cameron Highlands, the rain starts in the early afternoon and by evening the intensity has typically dropped substantially. Heavier rainfall in higher regions usually occurs in the mid-afternoon. Malaysia's islands receive relatively less rainfall during the afternoons because of a maritime influence. For instance, Penang and Labuan islands receive most of

The diurnal variation, expressed as a percentage of the mean annual rainfall for selected locations in Malaysia. The graph shows that the timing of the rainfall depends on geographical location and the influence of the monsoon.

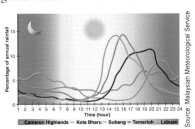

their rainfall between dusk and dawn. Over areas where the monsoonal influence is strong, the rainfall is more uniformly distributed throughout the day. In Kota Bharu, for example, the rainfall increases slightly during the early part of the night.

## Impacts

In Malaysia, rainfall is the most significant climatic factor that impacts on the social and economic activity of the country because it shows greater variation than other factors. Temperature and sunshine duration also have an impact, particularly on agriculture, but their affects are closely related to rainfall. For example, during rainy periods the skies are mostly cloudy. The clouds act as a blanket to incoming solar radiation, and provoke a drop in temperature and a decrease in sunshine duration.

The activity most susceptible to rainfall is agriculture. The distribution and choice of perennial, unirrigated crops are largely dictated by the rain. The regular dry season during the first few months in the year, that prevails in the northern parts of Peninsular Malaysia, discourages the cultivation of crops such as oil palm, cocoa and bananas, which require a regular and plentiful supply of water. However, sugar cane, which needs a dry period to ripen before harvesting, is well suited to such areas. Rubber is not favoured for cultivation in coastal areas because of morning rainfall during the monsoon, which is one of the reasons for a switch to growing oil palm in these parts. In recent years, oil palm cultivation has taken off on a grand scale in regions with high annual rainfall.

The heavy rainfall during the northeast monsoon also limits fishing in coastal areas facing the South China Sea because of flooding and rough seas associated with the strong, seasonal winds. For the same reason, outdoor sporting events, which are usually held in the west coast of the Peninsula, are usually limited to months outside the monsoon season, the preferred months being June to September when there is a rainfall minimum.

A fishing boat is beached off Kota Bharu, with well-developed storm clouds above. Socioeconomic activities, such as fishing, are disrupted at certain times of the year because of heavy rains.

Rainy days in Kuala Lumpur now and then. A man crosses Jalan Tuanku Abdul Rahman in the rain (top). Getting around during the 1926 floods was a slow process (bottom).

## Seasonal rainfall variation at selected locations

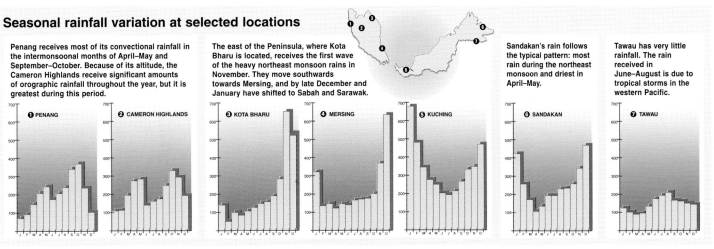

Penang receives most of its convectional rainfall in the intermonsoonal months of April–May and September–October. Because of its altitude, the Cameron Highlands receive significant amounts of orographic rainfall throughout the year, but it is greatest during this period.

The east of the Peninsula, where Kota Bharu is located, receives the first wave of the heavy northeast monsoon rains in November. They move southwards towards Mersing, and by late December and January have shifted to Sabah and Sarawak.

Sandakan's rain follows the typical pattern: most rain during the northeast monsoon and driest in April–May.

Tawau has very little rainfall. The rain received in June–August is due to tropical storms in the western Pacific.

# The Asian monsoon

*The word monsoon is derived from the Arabic* mausim *which means 'season'. Ancient traders plying the Indian Ocean and the adjoining Arabian Sea used it to describe a system of alternating winds which blow persistently from the northeast during the northern hemisphere winter and from the opposite direction, the southwest, during the northern summer. The monsoon dominates the climate of Malaysia and plays an important part in shaping human and economic activity.*

## Monsoon zones

The Asian monsoon is the most extensive of all monsoon systems. All areas within Asia and Australia that experience a tropical climate—an annual variation of both wind and rain—are influenced by the monsoon.

Winter monsoon, November–March: winds blow from the northeast.

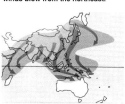

Summer monsoon, June–September/October: winds blow from the southwest.

Source: After Ramage (1971)

## The Asian monsoon

Monsoons are not single, aberrant storms, like hurricanes, but are wave-like air masses that move from sea to land, and from land to sea in recognizable cyclical patterns. They are the atmosphere's most impressive weather phenomenon, and are triggered by the tilt of the earth in relation to the sun. Two main conditions contribute to the monsoon seasons. These are the effects of different heating and cooling of land and sea (see box below), and the modification of atmospheric circulation by the Himalayas. The immensity of the Asian landmass and the massive Himalayan mountain range combine to produce the most dramatic and most extensive of the world's monsoon systems. The Asian winter, or northeast monsoon, is marked by cold, dry and windy conditions in northern Asia and heavy rain spells in equatorial Southeast Asia, including Malaysia. The summer, or southwest, monsoon is correspondingly drier.

## Wind and rain

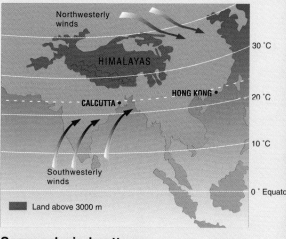

Land above 3000 m

## Seasonal wind patterns

The Himalayas act as a powerful windbreak. In winter, they shield northern Asia from warmer southern air and help maintain extremely low temperatures and intense high pressure in Siberia. Cold air travelling southwards is forced to skirt the Himalayas and blows as northwesterly winds towards China, from where it turns to northeasterlies before heading towards Southeast Asia. The appreciably cooler temperatures experienced by Hong Kong during the winter compared to those in Calcutta, which is practically on the same latitude, are directly attributable to the sheltering effects of the Himalayas on the Indian Sub-continent.

In summer, the Himalayas restrict warm air flowing north from Southeast Asia and cooler air from the north from reaching India. The prevailing winds are largely southeasterlies in the southern hemisphere and they turn to southwesterlies while crossing to the northern hemisphere.

## Monsoon mechanics: Land and sea breezes

Monsoons are created because of the broad temperature differences between land and sea surfaces. The sun's rays heat up land more quickly than water, which absorbs and stores solar heat. The concept of land–sea heating, seen in the daily patterns of land and sea breezes in the tropics, is duplicated on a much wider scale for the monsoon phenomenon. The Asian monsoon operates in two lengthy seasons over a large land area.

During the summer monsoon, long days and short nights mean the continental landmass warms up faster than the sea. As warm air rises, pressure falls. This causes cooler air from the sea to blow towards the land, creating a large-scale sea breeze. A reverse surface wind, flowing from the sea to the land, develops and persists throughout the summer.

Shorter days and longer nights in winter tend to cool the continent landmass more rapidly than the adjacent seas and oceans. This creates a higher pressure over the land compared to that over the sea. The higher pressure forces surface air to move from the cold land to the relatively warmer sea as a form of land breeze.

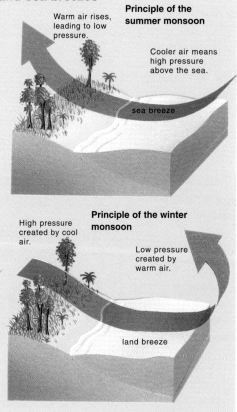

**Principle of the summer monsoon**

Warm air rises, leading to low pressure.

Cooler air means high pressure above the sea.

sea breeze

**Principle of the winter monsoon**

High pressure created by cool air.

Low pressure created by warm air.

land breeze

## Monsoon characteristics in Malaysia

In most parts of monsoonal Asia, the arrival of the monsoon signals the commencement of the rainy season. Lying within the Asian monsoon region, the seasonal rhythm of the Malaysian climate is very much dictated by the monsoon. The four seasons are the northeast monsoon (which lasts from November or early December to early March), the southwest monsoon (June to September or early October), and the two intermonsoon periods (April to May, and October to November).

Rainfall in the country is highest during the northeast monsoon which brings about 50 per cent of the country's annual precipitation. The monsoon weather systems, which develop in conjunction with cold air from Siberia, produce heavy rains which often cause severe floods along the east coast states of Kelantan, Terengganu, Pahang and east Johor in Peninsular Malaysia and in Sarawak. Following the southward march of the monsoon, Kelantan and Terengganu receive a mean monthly rainfall maximum (around 600 millimetres) in November, Pahang and east Johor (of similar magnitude) in December, and Sarawak (between 400 and 700 millimetres) in January.

The southwest monsoon is comparatively much drier throughout the country except in Sabah. During this season, most states experience a monthly

## Rainfall distribution during the monsoon

Except for Sabah, Malaysia receives relatively less rain during the southwest monsoon.

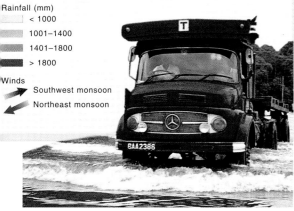

Malaysia receives most of its rainfall during the northeast monsoon which causes most of the floods.

Rainfall (mm)

- < 1000
- 1001–1400
- 1401–1800
- > 1800

Winds

- Southwest monsoon
- Northeast monsoon

A lorry makes its way along the road during monsoonal floods in Perak.

rainfall minimum of 100–150 millimetres. This is attributed to the relatively stable atmospheric conditions in the region as a whole. In particular, the dry condition in Peninsular Malaysia is accentuated by the rain shadow provided by the Sumatran mountain range. Sabah is wetter (exceeding 200 millimetres) because of the tail effects of typhoons, which frequently traverse the Philippines on their way to the South China Sea and beyond.

During the two intermonsoon periods, winds are light and variable. Morning skies are often clear, and this favours thunderstorm development in the afternoon. In the west coast states of Peninsular Malaysia, thunderstorms contribute to a mean monthly rainfall maximum (ranging from 160 to 280 millimetres in April, and from 200 to 380 millimetres in October) in each of the two transition periods.

## Monsoons and people

The first writings to document the monsoon originated largely from India and neighbouring areas. Reference to it was made in the Sanskrit classic *The Meghdoot* by the Indian lyrical poet Kalidas in the 6th century and by a Chinese Buddhist scholar Fah Hsien in 400 CE. From as far back as the 15th century, mariners and traders were exploiting the monsoons in the East Asian seas, particularly the South China Sea. The annals of the Ming Dynasty recorded a sharp increase in maritime commercial activity following the seafaring expeditions of Admiral Cheng Ho to Southeast Asian countries as well as to India, the Persian Gulf and Africa.

The socioeconomic activities in Malaysia are inevitably influenced by the monsoons. The northeast monsoon has most impact, as it brings half the country's annual rainfall. From time to time, strong outbursts of cold air from mainland Asia interact with cyclonic systems near the equator, resulting in strong winds, rough seas and heavy rainfall, particularly over the east coast states of Peninsular Malaysia and western Sarawak. Fishing is considerably curtailed, and the stormy weather and rough seas affect offshore oil drilling and exploration, as well as coastal shipping. The rain interferes with agricultural practices, such as preparing land for planting, applying fertilizers, rubber tapping and harvesting, and thus farmers avoid carrying out such activities during the period.

Heavy monsoonal rains provoke frequent flooding, especially over low-lying areas, damaging crops and property and occasionally claiming human lives (see also 'Flash and monsoon flooding'). The floods disrupt local daily activities, such as transportation, education and tourism. Schools may be forced to close and examinations postponed. Hotels experience their lowest occupancy rates during the peak wet period and promotion of major tourist events is limited.

Like all countries within the monsoon belt, the Malaysian way of life, particularly outdoor activities, is shaped by the climate's seasonal patterns. Activities are tied to the weather not only to minimize its negative effects, but also to benefit optimally from the monsoon's positive influence. Crop calendars, especially rice growing, follow the seasonal rainy and dry cycles closely. Land is prepared in the dry season and harvesting occurs just after the peak wet season so that crops benefit from initial rain, but escape the negative effects of the wet period. Occasional long, dry spells result in a reduction in available water and a slowdown in agricultural production.

Two views of Kota Bharu, Kelantan, under monsoonal flood waters. An aerial view of the town under water of between 0.3 and 1.3 metres, 21–27 December 1993 (above, top). A close-up of a Malay house surrounded by floods in which local children swim, 1988 (bottom).

Fishing is a seasonal activity, especially on the east coast of Peninsular Malaysia. These fishermen on Pulau Redang, Terengganu, are forced to hang up their nets during the period of heavy winds and rains of the northeast monsoon.

'Though the stem of the Meranti tree rocks to and fro (in the storm), Let the Yam leaves be as thick as possible, That Rain and Tempest may come to naught.'

Traditional Malay charm recited to try to allay the heaviest of downpours.

# Winds and storms

*In Malaysia, winds are largely attributed to large-scale phenomena such as monsoons and typhoons, and local influences such as land–sea breezes, thunderstorms and squall lines. Although Malaysia is almost exempt from direct typhoon hits, their aftereffects can result in serious flooding and destruction. Thunderstorms are prevalent throughout the year, with severe storms wreaking serious havoc.*

Although they can last as little as 15 minutes, freak storms can pose a serious natural hazard as they uproot trees, damage buildings and other public facilities, and cause flash floods and landslides.

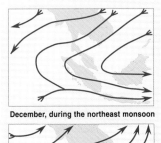

Source: Malaysian Meteorological Service

December, during the northeast monsoon

July, during the southwest monsoon

### Wind systems during the monsoons
In the northeast monsoon (November to early March), steady northeasterlies of 5–10 metres per second (10–20 knots) blow across the country. In the southwest monsoon (June to September or early October), the prevailing wind of 2.5–5 metres per second (5–10 knots) is mostly southwesterly.

Strong storms can cause disruption to daily life and services. The picture shows electric cables coming down along the track of the Klang railway line.

## Winds in Malaysia

Air flows from higher to lower pressures as a wind. The speed of the wind depends on the pressure differences; the greater they are, the faster the wind. Wind is observed whenever there is movement of air relative to the earth's surface and is generated by large- and small-scale (or local) weather phenomena. In Malaysia, winds are generally light, with average speeds ranging from 0.5 to 3.0 metres per second (1–6 knots). Winds are much weaker in the hinterland than along the coast where the effects of the monsoons and land–sea breezes are strongly felt.

In Malaysia, prevailing winds are strongly dictated by the monsoonal currents, which are modified, to a large extent, by topography and local meteorological conditions. Along the coast, land–sea breezes can act to strengthen or weaken the wind. For instance, along the east coast of the Peninsula during the northeast monsoon, the land–sea breeze reinforces the prevailing wind during the day and reduces the flow at night. Further inland, topography and frictional effect reduce the wind speed considerably. During the intermonsoon periods, the winds are generally light and variable. Inland, calm conditions prevail, particularly during the night. Along the coast and up to 20 kilometres inland, land–sea breezes are gentle (3–8 metres per second).

These characteristics represent the normally observed wind patterns. From time to time, the wind strengthens abruptly to several times its normal speed in rather gusty conditions. Such extremes are associated with outbreaks of cold air from Siberia during the northeast monsoon and

with storms. They usually occur at intervals of several days to two weeks corresponding to the surge–lull cycle of the monsoon. More violent winds are experienced in connection with typhoons, thunderstorms and squall lines.

## Tropical cyclones

Tropical cyclones are violent rotating storms, several hundreds of kilometres in diameter, that develop over the tropics. Typhoons, called hurricanes in North America and willy-willys in Australia, are a form of extreme cyclone and begin to appear in the western North Pacific as early as May. They increase in number and reach a peak frequency by September. The majority of the typhoons, in fact, develop in the area bounded by latitudes 5 °N and 20 °N and longitudes 130 °E and 170 °E. Once formed they normally move northwestwards and mature. While some land on the Vietnam and South China coasts, often passing through the Philippines on the way, others recurve northeastwards as they approach the Asiatic landmass and subsequently head for Korea, Japan and other neighbouring areas.

Intense tropical cyclones, such as typhoons, represent the most destructive of nature's phenomena. Any country struck by these storms has to contend with damaging winds, storm surges along the coast and torrential rains which can result in severe floods and landslides. Their presence disrupts many human activities, including shipping and aviation operations.

Cyclones are rare to the south of latitude 5 °N. The only recorded Malaysian cyclone is Tropical Storm Greg, which reached the west coast of Sabah in the early hours of 26 December 1996 and led to the death of 238 people (see box on the page opposite). In most instances, tropical cyclones generate large-scale, or distant, effects on Malaysia. In particular, cyclones travelling across the Philippines normally exert tail or fringe effects on Sabah in the form of strong winds and severe rainstorms. Occasionally, a typhoon located near the Vietnam coast, or even further to the north, has a similar impact on the northwestern states of the Peninsula. Tropical Storm Zita, for example, developed in the South China Sea close to Luzon Island on 21 August 1997. It moved slowly westwards towards southern China, where it arrived

## Storm Greg: Tracking a tropical storm

Tropical Storm Greg brought with its powerful gusts and whirling fury devastation that, on 26 December 1996, tore through Sabah, killing at least 238 people in its path. The worse affected area was Keningau.

1. Greg began as a low pressure area in the South China Sea, off the northeast coast of Peninsular Malaysia on 23 December 1996.

2. The low pressure system deepened and developed to storm intensity. By around 11 a.m. local time on 25 December, wind speeds were exceeding 34 knots. The storm reached Sabah's west coast around 2 a.m. on 26 December.

3. Strong winds, gusting to 90 kilometres an hour, swept inland along the coastal area, bringing destruction in their wake.

4. Intense rainfall was confined to the inland hilly areas, particularly Keningau. The heavy burst of rain caused abrupt swelling and overflowing of the Bayayo, Liawan, Pampang and Sinagang rivers. The flood waters swept away the flimsy settlements in their path, leading to loss of lives and property.

5. By 26 December, the storm had weakened and moved across Sabah towards the Sulu Sea.

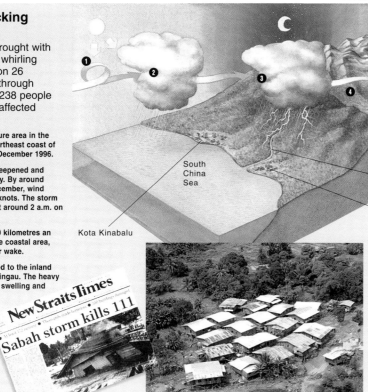

The path of Tropical Storm Greg (blue arrows).

*Sources: After the* New Straits Times *(1996) (illustration); Malaysian Meteorological Service (description)*

ABOVE: The burial of some of the 238 people who lost their lives.

LEFT: Aerial view over the area devastated by Tropical Storm Greg.

two days later. Even though it was 2000 kilometres away, the storm induced strong winds over the north of the Strait of Melaka between 21 and 23 August and intense storms occurred over the northwestern states of the Peninsula, causing scattered floods and six deaths.

### Thunderstorms

Thunderstorms are common in the tropics and in Malaysia occur throughout the year. Their peak frequency, however, falls in the intermonsoon periods. The early stage of a storm's development can be traced to the cauliflower-like cloud (cumulus) which is formed by convection in the early part of the day. The cloud grows laterally and vertically into a large and dense cumulonimbus cloud. In the mature stage of a thunderstorm, the cloud diameter can reach 3–5 kilometres and its top frequently exceeds 10 kilometres.

This stage, lasting 15–30 minutes, represents the most intense period of a thunderstorm when the frequency of lightning accompanied by thunder is at its peak. There is strong turbulence within the cloud and strong outflow, or downdraught, below its base. On reaching the ground, the downdraught spreads

Calm before the storm as ominous black clouds gather above Port Dickson, Peninsular Malaysia.

away from the thunderstorm as strong and gusty winds and, at the same time, brings along heavy rains below the cloud base. The final phase of the storm is characterized by a sharp fall in lightning activity, relatively calm conditions and fairly widespread light rain coming from layer clouds which spread out from the cumulonimbus.

### Squall lines

Squall lines is a term used to describe the moving lines of thunderstorms. They are hundreds of kilometres in length and they have a life span of several hours, which is considerably longer than that of their parent thunderstorms. The gusty winds and heavy rains that the squall lines generate are also more intense and extensive than individual storms.

Squall lines are often observed during the southwest monsoon along the west coast states of Peninsular Malaysia and coastal areas of Sabah and Sarawak facing the South China Sea. In Peninsular Malaysia, squall lines, referred to as 'Sumatras', are formed along the Strait of Melaka during the night and before dawn. The Sumatras tend to move inland in the morning mainly affecting the states of Perak, Selangor, Negeri Sembilan and Melaka. Squall lines in Sabah and Sarawak appear to exhibit the same characteristics. They develop offshore in the night before sweeping landwards in the morning.

### Tracking storms

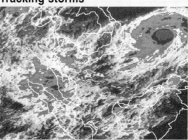

Enhanced satellite imagery captured by the Japanese Geostationary Meteorological Satellite at 8.30 p.m. Malaysian time on 30 October 1995. The central core of typhoon ZACK (9521) appears in red, top right.

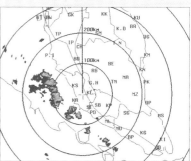

A radar map showing the presence of Sumatra along the Strait of Melaka, 18 August 1995. Use of remote sensing equipment, such as satellites and radar, means that meteorological stations can receive images and data which will pre-warn of forthcoming weather patterns.

# The El Niño Southern Oscillation

*Large disruptions to the pervading climate occur every few years in the east Pacific. Warm currents appear in the usually cool waters and the normal atmospheric pressures are reversed. This phenomenon of atmosphere and ocean variation is known as the El Niño Southern Oscillation (ENSO) system and it is credited as the cause of major climate-related natural disasters. The major droughts and floods experienced throughout the tropics, including Malaysia, have been attributed to ENSO.*

**Areas affected by El Niño**

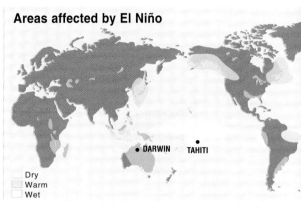

Dry
Warm
Wet

El Niño is the freakish, destructive disruption in the world's normal weather patterns. In the western Pacific, it interrupts the monsoonal rains of Malaysia and the rest of Southeast Asia creating periods of excessive dryness. It also leads to droughts in Africa. In contrast, the frequency of storms and floods increases in South and Central America.

One of the worst El Niño in 150 years hit the region in 1997. Some scientists believe that the increased frequency of the phenomenon in the 1990s and the most powerful one on record of 1997–8 could be due to global warming. The red and white areas on the satellite image indicate higher than usual sea surface temperatures.

## What is ENSO?

This is a combined atmospheric ocean system which is the result of a complex interaction between the atmosphere and the tropical waters of the Pacific Ocean. The intensity and duration of each ENSO varies widely, but typically they last for 9–18 months. An exceptional system, however, lasting nearly four years between 1991 and 1994, has been recorded as the longest. In the 20th century, there have been 23 occurrences of the ENSO. They are highly irregular and may present themselves at intervals anywhere between three and eight years.

The ocean component of ENSO is known as El Niño and the atmospheric component as Southern Oscillation. El Niño, which in Spanish means 'the Christ Child', was a term first used by fishermen in the 19th century to describe an episodic weak, warm, coastal current along the coasts of Peru, Ecuador and northern Chile which appeared during the Christmas period. Once every few years, unusually large warming takes place which extends beyond the coastal waters of South America to the eastern and central Pacific Ocean.

## How does it happen?

El Niño starts when easterly trade winds that blow from east to west across the equatorial Pacific Ocean slacken or sometimes change direction.

During normal years, the easterly trade winds push the warm surface waters away from the eastern boundary where the atmospheric pressure is high and piles them up on the western edge over a vast area about the size of Europe. This creates a tilt in the sea level so that the western edge of the Pacific Ocean becomes usually about 40 centimetres higher than the eastern edge. The warm tropical water fuels the atmosphere with additional warmth and moisture. This, coupled with lower atmospheric pressure, favours the subsequent strong rising motion of the moisture-laden air that condenses to form clouds and heavy precipitation in the western Pacific region, including Malaysia.

When the atmospheric surface pressure seesaws to a low over the eastern Pacific and rises to the west, the easterly trade winds in the equatorial belt relax, causing the warm waters piled over the west to flow to the east. Heavy rainfall and thunderstorms which form in the hot and humid tropical environment shift east along with the warmer waters, which are further enhanced by an overall increase in convective activity due to the exceptional rise in the water temperature. This causes tremendous amounts of rainfall over the central and eastern Pacific, where it is normally dry, and less rainfall over the western Pacific, where it is usually wet.

The abnormal weather pattern that occurs on either side of the Pacific is strongly related to the air pressure across the equatorial Pacific. The atmosphere above the eastern Pacific is dominated by a persistent high pressure region, while a low pressure zone dominates the west. When the pressure seesaws between the opposite ends of the Pacific, which is known as the Southern Oscillation, a pressure fall in the east is accompanied by a rise in the west, and vice versa. The pressure difference between Darwin and Tahiti at the two

## The Southern Oscillation Index

The intensity of any ENSO is determined by the Southern Oscillation Index (SOI) which is simply a numerical measure of the difference in mean sea level pressures between Tahiti and Darwin, two points at extreme ends of the Pacific. A strongly negative SOI indicates a higher than usual surface pressure over the western Pacific–Indian Ocean region and lower surface pressure over the eastern Pacific. This causes air to flow in the lower atmosphere from the Asia/western Pacific region to the east Pacific and vice versa in the upper atmosphere along an east–west orientation. Almost at the same time, the sea surface temperatures over the eastern and central Pacific Ocean are warmer than normal. During a strongly positive SOI, the reverse air flow takes place and during such an instance the sea surface temperature over the coastal regions of the South American coast in the east Pacific is much below normal. Such events have come to be known as La Niña which represents the opposite phase of El Niño. Notable El Niño events occurred in 1953, 1957, 1965, 1972, 1976, 1982/3, 1987, 1991–4 and 1997/8, with La Niña events in the mid-1970s and in 1988.

*Graph: Southern Oscillation Index vs Year (52 54 56 58 60 62 64 66 68 70 72 74 76 78 80 82 84 86 88 90 92 94 96)*

## The life cycle of an ENSO

Though each ENSO episode is unique in terms of intensity, spatial and temporal characteristics, a large number of similarities, linked to the annual cycle, exist. The life cycle can be divided into three phases: onset, maturity and decay.

### Onset

This starts around December when the easterly trade winds weaken over the western Pacific accompanied by a diminishing of sea surface temperatures in that region. The surface waters start flowing eastwards, raising the water temperature over the central Pacific and along the South American coast. Over these warm waters air starts ascending, which induces cloud development and thus precipitation in the same region.

### Maturity

The warmer surface temperatures over the South American coast continue to build up, reaching a peak between June and August, corresponding to a Southern Oscillation Index (SOI) minimum. The easterly trades by now have weakened considerably and extend further eastward over the equatorial Pacific region. The normal trade wind circulation along the equatorial Pacific region weakens, with the main area of large cloud development and rain shifting from the Asian and western Pacific region to the central and east Pacific.

### Decay

Almost a year from the onset, over the western Pacific the seasonal southeasterly trades begin to re-establish and strengthen in magnitude until a peak is attained. Responding to this, the cold upwelling in the east Pacific begins to return and normal conditions are re-established.

**Normal conditions**

Large-scale convention develops, bringing heavy rains to the western Pacific and Southeast Asia.

High above in the upper troposphere the winds return to the east.

Easterly trade winds push warm waters westwards and raise the sea level in the western Pacific.

surface easterly trade winds

equator

South America

Australia

40 cm
0

warm water

thermocline

cold water

200 m

0

50 m

**El Niño conditions**

Aloft westerly winds weaken.

Rainfall over the western Pacific and Southeast Asia is reduced.

The weakening of easterly trade winds and higher SSTs cause strong convection and heavy rains in the eastern Pacific.

The weakening of easterly trade winds causes warm water flow to reverse.

A thermocline is the depth where warm water near the surface meets colder, deeper oceanic waters.

SST stands for sea surface temperature.

Australia

equator

South America

30 cm
0

warm water

thermocline

cold water

200 m

15 cm
0

50 m

---

ends of the Pacific, either strengthens or weakens the trade winds that normally blow from east to west. The simultaneous wind circulation high above the surface of the Pacific Ocean is called the Walker Circulation.

## Impact on Malaysia's climate

The 1982–3 and 1997–8 ENSO events, regarded as two of the most intense in recorded history, brought about massive disruption in the normal climatic pattern in the tropics. Drought on a scale never seen before and torrential rains in usually arid regions plagued the region. In Malaysia, record-breaking temperatures and all-time rainfall lows were recorded in 1983 and 1998. Both Peninsular Malaysia and Sabah and Sarawak feel the impact of the climatic side effects of ENSO to varying degrees, but Sabah and Sarawak suffer the most. This difference may be attributed to the different affect of the sea surface temperature during ENSO over the sheltered seas of Southeast Asia, particularly that of the South China Sea.

In El Niño years, drought conditions in the region, notably in Indonesia, worsen and are prolonged.

Fires started in Kalimantan and Sumatra to clear cropland during the annual slash-and-burn agricultural cycle are enflamed by these drought conditions. With no monsoon rains arriving to dampen the fires, they start to burn out of control and produce billowing, black smoke that drifts across the region to Malaysia. The resulting haze that envelops the country was particularly severe in 1992, 1994 and 1997. Although these were all El Niño years, it would be wrong to suggest that El Niño years are necessarily accompanied by haze. If open burning were controlled, the haze would be minimized. Prior to 1990, severe haze was not reported in Malaysia during any El Niño year.

At the height of the haze in September–early November 1997, which El Niño helped to exacerbate, many Malaysians wore protective masks. Smog engulfed Kota Kinabalu (shown), grounding aircraft and disrupting other domestic activities.

### El Niño and rainfall

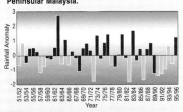

*ABOVE:* Average annual rainfall 1951–96 across Peninsular Malaysia.

*ABOVE:* Average annual rainfall 1951–96 across Sabah and Sarawak.

El Niño year    Normal year

Average annual precipitation over Malaysia during an El Niño year is dramatically lower than usual for the seasonal northeast monsoon or wet season of November to March. Rainfall anomalies are particularly marked in Sabah and Sarawak in El Niño years, indicating the greater influence of ENSO over these two states in comparison to Peninsular Malaysia.

71

# Temperature

*Malaysia's position close to the equator means it experiences an equatorial climate that is hot and humid all year round. There is little seasonal variation in the temperature and there are no seasons, such as summer and winter, to speak of. Any significant variations in temperature across the country are due to differences in altitude. With increased altitude, temperatures become cooler, making places like the Cameron Highlands and the Genting Highlands popular destinations for those seeking to escape the heat in the lowland areas.*

## Temperature and latitude

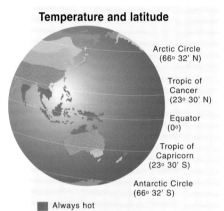

- Always hot
- Hot summer/warm winter
- Hot summer/mild winter
- Warm summer/cold winter
- Always cold

Distance from the equator affects temperature. Seasonal variation increases with higher latitudes. At the mean sea level, the average air temperature in Malaysia is about 26 °C compared to a global average of around 15 °C.

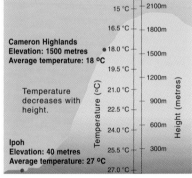

Cameron Highlands
Elevation: 1500 metres
Average temperature: 18 °C

Temperature decreases with height.

Ipoh
Elevation: 40 metres
Average temperature: 27 °C

Temperatures are influenced by altitude. The Cameron Highlands in the Titiwangsa mountain range has a cool, temperate climate, with temperatures around 7–10° cooler than towns in the lowlands. These ideal conditions for cultivating temperate crops make the area one of Malaysia's most important vegetable-, flower- and tea-growing centres.

## Defining temperature

Temperature, like rainfall, is a weather element to which living beings and vegetation are particularly sensitive. It therefore plays an important role in determining the conditions for life and agricultural productiveness in different parts of the world. Temperature is a quantity that measures the amount of heat energy any substance or matter possesses. Air temperature is the amount of energy the moving air possesses in the atmosphere. The primary source of all this energy comes from the sun in the form of solar radiation (see 'Solar energy').

## Factors affecting temperature

Malaysia's location in the equatorial latitudes causes little seasonal variation in the amount of solar energy received on the earth's surface, unlike in higher latitudes where the seasonal variation becomes larger with increasing distance from the equator. However, close to equinox—the two times in the year when the days and nights are of equal length—when the midday sun is directly overhead in Malaysia, the days are generally warmer. This general pattern is modified by altitude, distance from the sea—where the influence of land–sea breezes in moderating the temperatures becomes significant—and cloud cover in the rainy season.

The highlands of Malaysia have a cool, temperate climate because with increased elevation the temperature decreases at a rate of approximately 6 °C every kilometre. Cooler temperatures due to altitude can be seen in the Cameron Highlands which has an average temperature of 18 °C, compared to towns at low elevations where the daily averages are in the upper 20s. The hottest months, March–May in the Peninsula and April–June in Sabah and Sarawak, are due to a combination of increased solar radiation reaching the earth's surface and reduced cloud cover. The coldest months, December–February for most of Malaysia, are affected by the northeasterly monsoon winds that bring relatively colder air from the north as they blow over the

## Measuring air temperature

The two most commonly used units to measure air temperature are degrees Celcius (°C) and degrees Fahrenheit (°F) (1 °F equals 9/5 °C+32). Malaysia conforms to international practices and most commonly uses the Celsius scale.

Air temperature measurements are routinely taken from the mercury or alcohol in glass thermometers. Four such thermometers, the 'dry-bulb', 'wet-bulb', maximum and minimum thermometers are housed 1.5 metres above the ground in an instrument shelter called the Stevensons Screen. The dry-bulb registers the ordinary air temperature, from which, together with the wet-bulb temperature, the relative humidity of the air is calculated. The maximum and minimum thermometers are self-registering and are read at 8 a.m. and 8 p.m. respectively each day to record the extremes of air temperature for that calendar day.

The Stevensons Screen is painted white to shade the thermometers within from sunlight. The louvred sides allow air to circulate freely. The structure is raised off the ground at a height that is convenient for readings to be taken. The two instruments at each end are the thermograph and hydrograph which continously chart the temperature and relative humidity respectively.

country. The relatively high amount of cloud cover associated with the northeast monsoonal rains also reduces sunshine and significantly lowers day temperatures, particularly over the east coast states of Peninsular Malaysia and in Sabah and Sarawak. The same clouds that prevent the sun's radiation from reaching the earth during the day, act as a shield that reduces the amount of heat that escapes at night. This makes the days cooler and nights relatively warmer, in contrast to less cloudy months when the maximum temperatures during the day are high and minimum temperatures at night are low. Examples of such large extremes in the daily temperature range are Alor Setar, Chuping and Ipoh during January–March.

## Daily variation

The air temperature over any place in Malaysia goes through a cycle of change in a day, which is referred to as the diurnal (daily) variation. The sun's radiation starts warming the surface of the earth and the air above it from the time the sun rises. The intensity of the sun's heating increases until the sun is overhead and decreases thereafter until sunset, after which cooling, due to loss of heat from the earth's surface, takes place. Typically, the minimum temperature in Peninsular Malaysia occurs between 6 and 7 a.m., just before sunrise. The warmest part of the day in most places tends not to be at noon, but an hour or two after the midday sun has passed overhead.

The location of a weather station where temperature readings are taken, whether it be on an island, close to the coast, within an industrial area or in the middle of the countryside miles from a city environment, and the influencing effects of onshore winds from the sea, has a profound effect on the diurnal variation of temperature. Coastal locations,

## Temperature variations across Malaysia

Across Malaysia, there is a series of weather stations monitored by the Malaysian Meteorological Service where daily temperature readings are taken. The main stations are marked on the map; a graph is shown for those with a red dot. The graphs show annual variation of the minimum, average and maximum temperature for a range of locations.

In the Peninsula, the hottest months vary from west to east. The west coast states get hotter earlier, between February and April. Over the coastal areas to the east, it is hottest between April and June, which also coincides with the hottest months in Sabah and Sarawak. Over the interior of the Peninsula, it is generally hotter March–May. The coldest month in the Peninsula is December and in Sabah and Sarawak it is January. Both months coincide with the peak northeast monsoon over their respective areas. Island cities like Penang and Labuan show less seasonal variation and their minimum temperatures are higher than elsewhere.

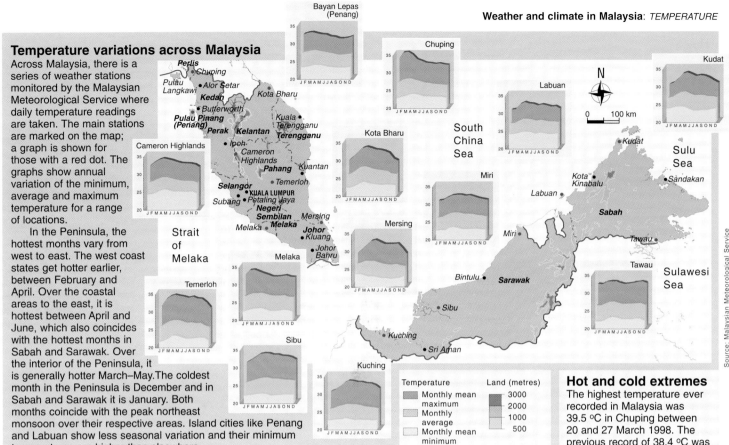

Bayan Lepas (Penang) · Chuping · Kudat · Labuan · Kota Bharu · Miri · Mersing · Melaka · Sibu · Kuching · Cameron Highlands · Temerloh · Tawau

South China Sea · Sulu Sea · Sulawesi Sea · Strait of Melaka

| Temperature | Land (metres) |
|---|---|
| Monthly mean maximum | 3000 |
| Monthly average | 2000 |
| Monthly mean minimum | 1000 |
| | 500 |

Source: Malaysian Meteorological Service

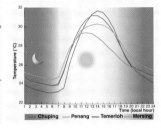

Source: Malaysian Meteorological Service

The diurnal variation of temperature at selected locations across Malaysia. The graph illustrates that the timing of the hottest and coolest temperatures are significantly influenced by proximity and distance from the coast. Annual temperature graphs for all four locations are shown on the map above.

such as Mersing on the east coast of the Peninsular, receive cool winds that blow in from the sea during the day, and thus have an early, and lower than average maximum temperature. Temerloh, a station in the interior, has the largest temperature extremes in a day with temperatures reaching their peak around 2 p.m. Malaysia's islands, such as Penang, seem to experience warmer nights and cooler days with evenly distributed temperatures.

## Temperature trends in Malaysia

Temperature records for most stations in Malaysia over the last 40–50 years show a rising trend, with most notable changes taking place after the mid-1970s. The level of increase is highest in the minimum temperatures as opposed to the daily average or maximum temperatures. This suggests that the so-called greenhouse gases, which act as blankets preventing heat energy escaping from the earth's surface, are on the rise. However, the chief factor contributing to the rise in temperatures is the overall increase in human activity and anthropogenic changes as Malaysia undergoes rapid change, especially in the urban and industrial sectors. It should also be noted that most of the weather stations in Malaysia are located in areas where rapid

growth is taking place. The temperature trend that the country is witnessing could be due to local effects and may, in fact, not be connected to the global warming hypothesis.

## Air temperature and human comfort

The human body needs to maintain a suitable body temperature to feel comfortable and this is strongly influenced by prevailing atmospheric conditions. In Malaysia, high temperatures accompanied by high humidity makes exposure to heat stress an obvious concern during the hot months. Temperature alone does not lead to comfort or discomfort, it is a complex combination of temperature and humidity which is called the effective temperature (ET) that determines the comfort level.

| COMFORT RANGE | EFFECTIVE TEMPERATURE (°C) |
|---|---|
| Above acceptable | above 24.5 |
| Upper acceptable | 22.8–24.5 |
| Optimum | 20.6–22.8 |
| Lower acceptable | 18.9–20.6 |
| Below acceptable | below 18.9 |

Comfort ranges and effective temperatures (ETs) for the Malaysian climate.

Source: Sham (1977)

## Hot and cold extremes

The highest temperature ever recorded in Malaysia was 39.5 °C in Chuping between 20 and 27 March 1998. The previous record of 38.4 °C was also at Chuping, on 18 April 1983. Both years happen to be the two most intense El Niño years of the 20th century. The impact of El Niño on Malaysian weather is reduced cloud cover which increases the amount of radiation from the sun that reaches the earth's surface so raising the air temperature.

The lowest temperature, 7.8 °C, was in the Cameron Highlands at an altitude of around 1500 metres on 1 February 1978.

The extreme range is the difference between the highest and lowest temperatures ever recorded for a particular location in a single day. The greatest such range is 18.6 °C, recorded at Alor Setar on 2 March 1973, and the lowest range is 5.8 °C, at Kuala Terengganu on 20 December 1969.

### Sarawak sunset

A dramatic and rapidly changing light show is seen daily over the Kuching River at dusk, as the sun steadily drops lower behind the horizon and eventually is lost from view (left to right).

# Solar energy

*As an energy source, solar power has much to recommend it on environmental grounds. Although it is not yet exploited widely in Malaysia, there are potentially broad applications for which it might be harnessed in the future, since Malaysia receives plenty of sunlight by virtue of its geographical position. Several trial projects are already underway, notably in rural areas where other power supplies are lacking.*

**Mitigating solar heating**
In the tropics, traditional houses have long been constructed with the local climate in mind (top). Material of low thermal capacity is used and the home positioned and constructed to minimize direct solar radiation. Large roof eaves act as sun shading and rows of full-length windows allow for plenty of ventilation.

In contrast, modern concrete and brick urban housing with lots of windows are baked by the sun and rely on air-conditioning systems to keep them cool. The powerful rays of the midday sun shine on the glass towers in Kuala Lumpur's business district (bottom).

## The source of solar energy

The sun is the source of light and energy that supports all life on earth. This solar energy is created through nuclear fusion at very high temperatures (15 000 000 °C) and pressures (340 billion times air pressure on earth). The energy particles are carried to the outer surface of the sun, the photosphere, from where they are released as light and heat. Solar radiation received on the ground is made up of beam, or direct, radiation and diffused radiation— sunlight passing through the atmosphere to the ground which is scattered by particles of water vapour and dust in the air.

## The Malaysian suntrap

Malaysia receives heavy doses of intense sunshine throughout the year, and is thus in a position to harness this source. However, the rainy conditions that prevail, particularly during the northeast monsoon, and regular cloud cover and tropical rain mean that the energy supply is regularly dampened. Peninsular Malaysia lies in the region receiving between 1620 and 1890 kilowatt-hours every square metre of solar radiation ($kWh/m^2$) and Sabah and Sarawak receive an average of 1380–1620 kilowatt-hours every square metre. This compares with an average of 1630 in Chile, 1950 in India and 2490 in Mali, Africa. The amount of solar energy received is affected by the weather and atmospheric conditions. Cloud cover and high turbidity, due to water vapour and suspended particulates in the air, interfere with the intensity and quality of solar radiation that reaches the ground.

In Malaysia, the average daily amount of radiation received at ground level is 4.76 $kWh/m^2$, roughly equivalent to the amount of electrical energy consumed by 47 100-watt light bulbs switched on for one hour. However, because of varying weather conditions, some days receive very much less than this. Within a month the range of energy levels vary widely. This puts severe limitations on the application of solar energy in industry, which requires a reliable and consistent energy source, and if solar power is used, then it needs to be supplemented by electricity or oil.

## The case for solar power

The sun is a vast energy source that costs nothing, is noiseless, non-polluting, free from political controls and unlikley to run out. In short, it is the environmentalist's dream energy source. Although it has been available to mankind since prehistoric times, it has not been harnessed as effectively as other sources until recently. Creating a system that provides a reliable supply from solar energy poses great technical challenges.

The availability of solar energy at the earth's surface varies daily due to the rotation of the earth on its axis, seasonally due to the tilt of the earth's axis, and annually due to the elliptical orbit of the earth about the sun, and because of cloud and atmospheric conditions or turbidity caused by dust and haze. The amount of energy falling on the earth each day is not very high compared to other energy supplies, which means that the energy needs to be collected over a wide area compared to other energy systems. The cost is also higher than more conventional sources.

In spite of these challenges, considerable progress has been made towards using solar energy to supply some of the energy

## Sunshine sectors

**Annual weather pattern**
In Malaysia, the average amount of diffused light received is 53 per cent of sunlight. The light is variously diffused by prevailing climatic conditions.

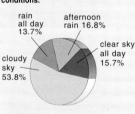

rain all day 13.7%
afternoon rain 16.8%
clear sky all day 15.7%
cloudy sky 53.8%

**Annual average amount of solar energy reaching ground level**
The regions of the globe where extreme highs of temperature coexist with dry conditions receive the greatest amount of solar radiation (darkest shading). Malaysia receives a global average amount of solar energy. Clouds near the equator reduce the amount of sunlight.

Maximum          Minimum

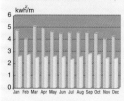

**Total and diffused solar radiation received in Kuala Lumpur**
▫ Total sunlight
▫ Diffused sunlight
The pattern is repeated throughout the country.

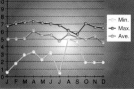

**Monthly variation of solar radiation in Sabah**
The widely varying amounts of sun received across Malaysia in any period means that, as a direct energy source, it is not wholly reliable.

- Min.
- Max.
- Ave.

# Solar energy in Malaysia

In Malaysia, solar energy has been traditionally used in the agricultural sector and fisheries, both for the drying of food crops, such as rice and fruits, fish products as well as rubber and cocoa. The domestic solar water heater has gained acceptance among more wealthy urban dwellers, and the photovoltaic solar power system has been introduced in the rural electrification programme, especially in Sabah and Sarawak, where the Ministry of Rural Development with the Ministry of Energy, Telecommunications and Post aims to introduce such systems to 2000 homes by the end of 1998. Trial systems have also been erected (and have now been dismantled) in three villages in Peninsular Malaysia, one each on Langkawi, Sibu and in Tembeling. There is large scope for the application in rural electrification.

As Malaysia continues to develop it is inevitable that more and more rural areas will receive electricity. The proposed Bakun Dam project in the remote upper Rajang, Sarawak, for example, was destined to generate electricity for Sabah, Sarawak and the Peninsula. As the electricity grid is extended to once remote rural areas, the photovoltaic system becomes obsolete unless it is relocated to even more remote areas.

## Traditional applications
In Malaysia, solar energy has mainly been reserved for agricultural use and relies exclusively on the weather's natural patterns.

Cocoa drying on a cement floor. Zinc roofing on rails is pushed over the drying beans when it rains.

## Modern applications
Solar panels are being used to power streetlamps in Penang and in the four applications shown.

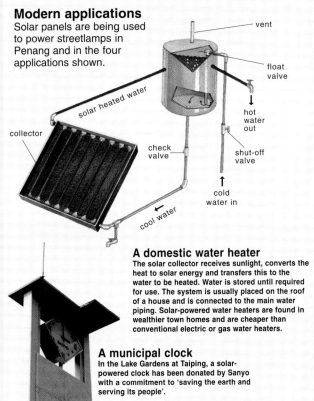

vent
float valve
hot water out
shut-off valve
solar heated water
collector
check valve
cold water in
cool water

### A domestic water heater
The solar collector receives sunlight, converts the heat to solar energy and transfers this to the water to be heated. Water is stored until required for use. The system is usually placed on the roof of a house and is connected to the main water piping. Solar-powered water heaters are found in wealthier town homes and are cheaper than conventional electric or gas water heaters.

### A municipal clock
In the Lake Gardens at Taiping, a solar-powered clock has been donated by Sanyo with a commitment to 'saving the earth and serving its people'.

### Roof panels
Solar energy is being used to power the Kek Lok Si Temple, Penang, Malaysia's largest Buddhist temple.

### Public telephones
These have been installed in some rural areas of Peninsular Malaysia, for example, in Kenong, Pahang. The battery is charged by a solar panel above.

Drying paddy in Langkawi.

Laying fish out to dry in the midday sun, Berserah fishing village, Terengganu.

---

needs of the planet because it is less environmentally harmful than fossil fuels and is inexhaustible.

## Solar photovoltaics
The direct conversion of solar energy into electricity is achieved through a process called the photovoltaic effect, carried out by the photovoltaic cell or photocell. This small device is capable of producing about one watt of electricity when exposed to bright sunlight. At the low-consumption level, such cells are used to power watches, calculators and toys. For large power applications, a number of cells are packaged together to form a panel which is capable of producing 10, 20 or 40 watts. Two or three such panels, together with a storage battery, would normally be sufficient to supply the electricity needs of a kampong house. The use of the solar photovoltaic system is limited only by the imagination of the user. Where there is a need for

Leaflets promoting solar heating panels in Malaysia for domestic and commercial use. They advocate the use of solar energy to heat swimming pools, hotels, hospitals and private homes.

electricity and it cannot be obtained from conventional means, photovoltaic electricity can be applied. The main obstacle is economic, as the cost of producing one unit of electricity using the photovoltaic system is about 20 times that of a conventional system.

Another important application of solar photovoltaic system is in powering remote communications systems such as microwave repeaters. Here photovoltaics have the advantage as there is no need to transport fuel to these remote installations. Telekom Malaysia Berhad, the main telecommunications company in Malaysia, has installed many such repeater stations. In the future, it may be viable to use photovoltaic panels as cladding on buildings to supply electricity during hotter months to run air-conditioning systems.

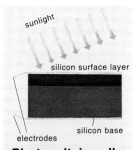

sunlight
silicon surface layer
electrodes
silicon base

### Photovoltaic cells
The direct conversion of solar energy into electricity is achieved by using the photovoltaic solar cell. As solar energy touches the wafer-thin top surface of the silicon cell, to which electrodes are fixed, it triggers an electric current.

Malaysia's first inhabitants lived in the forests and depended on its products for their survival. Rural subsistence lifestyles, including hunter-gathering, are still followed by many Orang Asli in Peninsular Malaysia and by some indigenous groups in Sabah and Sarawak. Rattan from the forest is woven into fish traps and baskets, and wood, bamboo and palms are used for forest homes.

The wooden longhouses of the Malaysian forest interiors are home to only a fraction of the population (left). More and more Malaysians congregate in urban settlements and new, modern housing estates spring up on city outskirts.
*RIGHT*: Bandar Sunway, near Kuala Lumpur.

The traditional back-breaking tasks of planting and harvesting rice by hand (left) are increasingly being replaced by modern methods that employ new technology and machinery.

# MAN AND THE
# ENVIRONMENT

Throughout the history of Malaysia, the link between man and the environment has been a close one. Descendants of the earliest peoples, such as the Iban and the nomadic Penan of Sarawak, still worship spirits that inhabit the natural world.

Since man has derived his food and shelter from nature, it is almost impossible to separate socioeconomic issues from environmental ones. Many forms of development erode the environmental resources upon which they must be based. Similarly, environmental degradation can undermine economic development. Poverty, for example, is both a major cause and effect of global environmental problems. Any discussion of environmental issues, therefore, needs to be seen in the light of both the biophysical and the socioeconomic aspects of the community.

In Malaysia, the natural environment is continually being transformed by human activities. During the 20th century, successive changes in land use have left their physical mark on the landscape. Commercial agriculture, mining, land development schemes, commercial logging, shifting cultivation and urban development have all been instrumental in bringing about such transformation. The once lush tropical rainforest is rapidly being replaced by rubber trees and oil palms that extend from the undulating coastal plains to the foothills. Tin-mining activities leave ugly scars in the form of widespread sand plains and man-made pools. Large-scale land development further reduces forested areas, while accelerated erosion due to deforestation contributes to the siltation of rivers and water channels. However, it is in the large and intermediate urban areas that the transformation of the environment has been greatest and thus the environmental implications most serious.

In the industrial-urban corridors like the Klang Valley, Penang/Seberang Perai, Johor Bahru and Melaka, development is rapidly altering the physical landscape. In the case of the Klang Valley, the Federal Capital Kuala Lumpur, for example, is expanding as part of a merging conurbation stretching from Port Klang by the Strait of Melaka in the west to the foothills of the Main Range in the east, a distance of close to 50 kilometres. Changes in land use will accelerate as the Malaysian economy continues to undergo structural adjustments. Already transport arteries, such as the North–South Expressway along the west coast of Peninsular Malaysia, are changing the mosaic of land use and influencing the patterns of human activities.

*ABOVE*: Wooden and stone figures, known as *Sinningazanak*, are found in the paddy fields around Kota Kinabalu, Sabah. These, like the stone megaliths found in the same area, are thought to be associated with historical property rights.

*RIGHT*: Malaysia opened up in the colonial era, with roads and railways stretching the length of the Peninsula to transport the tin and other ores mined from the landscape.

# Natural resources in daily life

*Malaysia's natural world, which is dominated by forests, meandering rivers and an extensive coastline, has been inextricably linked to the lives of its peoples for centuries. Fruits of the forest and lakes have been sources for physical necessities—food, clothing and building materials—as well as the actual locations for dwellings and communities. In addition, the natural world has been the inspiration for the spiritual and cultural development of different groups as can be seen in traditional rituals, folklore and crafts.*

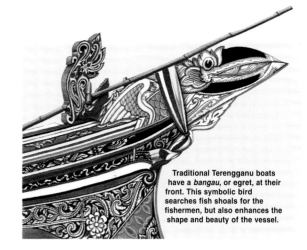

Traditional Terengganu boats have a *bangau*, or egret, at their front. This symbolic bird searches fish shoals for the fishermen, but also enhances the shape and beauty of the vessel.

Man has thrived on his interrelationship with the environment for millenniums, exploiting it for raw materials to serve his daily needs. This early 20th-century photograph depicts Sakai aboriginals.

## Nature's store

Man's basic needs can ultimately be linked to the physical environment. In addition to the most obvious needs of air and water, man relies on the riches of the natural world for his food, shelter and the materials to manufacture rudimentary implements. However, he not only interacts with his surroundings on the physiological level, but also responds to them culturally and spiritually. The earth and its riches are the basis on which traditional beliefs are built. Malaysia's indigenous forest dwellers have lived in harmony with their natural world for centuries. They take from nature's store cupboard only what they need for their own survival. Many rural societies or ethnic groups, particularly those who observe traditional animist beliefs, such as the Iban of Sarawak or the Negritos inhabiting the foothills of the Main Range, have a strong respect for plants and animals. They believe that these deserve the respect that should be accorded to any living being. Any 'disturbance' of animals and plants has to be preceded by man's placating or cajoling of the *semangat* or soul spirits that they possess. For example, when a tree is to be felled, signs of 'permission' must be obtained by reading the leaves, branches and the nodes of other large trees in the vicinity. When land is cleared to make way for a house, only the exact amount of land for the building is cleared and it is important that the surrounding area remains undisturbed.

The indigenous peoples also have deep respect for the sea and its creatures. Complex beliefs and

## The Malay house: Using natural materials

### Ventilation
Building materials with low thermal properties, such as wood, means that little heat is retained within or conducted into the house. Grilles and fenestrations fragment sunlight as it enters the house, and provide illumination whilst reducing the intensity of the sun's rays.

A bas-relief with floral designs found in a wall panel in a traditional Malay house.

Palms in a house compound are important for shade, fuel and making tools.

An *atap* roof made from natural material, such as *nipah* palm leaves, is cool and does not absorb excess heat.

*rumah ibu* (central area)

*serambi* (informal area or veranda)

*rumah dapur* (kitchen)

A carving with fenestrations is both aesthetic and practical, as it allows ventilation and light into the house.

Windows that open wide provide ventilation at body height.

A house on stilts keeps animals and floods at bay.

A Malay kampong house in Penang.

The traditional Malay kampong house is built from locally found materials and is constructed with the tropical climate in mind. It is a response to the needs, culture and lifestyle of its inhabitants. As such, aesthetic considerations are combined with appropriateness to the local climate and environment. The houses blend harmoniously into the natural setting from which they derive their materials. They are made of wood, the country's most plentiful natural resource; only occasionally are the buildings strengthened by stones. In the more remote areas, poles are taken from small trees, bamboo and hardy *nibong* palm are used as floor matting, the bark of hardwoods is employed for walls and the roof is of *atap* palm thatch. The tropical environment also dictates the shape and form of the buildings. A house is protected from the monsoon downpours, as well as from the sun, by a low-hanging roof.

rituals are observed in the construction and launching of their boats. A man embarking on a sea voyage or fishing trip is deemed to be intruding into the realm of the guardian spirits of the sea, and therefore he must seek their permission to do so.

## Traditional Malay dwellings

The basic design of the Malay house has given rise to many styles, from the intricate systems of longhouses in the interior of Sabah and Sarawak, to individual dwellings of the coastal Peninsular areas. The former has a common corridor where family members gather to weave, prepare their food or rest. The latter has developed different informal areas in which to receive guests and friends.

The natural colours of the wood and other construction materials are retained and what embellishment there is tends to be decorative carving on window panels, gables and door frames. The inspiration for many of the relief carvings of the Iban and the Orang Ulu is nature itself. They depict *naga* or magical snakes, crocodiles or beautiful flowering plants. The decorations on the homes of Malay Muslims are deliberately non-figurative as Islam forbids the depiction of the human and animal form in art, and homes incorporate floral patterns and designs such as *awan larat*, which are inspired by the clouds. The extent of such embellishments—whether they represent animate or inanimate forms—often denote the wealth and status within society of the resident of the house they adorn.

## Traditional crafts

The objects that people make are not only utilitarian, but are also expressions of aspects of their lives. Thus, Malaysian crafts, like traditional houses, combine functional and aesthetic features. A significant new recipient of Malaysian crafts is the visiting tourist. Traditional crafts play an important economic role and it can be argued that tourism has played a part in sustaining the Malaysian craft industry. Objects are made from a combination of

A woven basket from Kudat, northeastern Sabah.

A *wakid*, a bamboo and rattan basket made by the Kadazan people who live on the hills of Sabah's interior. It is used for carrying agricultural produce.

Traditional hats woven from brightly coloured *nipah* palm leaves.

A basket for transporting produce and rice, crafted by the Melanau peoples of Sarawak.

## Rattans and basketware

Forests, rivers and coasts all provide abundant material for crafts fashioned out of grass and plant fibres. The traditional Malaysian craft of rattan weaving can be perceived throughout the country. Treated leaves, stems and roots of plants are woven, plaited and coiled to produce a range of basketware. Mats, bags, rucksacks and household goods are decorated with various stylized ferns and birds. Rattan is still used by the indigenous peoples for making, for example, fish traps, food covers and baskets for their daily use. Traditionally, the weaving of these crafts has been a female activity. The women of Terengganu are particularly renowned for the fine quality of their work.

Baskets have existed as containers and retained their basic form for thousands of years. Back carriers are used by interior peoples and consist of rattan woven in a loose honeycomb pattern.

Basket weaving is a long-practised craft. In this early 20th-century photograph (left), women dye *pandan* leaves by boiling them in a dye pot. Their creative descendants, at the end of the century, gather to weave in a kampong home.

jungle creepers, bamboo, reeds and grasses. Many indigenous groups in Sabah and Sarawak also use bone, metal, stone, shell and clay.

Malaysians have depended, until relatively recently, exclusively on the wealth of the land and seas for their subsistence and economic growth. In the last quarter of the 20th century, such growth has been increasingly dominated by industrial and technological advances.

## Textiles: Embellishments inspired by nature

Textiles like *songket*, *pua* and batik are heavily dependent on the patterns of creepers, leaves and flowers, birds and butterflies for their motifs. Songket is decorated with gold and silver thread and is a heavy, elaborate cloth woven on a loom. Batik cloth, decorated with either traditional stamped designs or with hand-painted free-flowing styles, typically presents images of plants and brightly coloured flowers. The pua is dominated by geometrical or symbolic representations of reptiles and ferns.

*Kain songket* ( bottom right), luxurious handwoven silk shot with gold or silver thread, was once the prerogative of royalty, but is now worn by a wider population for weddings and formal occasions. Each piece is handwoven on warping frames, mainly by village women on small looms (left).

ABOVE: Batik started to be made in Kelantan in the 1930s, the art having been introduced from Indonesia.

Dayak men of Sarawak beat tree bast with water with a short wooden pestle. The resulting bark cloth is fashioned into shirts and jackets, which are now mostly worn only as ceremonial dress.

79

# Traditional attitudes towards the environment

*For the indigenous peoples of Malaysia's pre-industrial past, the relationship between man and nature was necessarily a very intimate one. It often involved a mystical view of the world where subsistence activities such as hunting, fishing or farming were perceived to be as much a ritual undertaking as they were a matter of practical technique. In many instances, especially in pre-literate societies without written records, ritual edicts served to codify traditional survival strategies, ensuring their successful transmission from one generation to the next by word of mouth.*

Penan hunters rest by the Tiga River, upper Baram, Sarawak. The Penan, an allegedly 'primitive' people leading a subsistence existence in the depths of the rainforest, have for many come to represent the archetype of natural man.

Carved Bidayuh male and female spirit figures are traditionally placed at the entrance to a village to ward off malevolent spirits.

## Animism

Many of Malaysia's indigenous peoples traditionally shared a common view of the world which may be described as animistic in character. Briefly, everything that exists, even inanimate or man-made objects, is believed to have a spirit counterpart, or 'soul', which participates in a kind of parallel universe that mirrors the mundane world of everyday experience. Though lacking in substance, this alternative 'reality' impinges upon the material world in that events occurring in the spirit realm have a direct effect on the physical world and vice versa. In the case of living things, it is this immaterial, and for the most part unseen, spirit 'essence' which causes them to be animated.

For human beings, this duality of body and soul is summed up by the Malay concepts of *tubuh* and *semangat*. The former term refers to the corporeal self and the latter refers to man's spiritual nature. These terms are part of an ancient web of ideas whose counterparts can be found throughout the Malay and Indonesian archipelagoes, testifying to a common Austronesian cultural inheritance. Naturally, this notion of a parallel world of spirit identities has played a crucial role in the way that people in the region have traditionally approached even the most practical of tasks, and in every aspect of life one finds evidence of ritual observances intended to influence events in the spirit realm.

## Corporate versus private ownership

The Penan are all too often depicted as simple jungle nomads who wander aimlessly through the forest of Sarawak in small groups, living from hand to mouth in a haphazard and desultory fashion. This is very far from the truth.

The Penan sense of territory and landscape is a very developed one, with rivers providing a framework around which this local knowledge is organized. Even the smallest trickle of water has a name and everyone in the group is aware of the precise location of these watercourses and the relationships between them in terms of size, the angle at which they flow relative to one another, their junctions and other significant topographical features such as waterfalls, rapids and pools. Within the home territory, well-maintained trails run between economically important sites, such as stands of sago palm or rivers well stocked with fish: known fruiting seasons and other periods of

## The soul of rice

Rice farming is central to the traditional economy of many of Malaysia's peoples and everywhere is surrounded by ritual practices and symbolic importance. Traditionally, supplications must be made to the deities of soil before clearing the land for cultivation, while subsequent stages in the agricultural cycle are prefaced by ritual observations intended to enhance the fertility of rice and protect the crop against pestilence and disease which are perceived in terms of malevolent spirit agencies. Rice itself is believed to have a soul which both animates the rice plant and is the source of agricultural fertility.

Agricultural rites frequently portray the natural increase of rice in terms of the fertility of women. In local mythologies, the first rice seed is depicted as having sprung from the body of a dismembered woman and ripening rice plants are typically said to be 'pregnant'. Significantly, in the Iban pantheon of deities, the wife of Pulang Gana, the paramount god of rice farming, is called Serentum Tanah Tumboh, which can be translated as 'Serentum, the fertile earth', while her daughter is named 'Seed dissolving in soil'. Here one sees a comparison made between the earth and the womb—both are containers for new life.

The correspondence between agricultural production and human reproduction is evident in the Iban planting rituals when it is always the women of the community who are allocated the task of placing the rice seed in the ground.

Dibbling is almost always done by men, the action of driving the dibble stick into the earth being metaphorically identified in ritual liturgies with sexual intercourse. The dibble stick itself is compared to the male generative organ.

abundance or scarcity will determine the pattern of movement from one location to another.

There are also clearly recognized rights of ownership, both private and communal, over natural resources. Tree species whose fruit are harvested only after they have fallen to the ground, for example, durian (*Durio zibethinus*) and several types of wild mango (*Mangifera* spp.), belong to the community as a whole, while those whose fruit is harvested when still on the tree belong to individuals who will mark them in some way to claim their ownership.

## An ambivalent view of nature

Traditional attitudes towards the natural world often are highly ambivalent. The forest is a source of food and raw materials, but it is also a place of danger where one can lose one's way or fall prey to snakes and other wild animals. This ambivalence is evident among the Ma' Betisék (Mah Meri) Orang Asli communities on Carey Island, off the coast of Selangor, who subscribe to two diametrically opposed views of the relationship between themselves and the natural world. On the one hand, they believe that plants and animals were 'cursed' (*tulah*) by their forefathers to become food for humans and that this legitimizes their exploitation by man which necessarily results in their death and destruction. On the other hand, the Ma' Betisék also claim that the killing and destruction of plants and animals is taboo (*kemali'*) and will bring about misfortune and death to those who do so.

These contrasting attitudes towards the natural world are not seen so much as contradictory, but rather as complementing one another, and they are summoned up according to specific circumstances. Tulah ideas, for example, predominate in hunting and agricultural rites, which highlight the economic usefulness of animals and plants, while kemali' ideas are prominent in healing rituals and rites to ward off misfortunes, especially natural disasters such as droughts, thunderstorms and whirlwinds. In the latter instance, plants and animals are generally referred to as ancestors which stresses an affinity between man and nature. Nevertheless, the natural world is without culture or morality—animals are incestuous and eat one another, and for this reason they were cursed by the ancestors of the Ma' Betisék.

## Iban stellar lore

The Iban, like other Southeast Asian peoples, make use of the movement of the stars as a calendrical device around which they organize their annual agricultural cycle. The Pleiades are particularly important in this scheme of things, the stars which make up this constellation being identified in Iban mythology as seven sisters. One story tells of how they were visited in ancient times by the culture hero Raja Tindit. He married the youngest of the

Atlas and Pleione are the father and mother respectively of the original seven sisters.

sisters and it was she who explained how they could be useful to him as a signal when to sow the rice crop. When the Pleiades first appear above the horizon at dawn is the time when the inaugural rites of the farming season should be held and the land cleared for swiddens. This is in early June. Later, in early September when the stars reach their zenith at dawn, it is time to begin planting.

Perhaps the most interesting aspect of Iban stellar lore, is evidence of its considerable antiquity. The Iban identify the Pleiades as being seven sisters, but only six stars in the constellation are visible to the naked eye. According to the Iban, the seventh sister variously committed incest and was pierced with a bamboo stake as tradition demands, or alternatively she tripped and fell to earth, being smashed to pieces and creating the Kapuas lakes in West Kalimantan in the process. The remarkable thing here, however, is that in the distant past there were indeed seven stars in the Pleiades group, but one burnt out at the end of the second millennium BCE.

## Blood, thunder and the mockery of animals

Ambivalent attitudes towards the natural world can also be discerned in a widespread ritual complex featuring thunder and lightning, blood sacrifice and the mockery of animals. The basic premise here is that certain types of behaviour constitute an offence against the natural order of things. This includes acts which compromise the dignity of animals, for example, laughing at them or dressing them up in clothes. The likely consequences of such rash behaviour are tempestuous storms, followed by a flood, with the offender typically being struck by lightning and often turned to stone. These ideas are common to all the indigenous peoples of Malaysia and are widespread throughout the region. There are remarkable parallels between the beliefs of the Penan of Sarawak and those of the Semang of Peninsular Malaysia despite the fact that the former belong to an Austronesian cultural tradition and the latter come from an Austro-Asiatic one. Often there is the accompanying idea that offences against nature can be paid for by an offering of blood drawn from the leg of the wrongdoer. In the case of Negrito Orang Asli groups in Peninsular Malaysia, hair, cut from the transgressor's head, is also included as part of the offering.

A Bukar Sadong shaman from Serian, Sarawak, performing the inaugural *langi julang* dance at a Bidayuh *gawai* festival. Gawai are held as a thanksgiving for the rice harvest and also to call upon the gods to bestow their blessings for the future prosperity, fertility and general wellbeing of the community.

A Negrito man takes blood from his leg to offer to the god of thunder, Kedah, 1920s. From Paul Schebesta's *Among the Forest Dwarfs of Malaya*, published in 1929.

The Iban of Sarawak, like many agrarian societies in Malaysia, are obliged to make offerings to the guardian spirits of the soil at the beginning of the agricultural cycle in order to compensate them for the use of land during the forthcoming farming season.

81

# Environmental ethics

*The attitude of Malaysian peoples to the natural world has been influenced at various times in their history by a combination of traditional belief systems and secular principles. Environmental ethics refer to a set of principles, values or norms relating to the ways in which an individual or a group interacts with the environment. In contemporary Malaysia, these values are established primarily through laws to protect the environment, made at both the national and international level.*

The Bobohizan Priestesses carry out important ceremonial duties after the rice harvest on behalf of their community in respect for the rice spirits.

Vital to the rites performed by the Bobohizans are their offering paraphernalia.

Primitive societies, still following a traditional lifestyle where individuals have inherent respect for the environment, usually have a more reverential approach to nature than urban dwellers.

## Origins and characteristics

Living in a multiethnic society, Malaysians possess a variety of ethical precepts, many of which call for a harmonious relationship between man and nature. All the major belief systems have certain tenets which refer to recommended modes of behaviour towards the environment. But in practice, such tenets are rarely translated into action beyond the level of ritual observance, especially among those who live in urban areas. Among rural dwellers, particularly those whose livelihoods depend on the environment, such as the aboriginal communities in Peninsular Malaysia and the numerous indigenous groups in Sabah and Sarawak, more reverential values pertaining to man–environment relationships are still observed (see 'Traditional attitudes towards the environment'). With continuing modernization it is not certain whether such transcendental values can be sustained. It is more likely that with the spread of secular education, old values, which are largely based on supernatural beliefs, will be gradually fused with new secular values based on scientific understanding of the environment.

As this change is taking place, a more specific and assertive version of environmental ethics pervades into local values through a global network of environmental action groups, such as the Malaysian Nature Society, Friends of the Earth and the Environmental Protection Society. Such groups are active about protecting the environment and are important awareness-raising bodies. They not only alert the public, but also help to place environmental issues firmly on the political agenda. Environmental ethics constitute a spectrum of values that vary under pervading cultural and historical circumstances and are not a single, fixed set of ideas.

Man's attitude to the environment evolved through four general stages in the history of Malaysia: animism, colonial mercantilism, post-colonial laissez faire administration, and environmental legislation after the mid-1970s. These stages do not represent mutually exclusive segments but only the dominant modes of thought for each period. In late 20th-century Malaysia, the emphasis is on using statutory law as a strategy for environmental management.

## Animist reverence for nature

Before the arrival of colonial rulers who brought in other immigrant communities, each with their own system of values, Malaysia's indigenous communities lived in river settlements and depended almost entirely on the natural environment for their survival. The Malays and most of the other tribal groups practised shifting cultivation and obtained food from the rivers and jungles. Their lives were vulnerable to attack from wild animals, diseases and other enemies, and were constantly subjected to the vagaries of nature such as floods, storms and droughts.

Although each adult member of the community would have acquired a great deal of folk knowledge on the environment, including the supernatural world, they had no acquaintance with the kind of scientific

An Iban seer makes predictions from the liver of a wild boar.

## The environment and religion

Religions practised in Malaysia advocate respect for the natural world and caution against its destruction.

*There is not an animal on the earth nor a flying creature soaring on two wings, but they are peoples like unto you.*      Qur'an, 6: 38

*The Earth dries up and withers. . . . The earth is defiled by its people, they have disobeyed the laws.*      Bible, Isaiah 25: 4–5

*Buddha law
Shining
In leaf dew*
            Issa, Buddhist meditator

*Part of myself is the God within every creature. . . . My energy enters the earth, sustaining all that lives: I become the moon, given of water and sap, to feed the plants and the trees.*      Bhagavad Gita

### Pesta Kaamatan: Placating the spirits

The rites and customs of Pesta Kaamatan, the Harvest Festival, are observed by most Sabahans, although they are specific practices of the Kadazan (Dusun) and Murut peoples. It is believed that the rice embodies a rice spirit, Bambaazon, that must be protected from harm. Such a task falls to the Bobohizan, Bobolian or Tantagas, ritual specialists of the locale.

The Bobohizan selects some rice stalks, which are left undisturbed until after the harvest when they are cut and carried to the paddy owner's house. This ceremonial homecoming of the Bambaazon may be marred if parts of the spirit are hurt or separated from the main mystical body because of floods, pests or man's carelessness.

It is the task of the Bobohizan to chant prayers to invoke the lost or damaged rice spirit. The ceremonial ritual, known as the Magavau, is commonly enacted indoors, and concludes with food offerings to the reformed Bambaazon, and general community merrymaking.

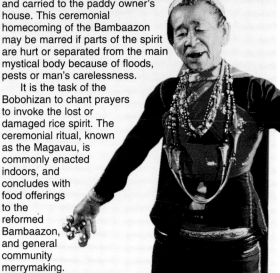

A Lotud Tantagas (female ritual specialist) offers prayers to the rice spirits. The Lotud inhabit the alluvial plains of Sabah's west coast, about 30 kilometres north of Kota Kinabalu.

A postcard from around 1908 showing a colonial couple at Crag Hotel, Penang Hill, making use of the environment for recreation.

understanding that modern man is exposed to. Consequently, much of the natural environment remained in the realm of the unexplored. Such widespread ignorance helped to perpetuate a general fear of the unknown, which in turn gave rise to a corpus of folklore and superstitions on a variety of environmental phenomena.

For the same reason, most ethnic cultures in Malaysia subscribed to the existence of supernatural beings. Taboos governed the individual's action in the environment so as not to disturb these spiritual beings, and numerous rituals and ceremonies were held to placate guardian spirits. It was customary to perform a ceremony (*tolak bala*) to ward off evil at the erection of a new house, or at the time of an epidemic or other calamity. Such ceremonies are still common among the Orang Asli and other indigenous groups in Sabah and Sarawak, where ritual cleansing of evil spirits before clearing the jungle for agriculture (*buka hutan*) and to appease sea spirits (*puja pantai*) is still being practised.

### Colonial mercantilism

As an ethical position this asserts that the interest of the nation, or the empire, overrules other considerations, and that this interest can be promoted through maximizing the nation's wealth through international trade. It was this motive that led to a succession of colonial powers taking control of new territories throughout the world from the 16th century. In Malaysia, colonial mercantile administration started with the Portuguese occupation of Melaka in 1511, and ended with the formation of Malaysia in 1963. In terms of

environmental ethics, the colonial usurpers did not respect nature as the native animists did, but treated nature as a gift from God to serve the interest of their motherlands. In essence, the colonial philosophy regarded the environment as a milieu from which valuable resources could be drawn to enrich the imperial coffer.

This perspective eventually led to land being parcelled out as a usable and exchangeable commodity, to be exploited with little regard for non-financial considerations. Land laws and ordinances were introduced to delineate nature reserves and wildlife sanctuaries, but mainly for utilitarian purposes—for recreational and scientific needs. Given the abundant supply of land during the colonial period and the near absence of man-induced environmental problems at the time, there was no need to pay attention to conservation issues beyond the enactment of housekeeping ordinances designed to regulate urban land use practices.

### Post-colonial administration to environmental legislation

When Malaya gained independence from the British in 1957, it inherited a system of administration which was designed to support the operation of a free market. Environmental matters such as public health care, urban sanitation, drainage, forest and wildlife management, fell under central government control. There was very little interest in conservation issues. This situation continued into the early 1970s when conservation concerns began to receive attention from politicians and policy makers worldwide. Prior to this, the newly established Malaysian government continued the previous policy of economic growth through the expansion of commodity production. The main concern was to develop rural areas as a strategy towards the eradication of poverty. By the mid-1970s, however, the traditional emphasis on commodity production began to be revised in favour of economic diversification. The waste produced by some industrial sites, together with the rural-based palm oil and rubber factories, began to create pollution problems which subsequently led to the promulgation of the Environmental Quality Act of 1974.

The 1974 Environmental Quality Act legislates for a cleaner, greener environment across Malaysia. Despite rapid expansion, Kuala Lumpur retains pockets of green space amidst its high-rise jungle.

### Legislating for the environment

The Environmental Quality Act 1974 (EQA) was the first attempt to use comprehensive legislation for the purpose of environmental protection. This act empowers the Department of Environment (DOE) to take polluters to task for damaging the environment, through licensing procedures which require factory or site operators to dispose of waste in line with prescribed standards. The effectiveness of this strategy depends on the capacity of the DOE to check that each industry is complying with the regulations. Although the impact of the EQA has been rather limited, its enactment has been valuable in terms of raising public awareness of environmental problems. Such awareness is one of the most important preconditions towards developing a greater appreciation of the true value of the environment in society.

# Early agricultural methods

*Societies with minimal contact outside their own community
derive their basic needs from resources found in their
immediate surroundings. This close man–nature relationship is
most obviously manifested amongst itinerant hunters and gatherers.
More settled communities establish their own sustainable forms of land
cultivation and, if they remain small, they too work with the land and
are not a threat to it. Hunter-gatherers and shifting cultivators were still
active in Malaysia in the late 20th century and remain in remote parts
of the country.*

Hunter-gatherers rely on the forest
and rivers for their food. Two men
return home after a successful
hunting trip with game strapped to
their backs.

The Negritos Bateq pursue a
nomadic existence in the north of
Peninsular Malaysia. They hunt and
gather small game, such as
squirrels and birds, with the
formidable blowpipe (*sumpit*). Made
from 2 metres of bamboo and
equipped with a wooden dart, the
blowpipe, when used by an
accomplished hunter, can impale
prey up to 36 metres away.

## Hunters and gatherers

Hunters and gatherers are nomadic people
without any permanent settlement base. Their
peripatetic lifestyle does not allow for any
permanent agriculture. They depend on
what they can gather from the forest, the
lakes and the rivers and what they hunt
from the land. They feed on wild
animals, such as pigs, monkeys and
birds, and gather leaves, shoots, nuts,
fruits, roots and tubers from the forest
floor. Whenever nature's store is exhausted and
needs time to replenish itself, the hunters and
gatherers move to new areas where they might
obtain the ingredients they require to survive in
their, literally, hand-to-mouth existence. Depending
on the availability of produce, they will stay for
several days. Their settlement is of the crudest kind
so it can be decamped with ease.

Several decades ago, the Semang community of
the interior rainforest of Peninsular Malaysia still
maintained themselves by gathering food from
forest resources. They wandered from one area to
the next once it had been
harvested. Some Penan in Sarawak
still follow such a traditional way of life
(see 'Traditional attitudes towards the
environment'). The territory covered by the
hunter-gatherers in their daily search may be
up to a few kilometres. It is possible that each
distinct group has its own area within which it
operates, and only moves into uncharted territory
when its own locality is completely exhausted
of produce.

The close link between the hunter-gatherers and
the environment is always maintained. The
communities take only that which is needed for
self-sustenance. As a result, they cause an
imperceptible amount of irreversible damage to the
surrounding area. Such a way of life is only possible
when a small population base exists which can
guarantee successful regeneration in the area.

## Major features in shifting cultivation

A more settled community requires a
continuous supply of food. A rudimentary form of
agriculture may develop as the community
interferes with the natural ecology by planting food
plants. Shifting cultivation is necessary where there
is limited information or technological resources to
counter the limitations of poor tropical soils. Being
dependent on the natural soil fertility, the
community utilizes the farm area until it cannot
support further planting. Subsequent cultivation has
to be done in a new locality. This warrants a shift in
the farm plots. The two forms of shifting cultivation
involve either the community moving to a new
locality when soil fertility cannot support further
planting, or a shift in the type of farming plots
while the community remains in the same area.

Although shifting cultivation is rare in
contemporary Malaysia, as recently as the 1970s this
practice was still seen amongst the Kadazan (Dusun)
of Kundasang in Sabah and the Iban of Sarawak's
interior, as well as amongst small indigenous
communities in the Peninsula's rainforests.

## The *sawah* ecosystem

A yet more settled community
develops more permanent
settlements and establishes long-
term agricultural regimes.
Amongst Malays of the
coastal plains and river deltas,
rice is the predominant crop.
Wet rice cultivation, known as
the *sawah* ecosystem, shows a
stable relationship between man
and his environment. Before
modern technology was widely available, paddy
(wet rice) growing in Malaysia's 'rice bowl' on the

A bamboo trap used by
farmers to catch fish in the
paddy fields. Held at the top
with both hands, the trap is
quickly placed over the
unsuspecting prey.

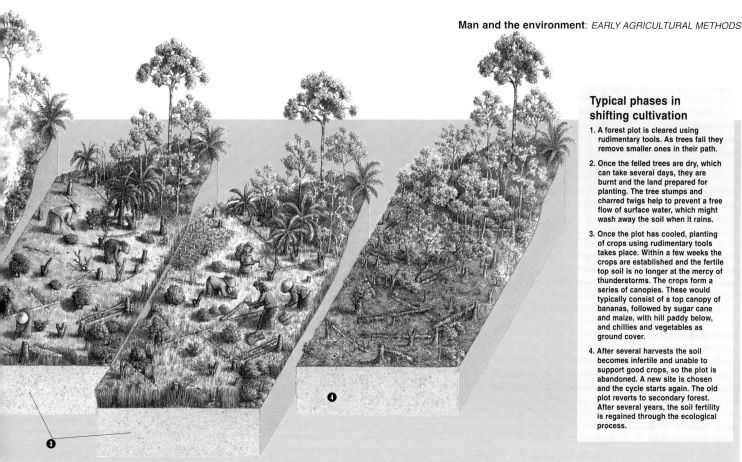

**Typical phases in shifting cultivation**

1. A forest plot is cleared using rudimentary tools. As trees fall they remove smaller ones in their path.

2. Once the felled trees are dry, which can take several days, they are burnt and the land prepared for planting. The tree stumps and charred twigs help to prevent a free flow of surface water, which might wash away the soil when it rains.

3. Once the plot has cooled, planting of crops using rudimentary tools takes place. Within a few weeks the crops are established and the fertile top soil is no longer at the mercy of thunderstorms. The crops form a series of canopies. These would typically consist of a top canopy of bananas, followed by sugar cane and maize, with hill paddy below, and chillies and vegetables as ground cover.

4. After several harvests the soil becomes infertile and unable to support good crops, so the plot is abandoned. A new site is chosen and the cycle starts again. The old plot reverts to secondary forest. After several years, the soil fertility is regained through the ecological process.

Kedah Plain and in the Kelantan Delta was a time-consuming process.

The wet paddy ecosystem is a unique system in which the farmer has a close control over water supply. He permits the growth of beneficial blue-green algae which fix nitrogen into the soil, thus enriching its fertility, and allows other non-harmful fauna and flora to thrive. Fish help control the populations of insects that can be harmful to the rice plants. Frogs, crabs and other aquatic life have similar roles and may also become an additional food source for the farmer.

The rice ecosystem is distinctive because the artificially created, hydromorphic paddy soil, which has been produced through tilling of soil, is submerged under water. The addition of organic matter, such as compost from weeds and paddy plants, helps to enrich the muddy ground. In earlier, traditional societies the wet paddy field was able to sustain a densely populated village. Rice was produced solely for self-consumption rather than for wider economic gain. The rice harvested and stored in one season was usually enough to meet the food needs of the community until the next.

## Living with nature

Hunter-gatherers do not create any noticeable changes to the physical environment since their

number is small and they take only those resources needed to maintain their simple lifestyle. The shifting cultivators may likewise have a minimal impact if their community is fewer than a dozen people. The sawah ecosystem shows how a well-managed relationship between man and his natural environment can work. If the community remains small, and the paddy is worked with traditional methods, the environment can be well preserved.

A *tuai* is traditionally used to cut ripened paddy.

## Wet rice cultivation: The *sawah* cycle

The farmer cleans the water canal, repairs and strengthens the bunds (embankments) to retain mud and water for the paddy-growing season. The land is ploughed (**1**), and flooded to several centimetres. Weeds are left to rot for a few weeks and later the land is raked to clear the soil of weeds. Paddy seedlings that have been sown and nurtured in a nursery are transplanted out in the field (**2**). The water level is regulated during the growing season to ensure healthy growth of the young plants, and the field is weeded to prevent them from being strangled. As the rice slowly ripens, the water in the field is gently drained. The ripened rice is harvested using sickles or *tuai* (**3**). After harvesting the field is left fallow until the next season, and the land often cleared by fire.

# Opening the Peninsula: Colonial impacts

*British colonial encounters with the Malaysian natural environment produced two contrasting outcomes. The colonial administration applied its knowledge and technology to exploit resources, ostensibly for the welfare of society back in Britain. The development of roads, railways, tin mines, and extensive rubber and oil palm plantations in the first half of the 20th century, are all legacies of Malaysia's colonial past. But, amidst the exploitation of resources the British also initiated environmental conservation through legislation and exemplary deeds.*

During colonial times, large acreages of pristine jungle were cleared to make way for new cash crops—rubber and later oil palm.

## Commercial exploitation of resources

A harmonious relationship between indigenous Malaysian man and his environment was the norm in pre-colonial times, when small-scale shifting cultivation and localized land exploitation for self-sufficiency, rather than wider trade, prevailed. This relationship was transformed through commercial exploitation of resources. The British imposed a new, market economy that immediately imbued the abundant local resources with economic values they freely exploited principally for the benefit, not of the local population, but of the coffers of the British Crown and a population thousands of miles away.

Malaysia's vast undulating terrain, especially that on the west coast of Peninsular Malaysia, parts of Sarawak and on the west coast of Sabah, was transformed. Thousands of hectares of virgin equatorial rainforest were logged and then cleared to carve out terraces for planting engineered rubber

### The rubber revolution

The extensive rubber plantations are perhaps the most obvious physical evidence of colonial changes to the Malaysian landscape. The sole goal of the British estate managers was to make profit. The estates were much vaster than the individual subsistence farms that had hitherto marked the pattern of agricultural land use. Rubber was the most important agricultural commodity in terms of hectares and people employed, and it soon became Malaysia's number one agricultural export, sweeping aside all other cash crops. In 1897, just 11 years after 'Rubber Ridley' received the first seeds of the *Hevea brasiliensis* at the Singapore Botanic Gardens, part of what was then British Malaya, only 137 hectares of land were under rubber cultivation. An agricultural report records that by 1909, some 82 064 hectares had been planted in Perak, Selangor, Negeri Sembilan and Pahang.

By 1930 two-thirds of the cultivated land area in Peninsular Malaysia was planted with rubber. By 1939 this had risen to 1.4 million hectares.

Nursery abutting a six-year-old rubber plantation, around 1907.

## Tin mining: The predominant methods

Opencast mining, used to mine both primary (older deposits) and alluvial ores, was favoured by Chinese miners. The alluvials are mechanically excavated from spiral terraces and once hauled to the surface, the cassiterite (tin) is removed.

clones on a commercial scale. Rubber was planted extensively and Malays, as well as new Indian immigrants, moved to work on the new colonially managed plantations. Others, persuaded by the commercial value of the new tree, grew it in independent smallholdings. Oil palm followed later. The forest clearance that began then, and which has continued and intensified through modern demands for land and timber (see 'Forest management'), helped destroy the forests' biodiversity, the unique gene pool of tropical forest species, a rich collection of medicinal plants and the habitats of wild animals that lived there.

## Tin mining

Under British colonialization, economic expansion progressed and exploitation of Malaysia's exceptionally rich mineral deposits, notably tin, commenced. Mining gave rise to new settlements and communication networks—roads and railway lines—to link the new pockets of population and provide adequate transportation routes for the marketable ore.

The present-day mining landscape in the Kinta Valley in Perak and the Klang Valley in Selangor, although now largely reclaimed areas with old mining ponds converted to recreational sites and duck farms, is still a good illustration of the dramatic changes to the original physical landscape that mining activities brought about. Malay, Chinese and European miners all left their mark on the landscape in the form of huge mining shafts and open pits. Traditionally self-sufficient cultivators and fishermen, the Malay miners' use of traditional mining methods, which reflected their low technological know-how, limited their impact on the landscape. They cleared the land and only worked the surface layers for tin.

Chinese miners mined tin by the opencast method. Using pumps to draw water from the pits, it was possible to mine deeper. With the availability

The dredge, introduced by the British, floats on water and draws up alluvium from under the water. Inside the dredge the alluvium is screened to remove the tin and any other minor minerals, and the waste then passes back into the water.

The primitive method of hand separating tin from gravels, known as panning, was practised by early Malay small, freelance mining operations. Earth and water are scooped into the pan or *dulang*, which is rotated so that the heavy cassiterite (tin) sinks to the centre and lighter sand and soil spill over the side with the water.

of the steam pump in the late 19th century, miners were able, at any one time, to work larger areas to a greater depth. The Chinese sluice box or *palong* was a common sight in the mining fields. But the most extensive and irreversible change to the mining landscape was brought about by European companies. Using modern machinery and methods of exploitation, large amounts of tin were extracted. The Europeans introduced new technology for lode mining, for mining in low and swampy areas, and for excavation. In the early 20th century, the dredge was introduced, allowing fast and extensive tin exploitation in swampy areas.

The overall impact of mining on the physical environment was widespread. Panning skinned the land surface leaving scattered scars, forest clearance induced erosion, sand tailings from dredges destroyed the landscape, and sand discharges into the drainage system modified river flows and changed the course of tributaries. A badlands topography emerged in place of the original landscape and man-made lakes, sand hills and mounds characterized the new dominant land features, which can still be seen today.

### Other new impacts

Apart from the cultivation of rubber and the mining of tin, gold and iron were also mined but they were

An aerial view of modern-day Ipoh tin mining, clearly showing the legacy of mining on the area's landscape.

limited to Raub, in the case of gold, and Bukit Besi in Dungun in Terengganu, for iron. Compared to the widespread mining and availability of tin, there was limited land degradation in those areas. Related closely to its commercial agricultural and mining activities, the colonial government initiated the growth of urban settlements, creating an expanded network of new roads and railways that were the communication arteries that transported the new exploited products—rubber and tin—about the country and to ports for export. These settlements completely transformed the original ecology to produce an urban ecosystem. In this urban, as opposed to predominantly rural, landscape the built-up townscapes tended to develop their own weather and climate. Commercialization of their economic activities had slowly drawn people to congregate in large numbers in relatively small areas. The high population density produced other related problems, such as household waste disposal and sewage discharge.

### Colonial conservation

Amidst these gradual and accelerated changes to the environment, the colonial administration initiated environmental conservation. As far back as 1879, the British had introduced the General Land Regulation with the purpose of controlling land exploitation. By 1895 the Mining Code was enforced giving the Warden of Mines the power to control mining methods. The colonial administration also introduced a number of enactments to regulate specific components of the environment. These included the Waters Enactment (1920), the Town and Country Planning Act (1927), the Forest Enactment (1935), and the Natural Resources Ordinance (1949).

These helped to formulate measures to make the population aware of the need to protect the equatorial rainforest, to minimize mining damage, and to care for wild animals. On the eve of Independence in 1957, Malaysia's landscape already possessed special reserved forest and protected water areas, but massive threats to the environment, to animal and plant species, did still remain. The development that ensued after Independence, at an even greater pace, provoked further detrimental environmental conditions, that in some cases proved irreversible.

## Development of the railway

Padang Besar
Alor Setar
Sungai Golok
Tumpat
Pasir Mas
Perai
Taiping
Port Weld
Enggor
Ipoh
Tronoh
Jalan Tapah
Kuala Lipis
Teluk Anson
Kuala Kubu Baharu
Batang Berjuntai
Batu Caves
**KUALA LUMPUR**
Ampang
Port Klang
Seremban
Gemas
Port Dickson
Tampin
Melaka
Johor Bahru
Singapore

----- 1893
---- 1900
----- 1910
—— 1939
⚒ Tin deposits

Source: After map in Hill (1979)

The pattern of development of Peninsular Malaysia's railway system was directly related to the tin-mining areas. The cities of Ipoh and Kuala Lumpur both developed from tin boom towns.

Batu Caves railway station, around 1907. The British introduced Malaysia's main networks of roads and railways.

The Great Waterfall in the Botanic Gardens in Penang, the first recreational park of its type to be established in Malaysia by the British. Lithograph by William Daniell from a painting by Captain Robert Smith (published 1821).

# Post-Independence developments

*Since Independence from the British in 1957, Malaysia has actively pursued policies to develop and modernize the country and to eradicate poverty amongst the population. Rapid development from the 1970s onwards is most obviously seen in urban expansion and in population growth. Such development brings changes that increasingly have a negative impact on Malaysia's natural environment.*

### The development route

Malaysia's socioeconomic development broadly follows the general model for a country occupied in shaking itself loose from the clutches of colonial influence.

Early years of Independence, concentration on modernizing society to achieve economic growth.

When growth is achieved, wealth is used to eradicate widespread poverty.

Economic growth is sustained and wealth is used for widespread infrastructural, social and economic development.

Environmental degradation issues surface and force governments into taking protective action.

### Oil palm and rubber

N

0    120 km

- Rubber
- Oil palm
- Jengka Triangle

Source: After Hill (1979)

In the years after Independence, oil palm cultivation (plantation shown above, top) increased substantially. In 1957, the crop covered 47 000 hectares; by 1972, this had risen to 887 000 hectares. Main FELDA oil palm and rubber schemes and the Jengka Triangle in Peninsular Malaysia are shown on the map (c. 1979).

## Modernization

After Independence, Malaysia's prime aim was to develop the economy and modernize society. This included resolving problems of inequality which the colonial period had perpetuated and raising the living standards of the population. In the first thirteen years after Independence, rural development programmes sat at the centre of the country's development strategy. The Federal Land Development Authority (FELDA) began to resettle the landless, rural poor in new land schemes (see 'Settlement patterns: Displaced people'), the largest of which, and the earliest, was the Jengka Triangle in Pahang. In addition, schemes operated by the Federal Land Consolidation and Rehabilitation Authority (FELCRA) and the Rubber Industry Smallholders' Development Authority (RISDA) extended the number of rubber and oil palm smallholdings. Improved drainage and irrigation of lands in Kedah, Perak and Kelantan led to increased farming of rice, and paddy production was extended commercially to Sarawak. In the 1970s, an increase of 3 million hectares of virgin forest was brought into agricultural production through regional development authorities.

## Industrialization and urbanization

From 1970, Malaysia made a major push to become an industrial exporter in order to increase economic growth and thus hasten socioeconomic development. Such efforts bore fruit—by the end of the 20th century, just over 40 years after Independence, Malaysia is the world's 19th largest trading nation with its industrial exports outstripping agricultural produce. Through various government incentives, foreign investors were attracted to the country to establish manufacturing industries. More roads, telecommunication systems and amenities were developed and industrial estates established on the outskirts of existing urban centres. Kuala Lumpur, as the country's central growth area, experienced explosive development, sending its urban areas sprawling out into the surrounding countryside to form a huge conurbation that now extends for 50 kilometres from the natural barrier of the Main Range to Port Klang on the coast of the Strait of Melaka. Penang and Johor Bahru also experienced expansion on a massive scale. State capitals grew to become regional centres. Urban immigration of rural workers contributed to the expansion of existing cities and towns and the rise of new industrialized towns in forested land.

## Sustainable development

All development efforts have, until very recently, been concentrated on socioeconomic progress. The development achievements, however, have not been without problems. Progress has introduced a new range of social problems, such as urban congestion, pollution and inadequate housing. There is a general consensus that economic development and social transformation should be accompanied by environmental conservation. To achieve sustainable development, Malaysia needs to develop its socioeconomy with regard to the country's ecology and not at its expense. Informed knowledge about the environmental consequences of development in the more socioeconomically advanced regions of the world serve as warnings to countries like Malaysia, driving home the urgent need for a harmonious relationship between man and the environment, lest Malaysia too should suffer the scorching effects of environmental degradation. The state provides an overall framework for environmental conservation with policies that legislate for sustainable development and management of the environment. Since the passing of the Environmental Quality Act in 1974, the state has played a primary role in ensuring socioeconomic progress continues with respect for the natural environment (see 'National environment policy'). The combined effect of the state's proactive role as the ultimate guardian of the Malaysian environment together with the policing acts of non-governmental organizations (NGOs) and increased public commitment to environmental conservation, makes the promise of sustainable development more of a reality.

In cities and towns, urban greening and the creation of mini parks help to reduce the impending threat of urban heat islands. There are organizations which clean, maintain and protect rivers from degradation through their 'Love Our Rivers' campaigns. Other groups cry foul of marine pollution and overexploitation of mangroves or excessive slope development. Urban dwellers are becoming impatient with acute traffic congestion and with the air pollution that arises from vehicle emissions and industrial wastes. Rural people have to grapple with chemical pollution from chemical weedkillers and consumers in general are turning towards organically grown food.

**Development deals to include clause on environment**

Make KL a garden city: Mahathir

Environmental issues are now firmly on the Malaysian political agenda.

# Some consequences of increased urbanization

## A growing urban population

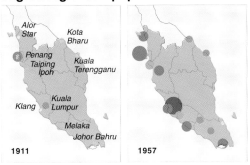

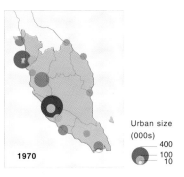

Urban size
(000s)
— 400
— 100
10

**1911** **1957** **1970**

People (000s)

Sarawak
Sabah
Peninsular Malaysia
Total

Source: UN *World Population Prospects*; *Information Malaysia* (1997)

The 1970s witnessed the first major urban and industrial growth in Peninsular Malaysia and saw the start of a rural–urban migration trend. The maps above show how selected towns developed in size from 1957 to 1970 and places this growth in the context of the preindustrial era of 1911.

### The making of a modern city
Kuala Lumpur was little more than a trading post in 1897 but developed rapidly in the 20th century to become a bustling international metropolis. The built-up area increased from one-third to 60 per cent of its total land area between 1966 and 1981 alone. The population of the city has risen equally dramatically as the graph shows.

Source: Hill (1979); Aiken et al (1983); UN (1995)

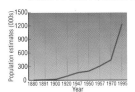

Population estimates (000s)

## Urban heat islands

**Parks, green areas and shady trees help to reduce urban temperatures and mitigate the heat island effect.**

An urban heat island refers to conditions when temperatures are warmest in a city centre and decrease towards suburbs and open land. Observations carried out in the Klang Valley from the 1970s suggest that built-up areas are usually several degrees warmer than the surrounding countryside. The average urban–rural temperature difference is 1–2 °C but can, during calm and cloud-free nights, be as great as 6–7 °C. City buildings tend to be made from materials that absorb rather than reflect heat: dark roofs, concrete and brick. Like tarmac roads, they have a high thermal capacity, which means they store heat during the day and release it slowly at night. Additional heat is generated by car fumes, factories and from people themselves.

Urban heat can impact not only on local climate and cause human discomfort, but can influence pollution concentration and dispersion which, in turn, affect the natural environment and human health. For example, emissions from vehicles and industry produce dust particles which contribute to urban pollution (see 'Air quality'). During an inversion, when normal atmospheric conditions are modified, circulation restrictions mean that dust-carrying air cannot escape. Dust particles absorb heat, thus also helping to raise temperatures and may contribute to hazy weather that causes asthma and interferes with business activities.

## Development in the Klang Valley
Increasing urbanization creates population pressures on land resources and growing competition for undeveloped land for agricultural, housing or industrial uses.
Agriculture is the most extensive form of land use in the Klang–Langat River basin, followed by forest which is located in the interior districts of Gombak, Ulu Langat and Petaling. Both agriculture and settlement are expanding at the expense of barren land and forest. The disused mining pools that scatter the landscape of the basin indicate that it was once a major tin-mining area. The pools account for the high acreage of water bodies. The rise in settlement is due not only to increased urban development to accommodate a growing population, but also to recent recreational additions, such as golf courses. Settlement will continue to rise, since major projects, such as the projected Multimedia Super Corridor, new international airport (open June 1998), new township of Putrajaya, express raillink, ring road, highways and industrial areas all fall within the river basin. The population in the area has grown from 1.5 million in 1970, to just over 2 million in 1980 and up to 3.2 million in 1991. The North–South Express-way facilitates growth of more urban settlements to accommodate overspill from the Federal Capital.

*LEFT*: A view across medium-cost housing in Petaling Jaya.

*BELOW*: A snapshot of Malaysia's most developed region between the years 1974 and 1990 shows how quickly changes to the land can occur as the pressure on resources from a growing population and industrial development increase.

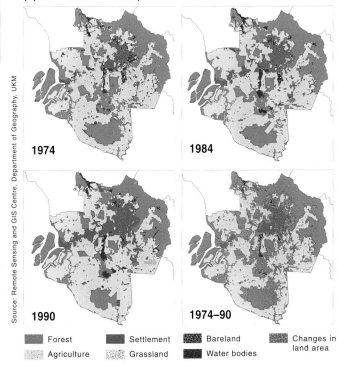

**1974** **1984**

**1990** **1974–90**

Source: Remote Sensing and GIS Centre, Department of Geography, UKM

Forest · Settlement · Bareland · Changes in land area
Agriculture · Grassland · Water bodies

# Changes in land use

*Malaysia's landscape has been subject to great changes in the 20th century as the country has advanced through various stages of economic development. The dynamics of land use changes are complex and largely driven by economic forces. Wide tracts of forest were transformed into rubber and oil palm plantations earlier this century, and agricultural land is now, in turn, being transformed by urban, industrial, commercial, residential and recreational development.*

The three main communication arteries that opened up the two parts of Malaysia to urban and industrial growth: rivers, roads and railways. The area shown is near Bukit Merah in Perak.

## A brief overview of land use

Before land was cultivated on a permanent, settled basis, farming was a small-scale, localized activity. A forest collector gathers *petai* pods (*Parkia speciosa*) in Kuala Kubu Baharu.

Relatively permanent human use of land in the Malay Peninsula began with mining in the mid-19th century, after the discovery of tin at Larut in Perak, and was followed, by the end of the 19th century, by agricultural production and the first rubber plantations. A world boom in rubber prices launched a scramble for land at the start of the 20th century and between 1910 and 1930 hundreds of rubber plantations were carved from Malaysia's tropical forests in the more accessible areas of Selangor, Perak, Penang, Melaka, Negeri Sembilan and Johor. Oil palm played a similar role in large-scale agricultural pioneering. From the 1940s, official encouragement of *sawah* (wet rice) production led to the reclamation of suitable wetlands in Kedah, the Kelantan delta, Melaka and the riverine valleys of Negeri Sembilan.

Political Independence in 1957 signalled a change from the deliberate, opportunistic land use under the British, to more planned land development that was linked more closely to the social needs of the population. Since Independence, large tracts of land have been opened up for agricultural settlement through regional development schemes on a scale comparable to the plantation expansion that was orchestrated by the British. The FELDA (Federal Land Development Authority) approach ranges from individual farming schemes to regional complexes. The rate of expansion in agricultural land use reached peak levels in the 1970s. Such expansion cannot, and does not, continue indefinitely; as competition for space from industry, tourism and other amenities increases, agricultural land may be converted to other uses.

## Urban industrial development

Development, especially in the Klang Valley, Penang/Seberang Perai, Johor Bahru, Melaka and other urban centres, is rapidly altering the face of Malaysia's economic, and thus also physical, landscape. Industries create employment and encourage population shifts from rural to urban centres, which in turn induce increased demand for housing and commercial services, social amenities (health, educational and recreational), and infrastructure (transport, water and electricity supplies). Rapid urban growth takes place often as existing and newly established industrial, commercial and residential areas expand and merge. Transport arteries, such as

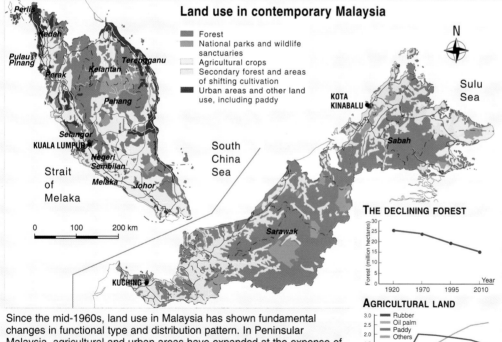

### Land use in contemporary Malaysia

- ■ Forest
- National parks and wildlife sanctuaries
- Agricultural crops
- Secondary forest and areas of shifting cultivation
- ■ Urban areas and other land use, including paddy

0    100    200 km

#### THE DECLINING FOREST

Forest (million hectares) — 1920, 1970, 1995, 2010

#### AGRICULTURAL LAND

- Rubber
- Oil palm
- Paddy
- Others

1970 1975 1980 1985 1990 1995 2000
Year

Others includes major cash crops: coconut, pepper, cocoa, pineapple and other fruits and vegetables.

Sources: The Malaysian Timber Industry Development Council (1994) (map); *Information Malaysia* Yearbook, various years, and FRIM (1987) (statistics)

Since the mid-1960s, land use in Malaysia has shown fundamental changes in functional type and distribution pattern. In Peninsular Malaysia, agricultural and urban areas have expanded at the expense of forests, dramatically in the case of the latter. Between 1966 and the early 1980s, urban and associated uses doubled in area from 74 000 to 150 000 hectares and forest areas contracted by 25 per cent, from 8.8 to 6.5 million hectares. Across Malaysia, in the last three decades of the 20th century, land has been converted to agriculture more than to any other use. In Sabah, the total land area under agricultural cultivation has almost quadrupled, from 175 000 hectares in 1963 to 687 300 hectares in 1990. In the same period, forests were reduced from 5.9 million hectares (1963) to 4.4 million hectares in 1990 (a decline from 80 to 60 per cent of the total land area). In Sarawak, agricultural land doubled, from 280 000 hectares in 1963 to 570 000 hectares in 1990 and forest declined from 9.1 million hectares in 1963 to 8.7 million hectares in 1990.

# Phases of land use expansion

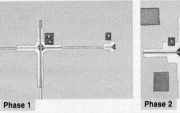
Phase 1

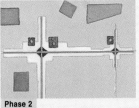
Phase 2

Phase 3

Phase 4

Phase 5

- Small agricultural holding
- Plantation
- Malay reservation
- Mining area
- Urban area
- Forest
- Forest reserve
- Road
- Path

Agriculture is by far the greatest encroacher on primary forest land in Malaysia. In the early 1990s, the total agricultural area in Peninsular Malaysia alone exceeded 4 million hectares. The expansion of agricultural land use in most parts of Malaysia followed a standard statistical or economically influenced pattern, each stage of which is characterized by localized spatial patterns. The phases occurred at different rates for different areas. Districts with more established urban centres, such as Kuala Lumpur, Penang and central Melaka, underwent the sequence more rapidly (and earlier) than less densely populated states.

The process can be characterized by five phases. In phase 1, rural and urban pockets are clearly defined. These become progressively less distinctly delineated as Malaysia progresses through the 20th century. By phases 4 and 5, urban sprawl has expanded and encroached upon former forested and agricultural land.

**PHASE 1:** Agricultural land use evolves around a settlement or mining camp at the initial stage of pioneering.

**PHASE 2:** Cultivation by peasants spreads out linearly along newly built roads or paths providing easy access to undeveloped areas in more remote districts. Virgin forest remains relatively undisturbed. As more land gets adopted for agriculture, gazetting of forested areas as reserves is introduced.

**PHASE 3:** Rapid diffusion of plantations on large tracts of land, mainly in the west coast states of Peninsular Malaysia. After Independence, development spread to less developed parts of Peninsular Malaysia, Sabah and Sarawak, in the form of government land settlement schemes.

**PHASE 4:** Areas suitable for agriculture are nearly exhausted leaving random parcels of land for farming by smallholders.

**PHASE 5:** Agricultural land begins to contract in area as it comes under pressure for conversion by a growing range of non-agricultural uses, such as urban and industrial development.

## The extent of development across Peninsular Malaysia (1984)

Phase
- 3
- 4
- 5

By the early 1980s, all districts in Peninsular Malaysia can be seen to have developed through phases 1 and 2 and can be placed under phases 3–5. More accessible, less hilly coastal areas are unsurprisingly more developed and have larger pockets of urban development than areas further in the interior.

After Independence, changing social conditions required a development strategy which gave priority to social justice, economic equality and poverty redressal. Pioneer FELDA (Federal Land Development Authority) settlements were introduced in the late 1950s.

From the early 20th century, freshwater swamps began to be transformed into distinctive paddy landscapes, characteristically dotted with small towns, kampongs, and drainage and irrigation canals. A contemporary view of paddy and vegetable fields near Kuala Selangor.

A few miles from Ipoh, this scene provides a good example of the patchwork nature of the landscape in developed regions. The limestone hills act as a natural barrier, preventing further spread of plantations and encroaching urbanization of the natural landscape.

The highland valley of Bareo in Sarawak is home to the Kelabit and still presents a landscape of low-impact development: small plots of paddy surrounded by virgin forest.

the North–South Expressway along the west coast of Peninsular Malaysia, are changing the mosaic of land use. Highways serve as growth corridors along which urban and housing complexes, new towns, industrial estates, golf courses and other resorts develop. These new features are replacing agricultural land in a process of re-allocation of productive resources from low- to high-income yielding uses.

## Future trends

Changes in land use will accelerate as the Malaysian economy continues to undergo structural adjustment and makes the transition from an agricultural to an industrialized and urbanized county. Land use patterns along the west coast states will become increasingly diversified to meet the demands of the urban–industrial and service sectors. Cumulative industrial and urban expansion will give

rise to further metropolitan growth, which will be aided further by the influx of immigrants from rural, less developed, parts of the country. These population shifts, motivated by employment opportunities in the urban industrial sector, are contributing to a significant increase in Malaysia's urban population growth. The built-up areas of the Peninsula, for example, increased dramatically between 1966 and 1990, from 66 302 hectares to 186 654, an increase of more than 35 per cent. In Sabah and Sarawak, development opportunities afforded by still untapped land resources will continue to be translated into a regrettably progressive decline of forest areas.

Current trends indicate that Malaysia's forests will continue to decline as the world demand for quality timber shows no sign of slowing down.

Agrochemicals are used on Malaysian crops more and more to achieve better and more economic yields.

As Malaysia develops industrially, more and more factories, and their inevitable wastes, are appearing.

*LEFT BELOW*: Tin mining in Malaysia is carried out mainly in Perak, where large tracts of land have been cleared for this purpose.

Logging, particularly in Sabah and Sarawak, takes place on a large scale.

## Striking the right balance

Malaysia's economic and industrial progress can only be deemed to have been successful if it is achieved with respect to the physical environment. Maintaining a balance between exploitation and protection of the natural world is one of the greatest challenges facing the country as it prepares to enter the 21st century. There is already commitment, backed by political will, on the part of some organizations and companies to tackle pollution and to try and conserve the nation's biological riches for future generations. Development projects if pursued unchecked can lead to serious environmental problems.

This waterfront along the Rajang River bustles with a variety of harbour activities.

Communication links across the country are improved by a huge bridge construction project along the Karak Highway.

Kuala Lumpur and the Klang Valley are expanding at a rapid rate. Construction at Bukit Gasing, Petaling Jaya is shown.

# ENVIRONMENTAL CONSEQUENCES OF DEVELOPMENT

Hill slopes are eroded by deforestation and made unstable by over development.

Although Malaysia's development achievements over the last 25 years have been impressive, such rapid pace of change has not been without its detrimental effects on the natural environment. It is not feasible to build new hydroelectric dams, airports and city conurbations, for example, without incurring physical change. But, to avoid extensive and unpalatable destruction of the environment and to demonstrate real progress, any new developments should ideally improve materially on what they destroy. Developing, and protecting, an environment that can be viably sustained into the foreseeable future is precisely what has not been the modern pattern of development in Malaysia. Despite all the improvements development has brought to the material lives of Malaysians, almost all aspects of the environment have been affected by development activities. These range from deforestation to air and water pollution, from erosion and siltation to the dangerous discharge of hazardous and toxic wastes.

The area of natural forests in both the Peninsula and Sabah and Sarawak is fast being depleted. Major causes include large-scale land development schemes, dam construction, mining, shifting cultivation and commercial logging. These activities also destroy, or threaten to diminish, the nation's biodiversity. Malaysia's closed canopy forests contain more than 50 per cent of the world's total plant species and about 1,000 species of vertebrates and anywhere between 20,000 and 80,000 invertebrates, many of which are indigenous. Soil erosion is closely associated with deforestation and vegetation clearance on hillslopes. This is best illustrated by erosion scars on steep road cuttings which can be observed alongside Malaysia's major highways.

Water and marine pollution are also closely related to many development activities. Major sources include organic wastes (sewage and animal wastes), silt from erosion and discharges from industries. Logging activities contribute to the siltation of rivers and the pollution of watercourses. Rivers which run through urban industrial areas contain heavy metals such as mercury, lead and zinc, and in many locations exceed World Health Organization standards. In coastal areas, oil and grease and suspended solids are major contaminants.

Air pollution is an additional problem, especially in urban industrial areas. Major sources include industries and motor vehicles. Kuala Lumpur and the Klang Valley are among the worse affected areas, with prolonged haze episodes occurring during dry months. Toxic and hazardous wastes are unavoidable by-products of industrialization. Their swift, safe and efficient disposal and greater enforcement of anti-pollution regulations should be national priorities.

# Forest management

*Malaysian tropical forests are acknowledged to be amongst the most species-rich on earth. They are exceptionally well stocked with trees of the Dipterocarpaceae family, which are valued for the high quality of their timber. As the forests face unprecedented pressure from human activity, such as conversion to other land use and timber harvesting, achieving a balance between economic exploitation and ecological preservation is a major concern. To prevent the forests disappearing altogether, sustainable management practices have been introduced.*

## Charting destruction

The rainforest is the most important ecological resource to have suffered heavily in Malaysia's pursuit of economic advancement. Between 1986 and 1990, 950 square kilometres of forest (or 1.6 per cent) a year were lost. These charts show the reduction in forested areas across Malaysia during the 20th century and the projected decline by the year 2010 if the current trend continues.

**1920** — 23%, 19%, 30%, 28%

**1970** — 28%, 19%, 29%, 24%

**1995** — 42%, 14%, 18%, 26%

**2010** — 54%, 12%, 16%, 18%

Forested area as % of total land area:
- Peninsular Malaysia
- Sabah
- Sarawak
- Unforested area as % of total land area

## Forest reduction

In Malaysia, forests have regularly been converted for agricultural use, but never before on the scale at the start of the 1970s. Cash crops, such as rubber, oil palm and cocoa, were heavily developed and landless villagers employed in the new plantations. This resulted in an acute reduction of most of the timber-rich lowland dipterocarp forests across the country. With the loss of lowland areas, forestry became limited to the hill forests, which are relatively poor in timber and more difficult to manage. Although forests represent over 56 per cent of the total land area, the decline in virgin hill forests has been dramatic.

In Sabah and Sarawak, in addition to cash crop development, forest reduction is due to uncontrolled slash and burn agriculture. To exacerbate the situation, increased demand for good quality hardwood timbers at competitive prices since the 1970s, particularly from the Asia–Pacific and the West, led to overharvesting and bad management practices. This boom coincided with improved mechanized techniques, which meant trees could be extracted more swiftly and cheaply with bulldozers and chain saws and then turned into planks at mechanized mills.

## Other fruits of the forest

In Malaysia, the prevailing primary concern seems to be the utilization of forest resources for the production of timber because it is an important source material for the manufacturing industry and fetches good foreign exchange. The forests, however, yield many more, often termed 'minor', forest products. Despite the term, such products have a major impact on local rural economies. They include rattan, bamboo, *illipe* nuts, spices, fragrances (such as *gaharu*), resins, wild fruits, wild sago, palm sugar, honey, and animals for food and skins. Logging the forests may vastly affect indigenous populations by robbing them of these plentiful supplies. For example, game sought by local hunters is threatened. One study in Sarawak showed that hunting in logged areas produced an average of 1.1 kilogram per man-hour, compared to twice that amount in unlogged areas. Meat is an important source of protein, and the study estimated that it would cost the Government of Sarawak about RM40 million to introduce fish ponds to compensate for the hunting losses. Although logging may provide local populations with employment, increased communication systems via new roads, and money from the government in the form of a royalty of about 45 per cent of the value of exported logs, it also leads to resettlement, the undermining of a subsistence economy, as well as the decline in other activities as cited above.

The bark of the yellow flame of the forest (*Peltophorum pterocarpum*), locally known as *jemerelang*, produces a reddish brown dye used in the batik industry. Its tannin is used for tanning leather.

In one study, it was found that for the removal of 133 large 'selected' trees, a further 1,145 trees were completely destroyed and others damaged. This represents a huge loss in future productivity.

| DAMAGE TO TREES FROM HEAVY MACHINERY USED IN HARVESTING AND HAULING | | |
|---|---|---|
| CATEGORY | NUMBER OF TREES (0.3 m diameter in 40 ha) | % |
| Fallen/broken | 1,145 | 61.7 |
| Bark damage | 10 | 0.5 |
| Crown damage | 105 | 5.7 |
| Bark and crown damage | 215 | 11.6 |
| Undamaged | 485 | 26.1 |
| Removed in selective felling | 133 | 6.3 |

## Management practices

Current management is based on selective felling. This involves harvesting trees that have attained a minimum diameter. The trees are extracted using a crawler tractor-skidder system and special lorries.

Although considered the most effective felling practice, selective felling is a cause for certain concerns. At what is termed the first cut the best trees are removed, leaving behind genetically inferior ones; this can cause heavy logging damage and subsequent mortality of the residual trees; and it often results in poorer than projected growth responses from the residuals (destined for the second cut).

Lack of consideration for the young regeneration that will form the third cut is also of concern.

Selective fellings are nevertheless considered most suitable for the forests in steeper

The bearded pig (*Sus barbatus*) roams forests and is an important source of protein.

## The real cost of rainforest destruction

Hasty and bad forest management has led to environmental problems and the loss of long-term timber productivity, and threatens biodiversity. Indigenous forest dwellers are displaced and seasonal earnings from minor forest products, such as rattans and medicinal plants, lost. In addition to damage to vegetation, heavy machinery used in harvesting causes massive soil damage leading to erosion. Logging roads and skid trails increase surface runoff almost tenfold from the normal 60 millimetres

a year to 550 millimetres. Increased runoff causes almost 30 times more soil erosion in the first year when an area is logged. Erosion stabilizes after three years, when the exposed surfaces have new vegetation cover, but the recovery of the soil takes anything between 10 and 50 years. Totally compacted sites generally do not support regrowth for over 30 years. Repeated logging using heavy machinery simply removes a large area of the forest from productivity altogether.

### Logging: Good and bad practice

1. Damage to vegetation reduces biodiversity and destroys the natural habitats of wildlife. The forest ecosystem is undermined. The orang utan, sun bear, flying squirrels and riverine birds, such as kingfishers and forktails, are particularly at risk.

2. Logging roads, dump sites, log landings and soil tipped down hillsides harm the soil and contribute to serious erosion. Deprived of humus from rotting leaves, the soil becomes poorer. Logging roads also provide easy access for illegal hunters and poachers.

3. Over-logging and uncontrolled practices can render a site barren and totally unproductive for the future.

4. Harvesting using heavy machinery leads to massive soil damage, leading to erosion and interference with normal hydrological processes.

5. Water and soil enter the river systems immediately, considerably increasing the potential for floods, and damage to reservoirs, water filtration plants and irrigation channels downriver.

6. Rivers silt up, clogging dams and causing floods.

7. Without vegetation to soak up water, heavy rains may flood kampongs downstream. Where rubber and oil plantations have been introduced, these help reduce erosion and stem water flow.

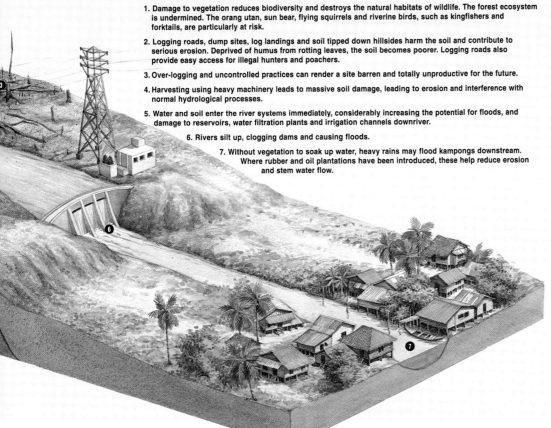

1. Over-logging, when cutting rates are higher than is permitted for maintaining sustainable growth, severely damages a forest habitat. It takes up to 50 years for a cut tree to be replaced. Logging roads and skid trails add to this destruction.

2. Good logging practices include a pre-felling inventory to provide reliable estimates of tree stock and species composition.

3. Other good practices include setting minimum cutting limits, based on tree diameters; directional felling, to minimize damage to the surrounding environment; reduced-impact extraction using cables or aerial techniques; a post-felling inventory to determine the status of forests after logging and to prescribe appropriate silvicultural treatments.

terrain, because soil erosion is minimized, wildlife is less affected, and biodiversity losses are not assumed to be too heavy.

## Preserving forests for the future

The problems in forest management have been clearly recognized, and major changes are being considered to introduce sustainable management. The hill dipterocarp forests, from altitudes of 300 to 750 metres, are now Malaysia's main source for timber production, and sustainable management practices are focused on them.

Under the National Forest Act (1984), forests have been gazetted for a variety of functions. These include permanent forest estates, which comprise over 30 per cent of the total land area in the country, that have been set aside permanently for forest use only and cannot be converted to other land use. The permanent estates have been subdivided into 'production land' and 'protection land'. Sizeable tracts of land outside the forest estates have also been designated important conservation zones in the form of national forest parks and game reserves. In Peninsular Malaysia, the largest areas of protected lowland forest are in Taman Negara and

the Endau-Rompin State Park that straddles Pahang and Johor.

Sustainable forest management has become conditional in Malaysia, following acceptance of the International Tropical Timber Organization (ITTO) Year 2000 Objective. Malaysia has developed management standards, called the Malaysian Criteria and Indicators (C&I), which address issues such as resource security, continuity of timber production, conservation of flora and fauna, environmental impacts and socioeconomic benefits. For the future, there are moves to independently audit the management of forests. Timber from a forest concession will have to be certified as originating from a sustainably managed forest in order for it to gain market acceptance. The essentials for managing forests on a sustainable basis are already in place; it is now a matter of commitment on the part of the people responsible for such management of the great natural assets that Malaysia's forests represent.

### Protected areas in Peninsular Malaysia

Areas gazetted under the 1984 National Forest Act. Protected areas include national parks, wildlife reserves and state parks.

Taman Negara

Endau-Rompin State Park

- Existing permanent reserved forest
- Proposed protected areas
- Existing protected areas

Source: Department of Wildlife and National Parks (DNNP) (1996)

# Wildlife at risk

*In the past, Malaysia's rich wildlife was sought by indigenous hunter-gatherers for food, and hunted as sport by colonial visitors. Today, the biggest threat comes from the destruction of the land the animals depend upon for shelter and nourishment. As forests are logged and converted to agricultural use, the rich diversity of fauna is seriously threatened. To combat declining populations, reserves and sanctuaries have been set up by the country's wildlife departments.*

Extensive logging in the lowland tropical rainforest in Sabah has destroyed wildlife habitats and scarred the landscape with access roads and skid trails.

In colonial days, the detrimental consequences of shooting large game for sport were not considered.

### Why animals need protection

Extensive deforestation of Malaysia's land has resulted in the loss of certain animals' natural habitats. Large-scale forest clearance has continued from early beginnings at the end of the 19th century, for the construction of railways and roads, through to the 20th century, when forests were felled to make way for agricultural land and rubber plantations.

The most important wildlife habitats are tropical lowland rainforests, below 300 metres, and it is these that have been most depleted. In Peninsular Malaysia, over 200 mammal species are concentrated in such forests and some 60 per cent of the total bird species. When land is cleared and burnt for agriculture, invertebrates, amphibians and many reptiles are lost because they lack the mobility to escape. Displaced birds and primates often fail to re-establish themselves in neighbouring forests where a dense population already exists. Where forests are still intact they are often reduced and, thus, insufficient to support viable populations. Mammals may also get caught in electric fences erected by farmers to keep them from their crops.

Animals are being threatened with extinction, a fate which has already befallen the once freely roaming Javan rhinoceros and green peafowl in Malaysia. Statistics suggest that species under threat are increasing at an alarming rate. In 1996, the Department of Wildlife and National Parks of Peninsular Malaysia categorized a total of 85 species as endangered, vulnerable, or rare compared to only 21 in 1986.

### Trade in animals

There is a long history in Southeast Asia of using wild animals and plants for cultural, religious and economic reasons. Rhino horn and tiger bone have long been prized by the Chinese community for their medicinal properties and this has contributed to the demise of the Javan rhinoceros and the reduction in the Sumatran rhinoceros and the Malayan tiger. In the 1970s, Malaysia was a significant exporter of long-tailed macaques to research laboratories across the world, with an average sale of 10,000 primates per year. As a result of global concern for vulnerable species, large-scale trade in animals, from reptile skins of the cobra, python and monitor lizards, swiftlet nests to live parrots and parakeets, is now restricted and monitored,

In Peninsular Malaysia alone, over 4,700 wildlife related offences were uncovered in 1995. Although the majority of offences involved the keeping of protected long-tailed macaques, leaf monkeys and other such animals without a legitimate licence, 100 were more serious cases involving the poaching of threatened species and the setting of wire traps to ensnare unsuspecting animals. To combat the trade in threatened wildlife, Malaysia is party to the Convention on International Trade in Endangered Species of Fauna and Flora (CITES). Through regulation, only certain licensed species are permitted to be legally traded.

## Endangered species

Once widespread throughout mainland Southeast Asia, the **Sumatran rhinoceros** (*Dicerorhinus sumatrensis*) is now a very rare sight. Just 121 individuals were recorded in Malaysia in 1997, scattered over isolated areas in Sabah and the Peninsula. The largest herbivore that lives exclusively in the tropical rainforest, each animal needs at least 10 square kilometres to roam in, thus, a large area of undisturbed forest is required for a healthy population to have any chance of survival.

Small populations of the plant-eating marine species **dugong** (*Dugong dugon*) with flipper-like forelimbs, are found exclusively off the coast of Sabah. Although they are thought to be capable of travelling long distances in search of food, they are seriously in decline.

Found in lowland forest, tree-lined swamps and riverine habitats of Sabah and Sarawak, the **Storm's stork** (*Ciconia stormi*) is now a rare resident, totalling fewer than 200 individuals.

Exclusively a forest dweller, the **clouded leopard** (*Neofelis nebulosa*) feeds on squirrels, birds and monkeys, including young orang utan which are themselves a protected species. Its survival is seriously threatened. Only very few recent sightings have been made in isolated forests.

In 1992, 113 **Asian elephant** herds (*Elephas maximus*), totalling 1,000 animals, existed on the Peninsula. In Sabah, the same number survive (1997 survey), the only significant wild population in Borneo. The clearing of lowland forest for agricultural use has fragmented habitats and elephant populations. As a result, the amount of food and cover will diminish and the chances of breeding will be reduced. The elephants pose problems by roaming into their former ranges, now cultivated with oil palm or rubber, looking for food.

## Protection

Malaysia realizes that wildlife has an important role in the natural ecosystem and that it needs to be conserved. A series of protected areas in the form of national and state parks, wildlife reserves and marine parks, comprising a total area of 1.5 million hectares, has been established. The first, Chior Wildlife Reserve in Perak, was established as early as 1903.

It is recognized that a balance has to be met between the human and animal populations so that they might exist for each other's mutual benefit. The Malayan tiger, elephant, tapir and Sumatran rhinoceros, for example, are managed in their natural habitats, which also serve as important biodiversity research areas and tourist sites. Before 1972, when the Malaysian government put a stop to the killings, elephants were being slaughtered for straying from their natural, damaged lowland forest habitats into crop land. To improve conditions for both the farmers and the crop-eating beasts, an active translocation programme was established. Between 1974 and 1995, over 300 wild elephants were transferred to larger, more secure habitats like Taman Negara, the Endau-Rompin State Park and the Belum forest bordering southern Thailand. The Sumatran rhinoceros has also been targeted for relocation.

## The Malayan tiger

Malaysia's national animal, a prancing pair of which adorn the country's crest, is now under threat. The Malayan tiger was long considered a livestock-preying pest, and was a popular target at the turn of the century for recreational hunters. But, because of the large-scale clearance of lowland forest, which also supports the greatest proportion of the animal's prey—wild boar and sambar deer—and more recently the demand for tiger products in Chinese medicine, the tiger population has been in serious decline since the 1960s. A once healthy population of 3,000 tigers in 1952 was decimated by 1976 to 300, the year the Malaysian government declared the tiger a fully protected species under the Protection of Wildlife Act (1972). Special tiger units, to monitor the tigers, were created at state level, and, due to *in situ* conservation measures, the 1991 population rose to around 490 animals, located in 272 sites.

| DISTRIBUTION OF TIGERS IN PENINSULAR MALAYSIA | | |
|---|---|---|
| AREA | NO. OF LOCATIONS | POPULATION |
| Kedah | 12 | 14 |
| Perak | 51 | 81 |
| Kelantan | 39 | 65 |
| Terengganu | 54 | 109 |
| Pahang | 48 | 84 |
| Johor | 26 | 38 |
| N. Sembilan | 6 | 9 |
| Selangor | 9 | 10 |
| Taman Negara | 27 | 81 |
| **Total** | **272** | **491** |

Source: Department of Wildlife and National Parks of Peninsular Malaysia (1991)

During the 1980s and 1990s, the Department of Wildlife and National Parks of Peninsular Malaysia and the Wildlife Department of Sabah embarked on an *ex situ* conservation strategy through a captive breeding programme. Twelve individuals, with little chance of survival in the wild, were caught and constitute the nucleus of breeding populations at the Sungai Dusun Wildlife Reserve in Peninsular Malaysia and Sepilok in Sabah.

Malaysia restricts large-scale trade in wildlife products.

## State Parks and Wildlife Sanctuaries in Sabah and Sarawak

Large areas of the magnificent rainforests of Sabah and Sarawak have been gazetted as protected areas, where all commercial logging activities are banned. In addition to the conservation of wide tracts of virgin forest, specialist centres have been established, and more are planned, that protect particularly vulnerable species.

**2. Turtle Islands Park**
The three islands that form the park are visited by marine turtles, which come ashore to lay their eggs. To prevent over-exploitation of the edible eggs of the green and (endangered) hawksbill turtles, hatcheries were set up in 1964.

**3. Sepilok Orang Utan Rehabilitation Sanctuary**
Opened in 1964, this field station cares for orphaned and illegally kept orang utan and prepares them for life back in the wild. There are an estimated 10,000–20,000 orang utan in Sabah and 500–2,000 in Sarawak.

**4. Danum Valley Conservation Area**
Mainly lowland forest, this outstanding area for wildlife supports all 10 Sabahan primates, the endangered clouded leopard and Sumatran rhinoceros, and more common species, such as the bearded pig (shown).

**1. Bako National Park**
Established in 1957, this is Sarawak's oldest and smallest park. The landscape is dominated by sandstone formations and a sheltered coastline of deep bays and narrow sandy beaches. Bako residents include the bearded pig, long-tailed macaque and the silvered leaf monkey (shown).

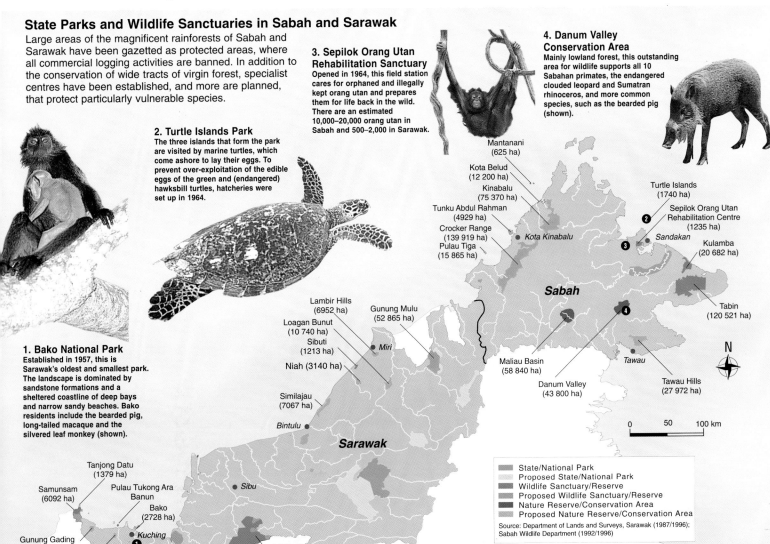

Mantanani (625 ha)
Kota Belud (12 200 ha)
Kinabalu (75 370 ha)
Tunku Abdul Rahman (4929 ha)
Crocker Range (139 919 ha)
Pulau Tiga (15 865 ha)
Kota Kinabalu
Turtle Islands (1740 ha)
Sepilok Orang Utan Rehabilitation Centre (1235 ha)
Sandakan
Kulamba (20 682 ha)
Sabah
Tabin (120 521 ha)
Maliau Basin (58 840 ha)
Danum Valley (43 800 ha)
Tawau
Tawau Hills (27 972 ha)
Lambir Hills (6952 ha)
Gunung Mulu (52 865 ha)
Loagan Bunut (10 740 ha)
Sibuti (1213 ha)
Miri
Niah (3140 ha)
Similajau (7067 ha)
Bintulu
Sarawak
Tanjong Datu (1379 ha)
Samunsam (6092 ha)
Pulau Tukong Ara Banun
Bako (2728 ha)
Sibu
Kuching
Gunung Gading (4106 ha)
Kubah (2230 ha)
Semonggok (740 ha)
Lanjak Entimau (168 758 ha)
Batang Ai (24 040 ha)

0 50 100 km
N

State/National Park
Proposed State/National Park
Wildlife Sanctuary/Reserve
Proposed Wildlife Sanctuary/Reserve
Nature Reserve/Conservation Area
Proposed Nature Reserve/Conservation Area

Source: Department of Lands and Surveys, Sarawak (1987/1996); Sabah Wildlife Department (1992/1996)

# Biodiversity management

*Malaysia possesses extraordinary species diversity. But, as the country's landscape continues to be extensively transformed in the name of development, many of its plants and animals are threatened with extinction. Steps are now being taken to protect this rich natural heritage. A combination of* in situ *and* ex situ *projects have been introduced to help ensure continued biodiversity for the future.*

## Threats to biological diversity

From the 1970s, Malaysia has witnessed unprecedented development. In the process, the country has sacrificed many of its pristine habitats and ecosystems. The reduction in forested areas has led to changes in soil structure, the water table level, vegetation cover and climate, and means a loss of flora and fauna.

### Habitat loss

Rubber and palm oil plantations have developed at the expense of lowland dipterocarp forests, home to Malaysia's most rich and diverse biodiversity, including some of the country's largest mammals. Large-scale agricultural schemes also have a detrimental effect on crop biodiversity.

### Unsustainable use of resources

Forests started to be extensively exploited for timber in the 1970s. Logging, particularly in Sabah and Sarawak, continues at a rate that will have dramatic future effects on the quality of the environment and, in particular, its biodiversity.

### Socioeconomic development

Schemes to improve the economic status of rural populations mean millions of hectares of forest have been converted to agriculture and settlement use, displacing much of the fauna and destroying flora. Massive man-made reservoirs, such as Lake Kenyir in Terengganu (shown above), have displaced animal species and obliterated plants and insects.

## Why is biodiversity important?

Individual life forms coexist in natural ecosystems which, if left unmolested, help moderate climate extremes, degrade wastes, recycle nutrients, create soils and control disease. The richness, or biodiversity, of an area is an indicator of the state of the biological resources within that environment. Biodiversity protection is necessary to stop species slipping into extinction and to preserve them for future generations, so they may continue to benefit from them aesthetically, scientifically, medicinally or economically. Protection maintains ecological balances and preserves a gene pool of the widest range of species.

## *In situ* and *ex situ* conservation

The two types of biodiversity conservation are *in situ* (or on-site) and *ex situ* (off-site).

Since habitat loss is a major cause of the loss in biodiversity, setting aside protected areas is the major *in situ* method to help preserve species. In Malaysia, 4.5 per cent of the total land area is designated as protected land. This incorporates 3.39 million hectares of forest of which 1.5 million hectares are national and state parks, wildlife sanctuaries and marine parks (see 'Wildlife at risk'). Non-protected areas, such as agricultural and forest lands, also require conservation. Retaining traditional systems of agriculture helps maintain crop genetic diversity. Some of the traditional conservation methods applied by indigenous people through their respect for the environment have been extremely effective in sustaining diversity. For example, many exotic varieties of fruit and tree species have survived under small-scale rural cultivation or semi-wild in the secondary forests and may serve as gene pools for future improvement of commercially grown fruits and vegetables.

Although *in situ* conservation is regarded as the most efficient way to preserve species in their natural habitat, *ex situ* methods are becoming increasingly important. They include botanical gardens (there are nine in Malaysia), zoological parks, gene banks and other laboratories where artificial

## Malaysia's megadiversity

Malaysia's humid, tropical location provides excellent conditions for thousands of plant species to thrive and evolve, and places it amongst the 12 countries internationally recognized as possessing megadiversity. These 12 countries act as an index for species richness around the world. A major part of diversity is endemism as this reflects the uniqueness of an area. Endemic species are those that have localized distribution and that have usually evolved after prolonged geographical isolation. Countries with a high number of endemic species, such as Malaysia, are globally important in terms of conservation because loss of these species locally would signal their worldwide extinction.

insemination and genetic engineering take place. *Ex situ* conservation also includes awareness campaigns and the promotion of scientific research in biodiversity and its management.

## Biodiversity management for the future

For sustainable management of Malaysia's rich biodiversity, a combination of both *in situ* and *ex situ* methods is recommended. As habitat requirements differ from one species to another, and in size, range and niche, *in situ* methods prove uneconomic and unattainable when land is scarce and required for development. Current protected areas are not extensive enough to capture the representative variety of most species. The *ex situ* approach is economical, but scientifically unproven.

Successful biodiversity management requires ongoing assessment of Malaysia's habitats to gauge the success of existing conservation schemes and to plan for new ones. If the forests across the country were thoroughly assessed in terms of their conservation and short-term use, a general

## Biogeographical realms of the Asia–Pacific

Between them the three biogeographic realms of the Asia–Pacific harbour the world's highest mountain system, the second largest rainforest, more than half the world's coral reefs and tens of thousands of islands. It is the centre for diversity for crops such as rice and sugar cane and a wealth of medicinal plants. In the middle of this rich region is Malaysia, one of the most species-rich countries in the world.

Source: S. Braatz, *Conserving Biological Diversity* (1992)

The white-handed gibbon (*Hylobates lar*), right, locally known as the 'wak-wak', is a common inhabitant of the Malaysian rainforest.

### ENDEMIC AND TOTAL SPECIES FOR MALAYSIA AND OTHER ASIAN COUNTRIES (estimates)

PR of China
Indonesia
India
Malaysia
Thailand
Vietnam
Philippines
Laos
Myanmar
Cambodia

■ Total number of species
□ Number of endemic species

Number of species, (0000s)
500  1000  1500  2000  2500  3000  3500

Source: World Conservation Monitoring Centre (1992).

## Malaysia's biodiversity in context

Below are conservative figures for the total number of species found in Malaysia for specific plant and animal classifications. The diversity of vertebrates and higher plants is well documented, and although reliable estimates of species number for some groups, such as mosses, liverworts, hornworts, lichens and fungi, insects and invertebrates are not known, their abundance and contribution to Malaysia's forest biodiversity is not in doubt. Botanists and zoologists are continually uncovering new, hitherto unrecorded varieties and species.

## Species loss

The extent of species and genetic diversity loss, and the knock-on consequences for the wider environment, are difficult to assess because a complete inventory of all Malaysian species is not available. However, it is undeniable that once a species is allowed to become extinct, it will be gone forever.

### BIODIVERSITY IN MALAYSIA

| CLASSIFICATION | NO. OF SPECIES |
| --- | --- |
| Flowering plants | 12,000 |
| Trees | 2,650 |
| Mammals | 280 |
| Birds | 624 |
| Frogs and toads | 165 |
| Snakes | 162 |
| Tortoises and turtles | 22 |
| Crocodiles | 2 |
| Lizards | 143 |
| Corals | 150 |

### SPECIES UNDER THREAT IN MALAYSIA

| CLASSIFICATION | NO. OF SPECIES |
| --- | --- |
| Plants | 522 |
| Mammals | 23 |
| Birds | 35 |
| Reptiles | 12 |
| Amphibians | 0 |
| Fish | 6 |

Source: World Conservation Monitoring Centre (1992)

management plan could then be adopted to prevent their continued detrimental transformation.

Tangible evidence of Malaysia's commitment to sustainable use of natural resources is the launch of a National Policy on Biological Diversity in May 1998. After the Earth Summit held in Rio de Janeiro in June 1992, a national committee on biological diversity was set up to formulate this policy. The international Convention on Biological Diversity signed at Rio has three main objectives: the conservation of biological diversity, the sustainable use of its components, and equitable sharing of benefits arising from the use of genetic resources. For the latter, this implies that conservation of biological diversity in developing countries, such as Malaysia, should be aided by biotechnology and expertise from developed nations. In addition, the Langkawi Declaration on the Environment, signed in October 1989 by Commonwealth heads of state, pledges to 'support activities related to the conservation of biological diversity and genetic resources, including the conservation of significant areas of virgin forest and other protected natural habitats'.

There are over 100 species of *Dendrobium* orchids in Peninsular Malaysia. *Dendrobium anosmum* is shown.

### *Ex situ* conservation

1. & 2. Seed orchards and nurseries provide seedlings for forest regeneration.

3. Malaysian zoos intend to help to regenerate indigenous wild animal populations through breeding programmes in captivity.

# Settlement patterns: Displaced people

*Human migration from one area to another in contemporary Malaysia is an extensive, ongoing process, and reflects the standard population shifts for any rapidly developing nation: major cities get larger and rural areas decline. The Federal Government has introduced various resettlement schemes, by which communities are moved piecemeal or in their entirety, primarily for economic or security reasons.*

In Malaysia, there is a marked increase in urban populations and a decline in rural settlements.

## Why do people relocate?

Populations primarily relocate because of economic criteria, which are closely linked with political issues. Climatic factors can also lead to permanent or temporary relocation as a matter of expediency. If an area is at risk from floods or landslides, for example, evacuation is necessary as a safety precaution. Where a resource is exhausted, for whatever reason—natural phenomena, pollution, human intervention—whether it is the decline in available fish or wildlife stocks on which one of Sarawak's indigenous groups depends for their existence, or the closure of a once productive tin mine, the affected population is required to seek a livelihood elsewhere. Relocation in Malaysia is primarily a response, either by individuals or by the government of the day, to employment opportunities.

Malaysia is witnessing a reduction in its rural population and a shift of people to urban centres as it works towards becoming a fully developed nation. Population shifts are reflected in different settlement patterns, such as the implementation of new settlements, or the expansion of old ones. In times of economic growth it is often easy to ignore the non-economic implications of human transfers. In their resettlement programmes, the Malaysian government has tried to be sensitive to the domestic, social, and environmental needs of the communities it moves, and to the wider physical environment.

### Moving house: Necessary relocation

The Malaysian state oil company, Petronas, has displaced populations and provided new housing so it can construct new industrial plants and oil refineries, for example, in the coastal area in central Melaka in the 1990s.

A resident surveys her damaged home, destroyed by soil erosion after a bout of heavy rainfall. Enforced resettlement can result from natural phenomena, such as this, or from the intervention of corporations or governments.

## FELDA: Replanting and resettlement

When it was established in the 1950s, the objective of the national Federal Land Development Authority (FELDA) was to develop forested land for agriculture and to resettle the country's rural poor. Large-scale resettlement and land development followed.

By 1992, FELDA had established 478 schemes (including 59 in Sabah and 6 in Sarawak) covering 897 143 hectares, representing 16 per cent of the country's cultivated area and a total of 117,491 families. The main crops are oil palm, rubber, sugar cane and cocoa. The FELDA schemes vary in size, but average 1500 hectares for rubber and 2000 hectares for oil palm, each with a settlement comprising about 200 families. These schemes are dispersed individually or grouped in designated areas under the charge of development authorities. Planned land development has almost completely redefined the tradition of smallholding agriculture in Malaysia. Hundreds of thousands of families have been uprooted, willingly, and resettled in different places thus creating new settlements in areas formerly uninhabited. The schemes are mainly found in the central foothill regions of Peninsular Malaysia and the more accessible former forested areas of Sabah and Sarawak.

**Distribution of Regional Development Authority areas and FELDA land schemes in Peninsular Malaysia.**

● Land Scheme
■ Regional Development

## Development and resettlement

The major resettlement projects in Malaysia relate to agriculture and industry. Development will always be accompanied by change, which often improves conditions for communities. Where settlement patterns are concerned, physical development will often lead to two related results: the abandonment of existing settlements and the creation of new ones. Socioeconomic development may lead to the expansion and diversification of established settlements as is the case of suburbanization, conurbation and the development of new towns, slum areas and squatter settlements.

Development of an area is usually seen in a positive light because of the increased benefits in the form of economic or technological advancement that it brings to those in the 'developed' area. Change, however, can work both ways. While development may bring tangible physical improvement, it may also upset the prevailing economic and social patterns of a region. In Malaysia, communities have been displaced as a direct result of development projects. These include the transfer of land to new uses, for example, the movement of self-sufficient cultivators to cash crop plantations. Other projects involve the building of dams and highways and major industrial construction.

## The effects of industrial development

In its efforts to become a Newly Industrialized Country (NIC), Malaysia has shifted the focus of its industrial policies several times. For example, the import-substitution policy of the 1960s was replaced by export-oriented activities in the 1970s

A traditional FELDA dwelling. Each new settler would receive a house such as this with a specified land plot, as shown in the illustration opposite.

## A typical FELDA plot

1. Settler's house
2. Latrine
3. Livestock
4. Hen coop
5. Oil palm
6. Vegetable plot. This would typically include spinach, long beans,

aubergines, lady's fingers and cabbage.
7. Orchard. Trees would include sugar cane, papaya, banana and durian.

A new house being built on a FELDA scheme in Negeri Sembilan. Many settlers have enjoyed a significant improvement in their incomes as plantations are converted to oil palm. This new wealth is often invested in the construction of new homes.

which were further strengthened in the 1980s. It also witnessed a switch to the production of capital goods and a concentration on heavy industry.

Ideally, industrial development should develop with, if not be preceded by, infrastructural changes. Construction of roads and highways may result in the displacement of people in their proposed path. Construction of industrial estates and hazardous plants may also lead to relocation and resettlement of those affected by what are known as the right-of-way or proximity effects. A classic example is the land acquisition issue involving 87.8 hectares of land at Pantai Tanah Merah and Pantai Kundor in the coastal area of central Melaka. The issue dragged on for more than three years from the early 1990s as villagers demanded adequate compensation for vacating the area, which had been gazetted as a danger zone because of the proximity of the multi-billion ringgit Petronas oil refinery located there.

To ease the burden on the state and to provide housing options, the Melaka State Government sought Petronas's assistance to build a new housing scheme for the residents. A 22-hectare site at Tanjung Kling/Tangga Batu, about 3 kilometres from the refinery, was made available. However, not all of those affected approved of the new site. The problems of land acquisition, relocation and resettlement for this particular development scheme illustrate how resettlement can give birth to new centres of population. Such schemes may lead to the demise of an existing village whilst giving rise to a new one. Settlement may also be transformed from one of sparsely scattered housing to one which is nuclear and provided with common amenities.

## Mega development projects: The Bakun Dam

Mega development projects may become the source of population displacement. They are usually controversial, as in the case of the Bakun Dam hydroelectric project (postponed in 1997 because of funding difficulties), where voices for and against the schemes have been debating vociferously.

Model of the proposed Bakun Dam

Supporters think the dam will be the answer to the country's electricity needs, providing Malaysians, across the Peninsula as well as in Sabah and Sarawak, with greener and cheaper energy. In the short term, the project provides construction work for local people. Long-term implications are that it will open up Sarawak's interior and improve communications for local communities, providing them with opportunities to ply their goods in a wider market downstream.

However, environmentalists claim that the dam will drown a natural forest about the size of Singapore, and putting a high block of concrete across the Rajang, Malaysia's longest river, will certainly have serious implications on the people living downstream. More than 15 communities comprising 10,000 people living around Bakun will have to be displaced. Their social and cultural sensitivities were claimed to be ignored. Not only will they be moved physically from their existing homes, but their whole lifestyle is likely to undergo profound change. The affected people are those furthest from 'civilization', pursuing most traditional rural lifestyles, inhabiting longhouses in the remote upper reaches of the Rajang River. Such movement of a rural and racial minority with no significant political voice for the 'good' of the wider population, is perceived by some detractors as a dangerous precedent.

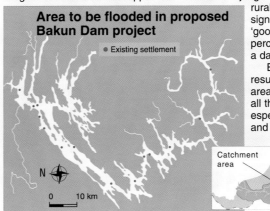

### Area to be flooded in proposed Bakun Dam project

● Existing settlement

Catchment area

N

0    10 km

Environmental damage may result from flooding such a large area. Rainforest destruction and all the associated problems, especially erosion, river siltation and the detrimental atmospheric implications on the wider, transboundary scale, could be immense if the project does go ahead at some future date.

# Water quality

*As Malaysia continues to develop industrially and its urban populations increase, the pressures on the country's water intensifies. More clean water is needed and expected, whilst at the same time more potential sources of pollution are appearing. Domestic sewage, factory discharge, oil spills and soil all contribute to the pollution of Malaysia's rivers and seas, often with dire consequences for wildlife and human health.*

Water bodies of excellent quality are those found in the national parks, forested water catchments and uninhabited areas.

Source: Department of Environment Malaysia (1994)

## Status of Malaysian rivers

The Department of Environment of Malaysia (DOE) monitors between 116 and 119 major rivers annually under the River Water Quality Monitoring Report. The 1996 report revealed that overall river quality had deteriorated at a rate of 0.5 per cent since the previous year.

### SOURCES OF POLLUTION

| 72% | 15% | 13% |
Agro-based and manufacturing industries (% of biochemical oxygen demand in the water)

| 39% | 30% | 31% |
Livestock farming and domestic waste (% of ammoniacal nitrogen in the water)

| 29% | 14% | 57% |
Earthworks and land clearing (% of suspended solids in the water)

Water quality is assessed by measuring certain aspects of a river. These include its temperature, pH value and levels of dissolved oxygen, chemicals and metals in the water, as well as its microbiological and aesthetic nature. 116 rivers with a combined length of 7599 km were monitored.

### EXTENT OF POLLUTION

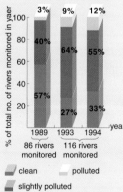

% of total no. of rivers monitored in year

| year | 1989 | 1993 | 1994 |
|---|---|---|---|
| (top) | 3% | 9% | 12% |
| | 40% | 64% | 55% |
| | 57% | 27% | 33% |

1989 — 86 rivers monitored
1993, 1994 — 116 rivers monitored

■ clean    ▨ polluted
■ slightly polluted

In certain rivers, the mercury, lead, cadmium, zinc and copper levels exceed the nationally set standards. Heavy metal pollution in rivers is caused mainly by industrial discharge or mining. The Damit/Tuaran River in Sabah is particularly polluted, exceeding standards for all heavy metals.

## The status of Malaysian rivers

To survive, all living things require water—clean, unpolluted water. We all ultimately draw from the same water supply, which is replenished over and over again through the hydrologic cycle. However, as societies develop more needs and sophisticated technologies, the quality and quantity of water declines, as societies' new activities generate pollutants that degrade the water.

Despite the government's 'Love Our Rivers' campaign, initiated in 1993 to raise public awareness about the importance of keeping rivers and their surroundings clean, the level of pollution in Malaysia's rivers continues to rise year by year. As Malaysia develops from an agricultural nation towards industrialization, the country has undertaken many development projects, such as the building of new highways, industries, office complexes, new towns and an international airport in Sepang. All these activities are affecting the water quality of rivers and the seas surrounding the country. Existing water treatment plants are unable to cope with demand and although measures are in place, it is difficult to enforce non-discharge of dangerous effluents from factories and domestic sites.

## The threat to human health

Polluted water can be a source of unhealthy drinking water, and any diseases or harmful chemicals may be ingested by fish which are then taken as food by man. In the dry season of 1997, the industrial effluents and sand discharged near the Dungun River in Kuala Terengganu resulted in yellowish, salty water for the local population, which they used for all domestic purposes: bathing, cooking and washing. The river had been polluted by discharges from a local oil palm factory and sandy sediments resulting from dredging activities along the river. These caused the river level to fall below the sea water level, forcing saline water from the sea to flow to the river and to render the water supply salty. This example illustrates how easy it is for water to become polluted and how immediate its affects on a local population can be. Changes to the usual pattern of water supply can be inconvenient and particularly uncomfortable in hot, tropical conditions. In October 1997, for example, 6,000 gallons of diesel were accidentally spilt in the

Most polluted rivers are in Johor which has main industrial zones at Pasir Gudang and Gelang Patah, where discharges from factories and pig farms mostly account for the poor quality of water. Other polluted rivers include Sungai Penchala (above) in Petaling Jaya.

Langat River in Selangor, depriving thousands of people of water for a week. Water can also harbour some of the most serious diseases harmful to man. Because typhoid, dysentery and hepatitis germs are colourless, it is not possible to tell by looking whether water is contaminated by them. Popular recreational beaches, such as Pantai Batu Buruk in Terengganu, Batu Ferringhi in Penang, Pantai Telok and Chempedak in Pahang, have been found to be contaminated with faecal coliform, as have a number of river estuaries. Faecal coliform are germs which find their way into water from human faeces as a result of poor sanitation, making the water unsuitable for drinking and dangerous to swim in.

## Protecting water

The Department of Environment of Malaysia has established numeric limits that describe water quality requirements necessary to meet and maintain uses, such as swimming, other water-based recreation, public water supply, and the propagation and growth of aquatic life.

There is a recognition that the water resource problems involve biological as well as physiochemical and socioeconomic issues. Sophisticated and quantitative assessments based on ecological principles are more likely to protect water resources from the wide range of human actions that degrade those sources. The challenge for basic and applied ecologists in the next decade will be to ensure that ecological principles are used to improve the nation's programme to protect and manage water.

# Polluting Malaysia's waters

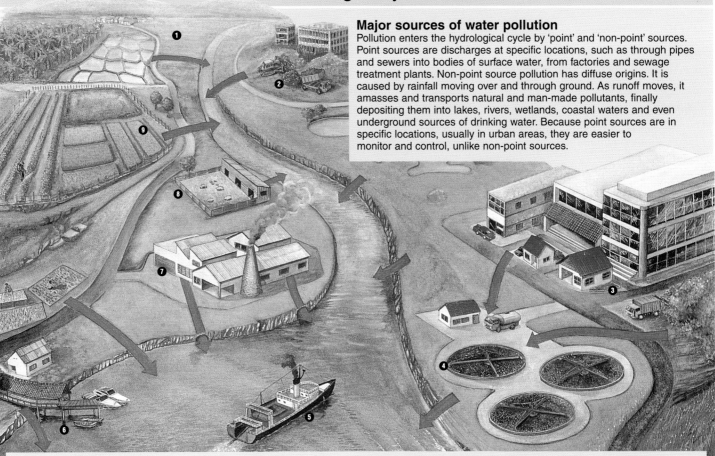

## Major sources of water pollution

Pollution enters the hydrological cycle by 'point' and 'non-point' sources. Point sources are discharges at specific locations, such as through pipes and sewers into bodies of surface water, from factories and sewage treatment plants. Non-point source pollution has diffuse origins. It is caused by rainfall moving over and through ground. As runoff moves, it amasses and transports natural and man-made pollutants, finally depositing them into lakes, rivers, wetlands, coastal waters and even underground sources of drinking water. Because point sources are in specific locations, usually in urban areas, they are easier to monitor and control, unlike non-point sources.

1. **Salt:** This is released by irrigation practices and abandoned mines and from salt water intrusion along coasts.

2. **Erosion:** Following alteration of landscape by agriculture, urbanization and forestry, sediments enter rivers. The muddied water harms aquatic life, degrading the quality of the river ecosystem, and downstream may cause siltation.

3. **Rubbish:** Humans generate huge amounts of rubbish, which can create toxic runoff. Recreational sites suffer from litter. It is not only unsightly, but may also interfere with natural drainage and harm aquatic life.

4. **Domestic waste:** Biodegradable sewage and waste water include detergents and household chemicals. Disease organisms, such as typhoid and cholera, may be carried in the sewage of those infected.

5. **Oil spillages:** Spills and deliberate dumping from oil tankers and platforms can cause serious damage to coastal waters and wildlife.

6. **Sea dumping:** Rubbish and untreated sewage are released from land or dumped by vessels at sea. Harmful chemicals may enter the food chain and be carried by fish that are then caught for human consumption.

7. **Toxic chemicals:** Most pollution from agro-based industries arises from crude palm oil mills and raw natural rubber processing plants either discharged deliberately, or accidentally, by factories. Metals, such as mercury and cadmium, can enter the food chain and oil and grease come from urban runoff and energy production.

8. **Intensive farming:** Bacteria and nutrients from livestock, pet wastes and faulty septic systems wash into rivers. Sludge from animal farming, largely from pig rearing, enters as untreated liquid manure.

9. **Agrochemicals:** Pesticides that do not decompose are carried by runoff from sprayed croplands and residential areas or seep into ground water.

## Oil spillages

Malaysia's coastal and marine waters are subject to pollution, predominantly from oil and grease, suspended solids and *Escherichia coli* (*E. coli*), a deadly food bacteria that causes fever, vomiting and diarrhoea. Spillages, whether accidental or from deliberate load dumping, of oil from tankers and platforms has a serious detrimental affect on the country's marine life and beaches. In 1989, there were 22 cases of oil spillage reported, and in 1994 alone, some 14 oil incidents in the combined territorial waters of the South China Sea, Strait of Melaka and Strait of Johor. Most of the incidents reported were due to oil sludge and oily waste discharges, and leakages during transfer and tanker cleaning activities. In January 1994, a Liberian-registered tanker dumped 900 tonnes of oily sludge off the Malaysian coast. High lead levels were recorded in the coastal waters off Perak, Penang and Kelantan, and high mercury levels observed on the coastal waters of Johor, which were in part attributed to the oil sludge dumping.

Source: After *World Environment Atlas* (1991)

More than 10 000 tonnes of oil, spilt from a tanker off Singapore in late 1997, flowed into Malaysia's western coastal waters to cause incalculable environmental damage to beaches and wildlife.

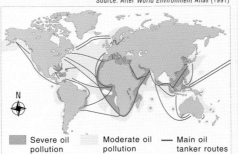

*RIGHT:* It is estimated that worldwide, several million tonnes of oil finds its way into the sea each year. Malaysia is located in the midst of one of the worst polluted areas.

N

| Severe oil pollution | Moderate oil pollution | — Main oil tanker routes |

## Protecting Malaysia's rivers

At both the federal and state level, authorities are recognizing the urgent need to protect the nation's rivers. For example, in Melaka the State Government has approved the setting up of a river management committee to oversee the effective management of the state's 98 rivers.

Government efforts are complemented by those of non-government organizations (NGOs), such as the World Wide Fund for Nature Malaysia who, in 1994, initiated a two-year project to clean up the polluted Sungai Penchala. The river, a tributary of the Klang River, flows through Petaling Jaya and was steadily choking under the rubbish, factory and household wastes that were flowing into it from industrial and squatter areas along its banks. The main aim of the Penchala Project was to raise public awareness about the state of the river and so instill better treatment of it. On a broader scale, all Malaysians are encouraged to participate in the ongoing 'Love Our Rivers' campaign which was launched in 1993 with a scheme targeted at local communities to 'adopt a river' in their vicinity.

# Coastal erosion

*Since the 1960s, Malaysia's long and attractive coastline has been increasingly threatened. The unabated development of commercial, industrial and tourism centres has directly and indirectly caused erosion along one-third of the country's 4800-kilometre coastline. Natural conditions combine with man-made influences to produce this serious situation, which is a costly drain on the public purse. Strict management of the coastal zone is needed to stem the flow of erosion.*

Because of coastal erosion, this house along Kelantan's coast is located too close to the shore and is exposed to storm damage.

A case of severe erosion on Sabak beach, Kelantan. A staggering 75 per cent of Kelantan's coastline is threatened by erosion, the highest proportion for any state.

### Breakwater intruding on a natural coastline

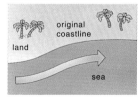

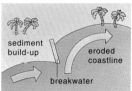

Top: Sediment is naturally transported along the coast.

Bottom: The breakwater interferes with the natural drift of the sea causing the current to erode the coast.

## Malaysia's eroding coast

Every state in Malaysia is affected by coastal erosion. The National Coastal Erosion Study carried out in 1997 estimated that about 1400 kilometres, or 30 per cent, of the total shoreline was subjected to erosion of varying degrees of severity. In areas of erosion, the average rate of shoreline retreat can range from anything less than 1 metre to more than 10 metres a year. Severe coastal erosion threatens settlements and livelihoods and upsets the natural balance of the rich marine life that exists offshore. Within 12 years, the number of sites identified as having serious erosion problems has increased from 47 in 1985, when the previous National Coastal Erosion Study took place, to 74.

Coastal erosion occurs naturally when high-energy waves and winds, such as those

## The process of coastal erosion

As waves enter shallow water they increase in height, become unstable and break on the shore. The resulting uprush rides up the beach and carries sediments back out to sea in the backwash. When the incoming destructive wave is followed by less steep constructive waves, sediment is removed more quickly than it is replaced. This leads to erosion of the beach.

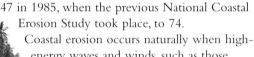

generated by a storm, stir up beach sediments, carrying them away from their existing location. When milder wave conditions prevail, sand is redeposited elsewhere along the coast. A natural balance of sediment transportation from sea to land and vice versa is maintained in a process known as accretion. The inherent dynamics of these sediment ebbs and flows ensure that the shoreline remains constant. Intensive and indiscriminate human activities on the coast, however, interrupt the process and cause severe erosion which needs to be arrested if disasters are to be avoided.

## Living on the edge

Communities who inhabit Malaysia's coastal areas are increasingly being confronted with the

## Going against the tide: The human contribution

Human activities along the coast disrupt the natural equilibrium of shoreline activity, introducing or provoking accelerated erosion. These activities include coastline development, land reclamation schemes, sand mining and river dredging.

During building projects to create new, or develop existing, coastal resorts, recreational facilities, fishing harbours or ports and shipyards, serious erosion can take place. Mass tourist developments which are not adequately planned bring destruction in their wake. In Port Dickson, on the southwest coast of the Peninsula, for example, most of the hotels have been located close to the beach, less than 30 metres from the shoreline. As a result, the shore has been critically eroded and 2 kilometres of beach have had to be restored at high cost.

Mangrove swamps, notable on the muddy shores on the west of the Peninsula and along the coasts of Sabah and Sarawak (see 'Mangroves'), are cleared during building and reclamation. These swamps are natural wave breaks that protect the beach from erosion. Their destruction has consequences for coastal ecosystems as they are important breeding habitats for marine species.

Sand mining involves the conscious removal of sand from the littoral zone. Silica sand minerals are mined for use in the growing glass-making industry and silts are removed to prepare the area for building or transported to landfill sites.

Dredging activities carried out near shore bars and shoals dramatically alter the usual wave patterns along the beach. These shoals and bars normally act as natural wave breaks, absorbing wave energy. Dredging, however, causes a concentration of high-wave energy which the natural features are unable to withstand, thus leading to erosion.

### Sources of coastal erosion

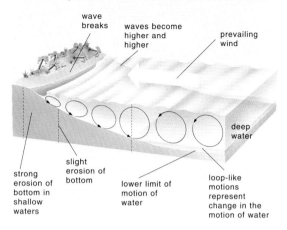

coastal reclamation of 50 hectares of mangroves

coastal resort

clearance of island mangrove swamps to build recreational facilities

inter-island or tourist ferry

destructive forces of coastal erosion. As their property is threatened and access to the seas for fishermen is denied through land reclamation, serious social and economic problems result. On the east coast of Peninsular Malaysia, houses have been damaged, forcing populations to relocate and thus removing their livelihood in the process.

Agricultural activities are particularly vulnerable to the effects of erosion. Bunds, for example, originally built to protect the coastline from the intrusion of the sea at high tide, have sometimes become ineffective as natural barriers because the shores have been so eroded. In Perak, coconut plantations have been flooded with incoming waters, thus turning the whole area barren and reducing it to unprofitable wasteland. In coastal riverine areas, a tidal flood is capable of penetrating 2 kilometres inland, damaging crops such as cocoa, oil palm and rice in addition to coconuts. Soil fertility is also reduced.

## Paying the price

Coastal erosion is both an ecological and an economic loss. It has taken its toll on public utilities and infrastructure. In 1996, approximately RM400 million was spent on repairs to eroded areas. This included engineering works, such as the construction of concrete sea walls and revetments (retaining walls). The beach at Pantai Kundor, Melaka, for instance, was eroded to such an extent that the sea bordered directly on the edge of the road. Extensive repair work was carried out at high cost to restore some of the beach.

Short-term remedial measures are necessary to correct localized problems, but if Malaysia's vulnerable coastal zone and its communities are to be safeguarded for the future, more long-term

solutions need to be sought. Proper land use, intelligent planning and respect for the fundamental regulations governing shore areas will help reduce the alarming statistics revealed by the National Coastal Erosion Study.

## Protection

Nature has its own way of maintaining a balanced coastline. Mangrove forests, with their interlocking root systems and ability to anchor sediments, provide excellent natural defences. Rocky foreshores and submerged sandbanks act as breakers against incoming waves, by dissipating the wave energy offshore rather than along the coast itself. Shorelines protected by protruding headlands, sediment transferred by inshore rivers to the coastal zone and longshore littoral drift are all nature's way of protecting beaches.

Before artificial coastal protection structures are put in place, the coastal processes of an affected area need to be understood. Failure to do so could mean designing weak structures that may collapse, or installing structures that are inappropriately placed and which might actually accelerate coastal erosion rather than mitigate it. Types of man-made coastal erosion protection structures include offshore breakwaters, notably in Kedah and Terengganu. Foreshores are protected by artificial headlands, bulkheads and sea wall constructions, and beach replenishment schemes.

**Protection structures**
Artificial banks are erected to help stem erosion, such as this barrier at Sungai Dungun, Terengganu (top). Retaining walls, called revetments (middle), are short-term protection structures. Mangroves provide a natural protection against erosion (bottom).

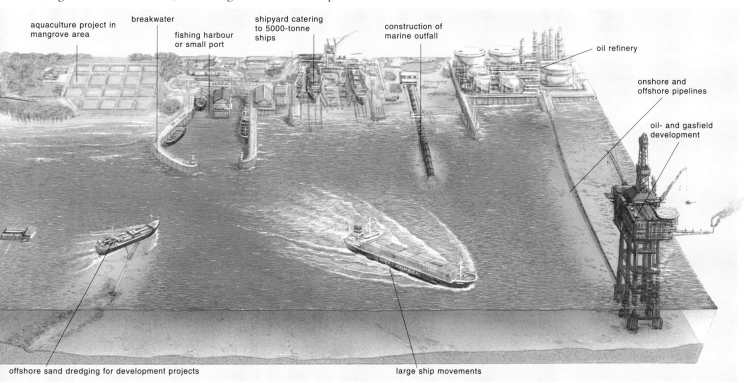

aquaculture project in mangrove area

breakwater

fishing harbour or small port

shipyard catering to 5000-tonne ships

construction of marine outfall

oil refinery

onshore and offshore pipelines

oil- and gasfield development

offshore sand dredging for development projects

large ship movements

# Hillsides

*Hillsides in Malaysia have been developed for reasons that are historical, practical and economic. A growing population needs somewhere to live. When flat land is fully built up, developers look to the highlands for expansion. Forest is cleared to make way for new access roads, housing and resorts, which have introduced major environmental problems to the prevailing climate and ecology. Such overdevelopment results in erosion, siltation and landslides.*

## Landslides

Landslides occur where a slope remains static for a long time and then fails in a single dramatic event. Within the six months from June 1995 to January 1996, there were at least 180 landslides across Malaysia, most of which disrupted traffic and caused damage to property. If the landslides were not directly caused by development projects, in many cases these were contributing factors to rendering a slope unstable.

### Types of landslide

**SINGLE ROTATION SLUMP**

upper surface tilts backwards to create a reverse slope

as the bedrock mass moves down the slip surface it rotates on a horizontal axis

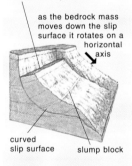

curved slip surface     slump block

**MULTIPLE ROTATION SLUMP**

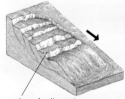

series of adjacent rotational slumps

**MUDFLOW**

flowing mass of fine-grained rock and mud

sediment fans out at the foot of the slope

## Threats to the environment

Rapid growth has taken place in Malaysia's hillside areas, sometimes with detrimental results. These include the destruction of the landscape, modification of the climate and the degradation of the quality of the soils and rivers. Deforestation and loss of vegetation cover have resulted in rising temperatures, which reduce the attractiveness of hill locations as cool getaways, but also may interfere with the prevailing agriculture of the area. Land clearing, to make way for new roads and buildings, significantly increases the rate of soil erosion and the mass movement of earth—soil creep—from one area to another. Costs involved in the mitigation of such problems, which include putting in place retaining walls and other control measures, and to continue maintaining such structures, are considerable. Development on hillsides increases the prospect of slope failure, or landslides, the problem becoming particularly critical in wet seasons. Landslides are likely to occur because of the combination of deep weathering and steep slopes. They cause severe property damage and can also lead to loss of life.

The different temperature and humidity zones naturally occurring in Malaysia's mountainous areas provide unique habitats for diverse plant and animal life. Changes in humidity and temperature due to anthropic (human) activities upset the delicate ecological balance of these habitats. Unique, and sometimes endemic, montane species of plants and animals are lost through development, thereby destroying the nation's natural heritage and ecotourism potential.

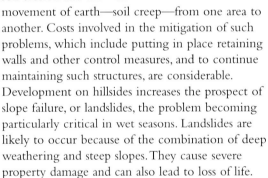

Slopes consisting of loosely consolidated rock can be protected by a concrete wall. Holes in the wall allow water to drain, to avoid any build-up of water pressure behind it.

Malaysia's hills and mountains are important water catchment areas. Bukit Melawati in Selangor is shown.

## Environmental considerations in hillside development

Mountains and hills of Malaysia are water catchment areas, where streams and rivers begin their long journey to the sea. These rivers are characterized by high erosion capability. In the tropics, where thick, loose residual soil, the result of deep weathering, can be easily eroded, transported and deposited, this capability is enhanced. As a consequence of erosion, river siltation during heavy rain is very high. Because of extremely deep weathering steep slopes are easily eroded by streams and rivers. This in turn increases the rate of mass movement, such as soil creep, slope failure and landslides. The high erosion capability, coupled with a high rate of mass movement, makes hillsides geomorphologically sensitive regions.

For physical development, suitability, safety and value for money are the most important factors. In hillsides, 'suitable' areas are limited, hence the necessity to build on steep slopes and other difficult terrain. In such situations site investigation needs to be carried out with extreme care in order to avoid man-induced hazards which can lead to loss of life. Not only will development on hillsides create difficulty in ensuring public safety, it will also pose problems to adjacent low-lying areas.

Siltation, flash floods and river bank erosion in the lowlands are often caused by uncontrolled and excessive development in the uplands. This phenomenon is often ignored when investigations into the causes of floods are carried out. In Kuala Lumpur, for example, events and activities nearest a flood are often cited as its cause when, in fact, its origins can frequently be traced to development on the surrounding hills.

## The engineering solution

Apart from avoiding further development on hillsides altogether, which in reality may not be a practical and economic solution, there are remedial measures to render slopes safer. These include cutting terraces (called berms), cutting back the slope, putting up retaining walls or anchor blocks, soil nailing and improving drainage by various methods. Wells driven into a slope pump out water, a perforated pipe driven into a slope collects water that then drains off away from the slope, or a concrete drain, excavated along the top of a slope, can intercept runoff and carry it away. Terraces may be cut into the slope to create greater stability. The 'steps' can break the journey of any earth slippage as it travels downwards. Slopes can also be graded into gentler ones to reduce landslide risk.

Such pre-emptive methods and treatments are very expensive, but to reduce risk and to protect the environment such investments are necessary. In any case, these solutions do not guarantee that disasters will not occur at hillside developments.

## Hillside development
In Malaysia, the physical development of hilly or mountainous areas takes place for four main reasons.

### Historical
Some hillside areas have been inhabited by indigenous people—shifting cultivators—over many generations. The adaptation to a modern lifestyle has made some of these areas permanent residential centres, such as Kundasang in Sabah, whose people practise traditional temperate climate agriculture.

### Encroachment
As low-lying areas get developed and thus more scarce, developers look to the foothills, and eventually higher slopes to expand. The granite hills in the north and west of Kuala Lumpur have been developed in the 1990s, with new executive condominiums springing up along the route to the Genting Highlands.

### Hill stations
These began as retreats consisting of small bungalows, where colonial masters would seek sanctuary from the towns and humid climate. They include Maxwell's Hill, Fraser's Hill and Cameron Highlands (the Lake View Hotel is shown) and cater to modern-day tourists. The Cameron Highlands, in particular, has experienced substantial development.

### Recreational
There is currently a strong demand for recreational and entertainment activities on the hills. One of the most developed areas is the Genting Highlands, which houses a casino, a theme park, luxurious hotels and privately owned apartments.

# Tales of overdeveloped hillsides

## Changing the face of Bukit Larut
Previously known as Maxwell's Hill, Bukit Larut, Malaysia's oldest and sleepiest hill resort, rises 1036 metres above sea level. With limited flat land, it has survived unaffected by new developments for 100 years. But not for much longer if a new improvement scheme gets the go-ahead. Observers worry about the ecological damage the proposed scheme may cause, as the area is particularly sensitive because of its limestone composition.

## Developing too fast
Fraser's Hill represents a well-balanced hillside development, but future plans for the area may end this. Condominiums, high-rise hotels and golf courses already dot the 2400-hectare site of this temperate hill station. The first sign of development-related trouble surfaced in 1994 when the foundation of an apartment was damaged due to slope failure. In addition, severe river siltation led to the temporary closure of a popular waterfall in the area, indicating that development has been too rapid and that the natural environment is unable to withstand further human infiltration.

*Fraser's Hill losing its 'novelty factor'*

A retaining wall has been erected to prevent erosion and landslides at Fraser's Hill.

## Landslide fury
Hillside development is susceptible to naturally occurring phenomena which can lead to disaster. Mud, boulders and debris flowing violently on the narrow gulley of the Genting Sempah area swept away a dozen vehicles on the slip road to the Genting Highlands, killing 21 people and injuring 22 others on the afternoon of 30 June 1995. It has been speculated that human activity in the area altered the natural characteristics of the slope and surface hydrology, rendering it vulnerable under wet conditions. The avalanche of mud and other debris, that naturally occur in mountain areas, was triggered by unusually heavy rain.

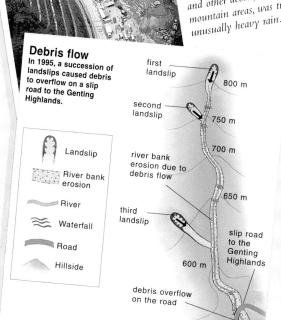

The aftermath of a fatal landslide in June 1995 in the Genting Highlands.

## Highway disaster
The North–South Expressway runs along the foothills of the Main Range. Although generally stable, some stretches traverse geologically difficult terrain. A major slope failure occurred in early January 1996 along a weak zone between Tapah and Gopeng, near Gua Tempurung. One driver was buried in the soft, orange mud that flowed down from the collapsed slope and spread out across the road for 300 metres. The freak accident triggered a general panic amongst the public, who began to worry about safety along the entire length of the highway. The landslide may have been caused by soil erosion and stagnant water at the top of the slope.

Landslides along the North–South and East–West (shown) highways are all too common occurrences, causing destruction and loss of life.

## Debris flow
In 1995, a succession of landslips caused debris to overflow on a slip road to the Genting Highlands.

first landslip — 800 m
second landslip — 750 m
river bank erosion due to debris flow — 700 m
— 650 m
third landslip — 600 m
slip road to the Genting Highlands
debris overflow on the road

- Landslip
- River bank erosion
- River
- Waterfall
- Road
- Hillside

## THE HIGHLAND TOWERS DISASTER
On Saturday, 11 December 1993, at 1.30 in the afternoon, Block 1 of the Highland Towers at Hillview Garden, Ulu Klang, Selangor, toppled, burying 49 people in its rubble. Believed to have been triggered by a period of intense and prolonged rainfall in the area, the collapse of the 12-storey building was caused by the landslide of the hill behind the condominium, involving some 50 000 cubic metres of earth. This disaster was the first to attract public attention, helping to open the eyes of many Malaysians to the importance of proper geological and geotechnical investigation and slope stabilization measures for hillside development.

A landslide behind Highland Towers in Selangor caused the collapse of the condominium.

# Air quality

*Until relatively recently, air pollution was not regarded as a significant problem in Malaysia. However, following rapid urban and industrial expansion, the quality of air, particularly in built-up areas, has become a major concern. For certain locations and during certain times of the year, the situation is serious. Haze and acid rain are the main problems and are threats to both the natural environment and the health of the Malaysian population.*

Open burning of fields in Rawang illustrates that it is not just urban centres that experience reduced air quality. Agricultural burning in the countryside contributes heavily to air pollution, especially haze.

Yellow smoke is churned out from a factory's chimney stacks in the Sungai Siput Industrial area, Perak.

The number of motor vehicles on Malaysian roads increased from 670,000 in 1970 to 6.3 million in 1994, making exhaust fumes one of the country's major sources of pollution.

## The quality of Malaysian air

The quality of air in Malaysia is very much dependant on the level and pace of urban development, most notably within the industrial corridor that extends south from Penang to Johor Bahru. There is a real danger that the quality of the country's air will be further harmed as both the government and private sector forge ahead in their concerted effort to turn Malaysia into a fully developed nation by the year 2020.

In urban areas, the two largest sources of air pollution are motor vehicles and industries. More than 90 per cent of emissions occur in the form of carbon monoxide, nitrogen oxides and sulphur oxides. In many places, the levels of total suspended particulates (TSP) well exceed the recommended Malaysian guidelines of 90 micrograms per cubic metre ($ug/m^3$). Cement and quarrying industries and open burning emit the greatest amount of particulates, and between 1987 and 1995 the contribution of exhaust fumes to pollution grew steadily, exceeding that from fuel burning and other industrial sources.

In rural areas, air quality deterioration occurs near quarries, palm oil mills, sawmills and paddy mills. The billowing black clouds that rise up from burning fields are also a serious contributor to the country's pollution.

## Contributing factors

Air is polluted by a potentially deadly cocktail of dust, dirt, odours and vehicle fumes. The severity of pollution is dependant on four main factors: topography, local climatic conditions, city effects, and the distribution and number of people and industries in an area.

The nature of the atmosphere and its ability to dilute and disperse pollutants determine what happens to air pollutants once they are released from their respective sources. Data from Malaysian meteorological stations show that the atmosphere is far less successful in dispersing pollutants than, for example, the atmosphere in Los Angeles, a city known for its high pollution, because ventilation and wind in the tropics is comparatively limited. Mountains and ridges, by confining circulations within valleys, also encourage high pollution concentrations, as in the Klang Valley.

## City effects

The problem of air quality in city areas is particularly complex. A phenomenon known as the 'heat island' exacerbates pollution. Urban activities produce a significant amount of heat, in addition to large quantities of fine particles that can affect radiation and heat balance; the heat is absorbed and retained by concrete buildings and surfaces. As a result, commercial centres are usually several degrees warmer than the countryside—on average 1–2 °C—and on calm, cloudless nights, the urban–rural temperature differential can exceed 5 °C. Pollutants are trapped in the heat island by an elevated inversion, an atmospheric condition in which air temperature rises with increasing altitude, trapping surface air below and preventing dispersal of pollutants.

## Acid rain

One way in which air pollution in Malaysia manifests itself is as acid rain. Its two major contributors are sulphur and nitrogen oxides which are released into the atmosphere through industrial processes, motor vehicles, power generation and other human activities. Acid rain is formed when the pollutants combine with moisture in the atmosphere.

In Malaysia, studies by the Meteorological Service show that, although it is not yet as critical a problem as in Western Europe, it is fast becoming of public concern. Prai, Petaling Jaya and Senai recorded low pH values, with annual averages as low as 4.40 between 1985 and 1987; pH is a value on a scale of 0–14 which gives a measure of acidity. A neutral medium has a pH7; less than pH7 is acidic. The extent of areas affected by acid rain is increasing, especially along the west coast of Peninsular Malaysia in Selangor, Johor and Perak.

Acid rain is detrimental to life and life-support systems, such as the aquatic ecosystem of lakes and rivers. Many species of fish will perish when their pH levels fall below 5.5. In addition to drought and ozone, acid rain contributes significantly to forest damage. In Malaysia, the effects of acid rain are evident in severe cases of metal corrosion. For

# Living with air pollution

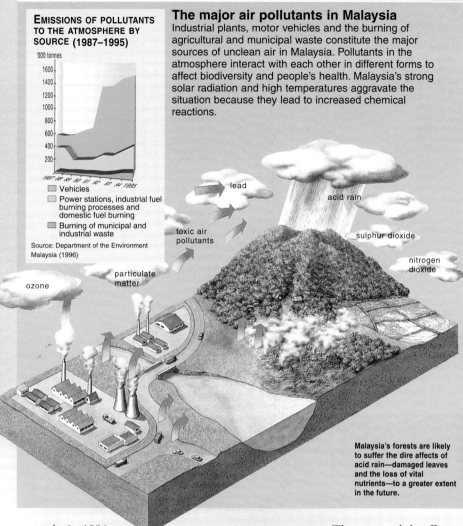

## The major air pollutants in Malaysia

Industrial plants, motor vehicles and the burning of agricultural and municipal waste constitute the major sources of unclean air in Malaysia. Pollutants in the atmosphere interact with each other in different forms to affect biodiversity and people's health. Malaysia's strong solar radiation and high temperatures aggravate the situation because they lead to increased chemical reactions.

lead · acid rain · sulphur dioxide · nitrogen dioxide · toxic air pollutants · ozone · particulate matter

Malaysia's forests are likely to suffer the dire affects of acid rain—damaged leaves and the loss of vital nutrients—to a greater extent in the future.

## Acid rain in Peninsular Malaysia

From 1985 to 1995, there has been a progressive deterioration in the air quality of many areas in Peninsular Malaysia, which has been directly attributed to acid rain. The most severe incidences occur in highly industrialized areas such as Penang, Selangor and Johor, as shown in the maps below. The reduced acid rain in 1990 resulted from a lower amount of pollutants in the air because of a slowdown in economic activity and particularly wet climatic conditions that year.

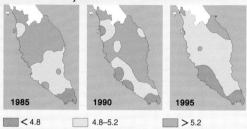

1985 · 1990 · 1995

☐ < 4.8   ☐ 4.8–5.2   ☐ > 5.2

The Malaysian Meteorological Service uses pH 5.2 as the parameter for acid rain caused by man-made activities. Areas recording a pH of less than 5.2 are deemed highly acidic.

Source: Malaysian Meteorological Service

example, in 1996 cars in Johor Bahru were reported to have been corroded by sulphuric acid.

## Other evidence of pollution

The haze phenomenon is another example of poor air quality (see 'The ominous haze'). Indirect effects are seen in the increased number of pollution-related health problems.

Haze has been gaining prominence in Malaysia, especially Kuala Lumpur and the Klang Valley, in the 1990s. Although haze occurrences were noted as early as the 1960s, they became a problem only relatively recently. The haze episodes between September and October 1994, and from September to November 1997, were particularly severe. These were both attributed to prolonged forest fires in Kalimantan and Sumatra, Indonesia, being further aggravated by the southwest monsoon and by the El Niño phenomenon. The latter has been identified as a major cause of disruption to the prevailing climatic conditions and occurs every few years in the Pacific (see 'The El Niño Southern Oscillation').

The more subtle effects of air pollution are seen in the way it affects the human body. Polluted air can irritate a person's skin and eyes, causing physical discomfort and reducing visibility. It can also be inhaled into the respiratory system, provoking serious health conditions, such as bronchitis, emphysema, asthma and lung cancer.

## Patrolling pollution

Pure, clean air is essential for plants to grow, for animals to survive and for human beings to remain healthy. Measuring pollution and finding alleviating solutions constitute one of Malaysia's greatest priorities. The control of dusts from roads and stricter enforcement on industrial sources to control the emission of pollutants have succeeded in reducing the TSP in certain regions. Legislation has resulted in lower lead levels, which in the Klang Valley region have shown a marked decrease since 1989. Switching of fuel energy supply, from oil- and diesel-fuelled power stations, saw a notable reduction in the amount of sulphur oxides emitted in 1989 compared to those in the previous two years.

Exhaust funes that cloud Kuala Lumpur's streets are a health hazard for pedestrians and roadside hawkers.

# The ominous haze

*Haze is a form of air pollution which is exacerbated at certain times of the year under specific weather conditions. In 1994 and 1997, Malaysia experienced two of its most severe haze episodes. The problem was especially intense in the Klang Valley, where it created poor visibility and contributed significantly to health problems.*

At the height of the haze episode in 1994, visibility of the Kuala Lumpur skyline was reduced to as little as 500 metres.

Visibility of the Kuala Lumpur skyline after the haze had dissipated after three weeks.

## Hazy perspectives

The haze phenomenon was first noted in the 1960s, but has now become a regular feature of the Malaysian environment, especially during the relatively dry months of February and March and from June to September or early October. The haze condition is considered severe when the level of suspended dust particles in the air are more than twice the average values usually observed in a particular area.

When haze covers the lower atmosphere it prevents sunlight from reaching the ground. This interferes with normal plant photosynthesis (food production) and can thus affect crop yields or destroy animal habitats. Haze poses a serious health risk, particularly to sufferers of asthma and bronchitis. Haze has also been responsible for flight cancellations and for the disruption of other businesses.

## Conditions favourable for haze formation

Haze is caused by the presence of a large number of minute particles suspended in the atmosphere. These particles, which are invisible to the naked eye, can be natural in origin, for example, soil dust, volcanic emissions and sea spray salt. They are also found in anthropogenic (man-made) sources, such as soot, smoke and other by-products from fuel burning and industrial processes. These particles absorb and scatter light, and in so doing, reduce atmospheric visibility and give the air an opalescent or hazy appearance.

Haze occurs particularly when there are high levels of air pollutants, especially particulates, hanging in the air, coupled with dry, stable weather conditions. The atmosphere's inability to disperse pollutants has been shown to be much greater in tropical cities, such as those in Malaysia, than in mid-latitude regions. This, combined with the near-total dependence on motor vehicles and the abundance of sunshine provide the necessary conditions for an intense smog, or haze, to form. Severe haze

Asthma cases increase during haze periods. Government-issued masks can help protect children from breathing polluted air.

## Significant haze episodes in Malaysia

According to the Malaysian Meteorological Service, severe haze episodes, lasting more than a week and causing visibility to be reduced to less than 1 kilometre, were not a feature of the 1960s and 1970s. They started to appear in the 1980s because of the rapid industrial growth that the country experienced from that period.

### BETWEEN 1983 AND 1997, SEVEN EPISODES OF SEVERE HAZE WERE REPORTED

| | |
|---|---|
| April 1983 | Peninsular Malaysia, Sabah and Sarawak |
| 15–30 August 1990 | Peninsular Malaysia and western Sarawak |
| 15–18 June 1991 | Peninsular Malaysia and Sabah |
| 10–22 September 1991 | Sabah and Sarawak |
| 27 September–11 October 1991 | Peninsular Malaysia and Sarawak |
| 15 September–6 October 1994 | Peninsular Malaysia, Sabah and Sarawak |
| August–October 1997 | Peninsular Malaysia, Sabah and Sarawak |

episodes occur primarily during the relatively dry period of the southwest monsoon, from June to September or early October.

## Measuring haze

Haze is measured on a scale of 0–500 by the pollutant standards index (PSI). This measures five specific pollutants in the air. The pollutant with the highest reading in any 24-hour period is taken as the PSI reading for the whole period.

| PSI LEVEL | RISK (TO NORMALLY HEALTHY PERSON) |
|---|---|
| 0–100 | Within acceptable level. No risk. |
| 101–199 | Persons with existing heart or respiratory ailments should reduce physical exertion and outdoor activity. |
| 200–299 | The elderly and persons with existing heart and lung disease should stay indoors and reduce physical activity. |
| 300–399 | The elderly and persons with existing diseases should stay indoors and reduce physical activity. The general population should avoid outdoor activity. |
| 400–500 | Everyone should remain indoors, keeping windows and doors closed and should minimize physical exertion. |

## The formation of haze

While many built-up areas in Malaysia are adversely affected by haze, it is especially serious in the highly industrialized Klang Valley where Kuala Lumpur, the capital and the country's largest city, is located. At its height, haze has resulted in poor visibility, disruption of flight schedules and marked increase in respiratory complaints, especially among asthmatic patients.

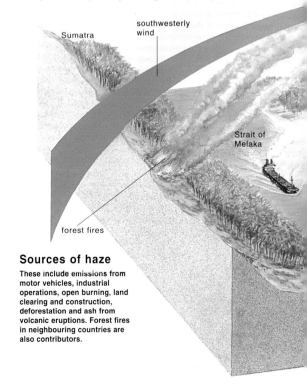

## Sources of haze

These include emissions from motor vehicles, industrial operations, open burning, land clearing and construction, deforestation and ash from volcanic eruptions. Forest fires in neighbouring countries are also contributors.

### Forest fires as haze contributors

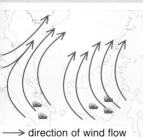

→ direction of wind flow

The haze episodes of 1991, 1994 and 1997 were associated with forest fires on the Indonesian islands of Kalimantan and Sumatra. The constant influx of soot and carbons from the fires, brought across by southerly winds, made it very difficult for the atmosphere to effectively disperse and dilute the particulates. At the same time, widespread air subsistence and temperature inversions further prevented the pollutants from being lifted into the higher atmosphere and dispersed.

Under normal conditions, warm air near the earth's surface cools upwards at a steady rate. As surface air is heated, its density becomes reduced and it rises, carrying any pollutants with it. These are then carried off by winds at the atmosphere's upper levels. However, sometimes temperature inversion occurs, where colder air sits near the surface with warmer air above. During such inversion, the lower, often more polluted air, cannot rise and be dispersed because it is blocked by the warmer air above.

Circulation restrictions in the Klang Valley, recipient of particularly severe bouts of the ominous haze because of its low-lying position, mean that polluted air cannot escape and fresher air from outside or above the inversion layer cannot enter. While emissions continue unimpeded, pollutants accumulate in this stagnant circulation system. Visibility declines rapidly as light scattering and absorption increase because of the rise in particle concentration. Particularly intense haze hovered over the Klang Valley in 1991, 1994 and 1997.

### Shifting the haze

Haze will ultimately dissipate when there is a decrease in particulate emission, or when heavy rain falls for several consecutive days. A change in the wind direction or a persistent strong wind in the lower atmosphere will also disperse polluted air and so reduce the haze.

For haze to shift there must be a strong enough convection air current to break through the inversion layer so that normal mixing of air and dispersion can resume. An external disturbance, such as an intense thunderstorm, is usually necessary to trigger such a situation. The intense updrafts in the thunderstorms draw large amounts of surface air up into the upper troposphere. The intense rainfall also creates downdrafts which spread out at the surface as gusts. The disturbance of the stable haze layer enables the large-scale wind to push the particle-laden surface air out of, for example, the Klang Valley, and so restore normal visibility.

### Haze, fog or mist?

Haze is often confused with fog or mist but there are distinct differences. Microscopic water droplets suspended in the air are responsible for reduced visibility in fog or mist. When haze occurs, however, the opalescent appearance of the atmosphere is caused by suspended microscopic dry particles, such as dust or soot. In fog, horizontal visibility drops to below 1 kilometre and the relative humidity in the air equals, or exceeds, 97 per cent. Mist occurs when humidity is more than 95 per cent. For haze, the humidity is lower at less than 95 per cent.

In the tropics, a mist or fog tends to disappear after sunrise as the sun's rays heat the ground and cause the accumulated moisture to evaporate. Haze can persist throughout the day and over consecutive days.

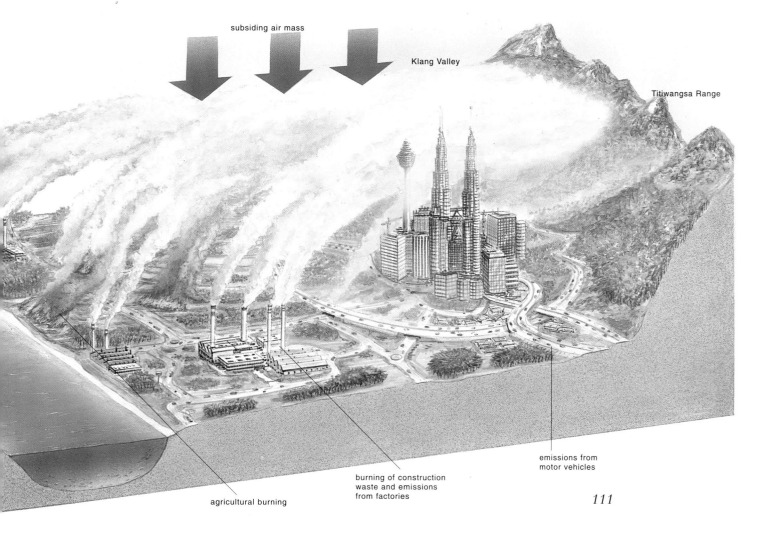

subsiding air mass

Klang Valley

Titiwangsa Range

agricultural burning

burning of construction waste and emissions from factories

emissions from motor vehicles

# Flash and monsoon flooding

*Floods are the most common natural hazard in Malaysia. They cause damage to property and crops and sometimes loss of life. Flash floods are swift, localized, highly unpredictable and are largely due to land use changes induced by rapid urbanization and economic development in major cities. Monsoon floods occur annually during the monsoon seasons and are more widespread and devastating.*

School children put their exercise books out to dry in a clear-up operation after flooding of their rural classroom in Selangor.

Top: Inhabitants of traditional Malay houses have learned to adapt to the seasonal monsoon floods. The houses are built high enough to prevent infiltration by the flood waters.

Bottom: Kuala Lumpur under water in January 1971 during one of Malaysia's worst floods. Even when the city was less developed it suffered some disastrous floods. Further urbanization is likely to greatly increase the risk of flooding.

## Causes of flash floods

Flash floods are largely due to environmental deterioration caused by human interference with the natural hydrological cycle. When land is overdeveloped, natural resources such as forests and hill slopes are depleted to such an extent that the natural river system cannot cope with slope runoff.

The increase in flash flooding in many urban areas in Malaysia in recent years is directly related to the inability of disturbed river systems to cope with sudden changes inadvertently induced, or deliberately carried out by people. Floating logs and vegetation debris from logging and related activities, and indiscriminate disposal of rubbish into drains and rivers block the free flow of water causing rivers and the natural or man-made drainage systems to overflow.

Other factors contributing to flash floods include excessive improvements to river channels which overtax the discharge capacity of their downstream stretches; siltation of riverbeds due to soil erosion and other sediment runoff from slopes and housing schemes which reduce the normal capacity of a river; low bridge crossings with insufficient clearance which interfere with the high flow of the river; infilling of tin-mining ponds and lakes for development; and the clearance of peatswamp forests.

## The perils of flash floods

Flash flooding is inundation usually caused by convectional storms accompanied by torrential rainfall over a short period of time. These storms occur most frequently during two relatively short intermonsoon seasons around April and October. Such storms usually last less than 24 hours. The resulting rainfall is too heavy to be absorbed by the soil, and in well-developed urban areas, where much of the land surface is composed of impermeable materials, most of the rainfall flows as surface runoff and very quickly enters the river system. The capacity of a river to carry the runoff discharge is soon exceeded, leading to floods.

Although flash floods are known for their rapid onset, they subside equally rapidly. The water level reaches its peak flow (flood peak) in a very short time, usually within half an hour of the start of a downpour and often within minutes in highly urbanized catchment areas. Because of this, flash floods are difficult to predict and often there is little warning (at best a few minutes), before flooding occurs. Despite their short duration, flash floods can cause considerable inconvenience, huge traffic jams in densely populated areas, damage to property, vehicles and public infrastructure, and loss of life.

## Monsoon floods

Monsoon floods are largely caused by natural factors, such as heavy seasonal monsoon rainfall and prolonged rain spells. Low-lying land, poor drainage in swampy areas, and other local factors have made certain areas extremely susceptible to flooding. Human factors, such as the location of early settlements near rivers—to establish transportation links and to be close to an essential source of water supply and drainage—and activities such as farming, mining and fishing, have also contributed substantially to the increased incidence of monsoon flooding.

These are brought by both the southwest monsoon (June–September) and the northeast monsoon (November–March). They are seasonal in nature, last longer, and are generally more extensive and severe than the average floods, especially during the northeast monsoon. In contrast, flooding during the southwest monsoon is relatively mild, as a greater part of Malaysia is sheltered from the winds by the islands of Indonesia.

## Peak periods of flooding in selected locations in Malaysia

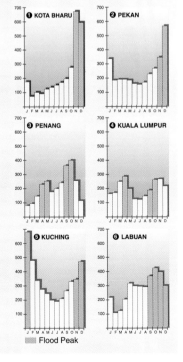

In Kota Bharu and Pekan, which are both exposed to the northeast monsoon winds, the flood peak periods coincide with two months of heavy rainfall in November and December. Kuala Lumpur and Penang on the west coast of the Peninsula, however, are sheltered from the monsoon winds. Here rainfall is fairly evenly distributed throughout the year, but flash floods generally occur during the intermonsoon periods of April/May and September/October when heavy convectional rains are common.

Kuching is also exposed to the northeast monsoon winds and experiences heavy rainfall, leading to floods, from November to February. Labuan receives rain all year round, but floods tend to occur between September and December.

# Comparison of flood potential in forested and urban areas

### Forested areas

In a forest ecosystem, rainfall passes through several processes which absorb part of the moisture and reduce the speed of the water's natural journey into the river. Only a portion of the original rainfall ends up in the river because a significant part is absorbed by vegetation and soil. Dense tropical vegetation acts as a 'sponge' which soaks up much of the rain, which means floods are unlikely.

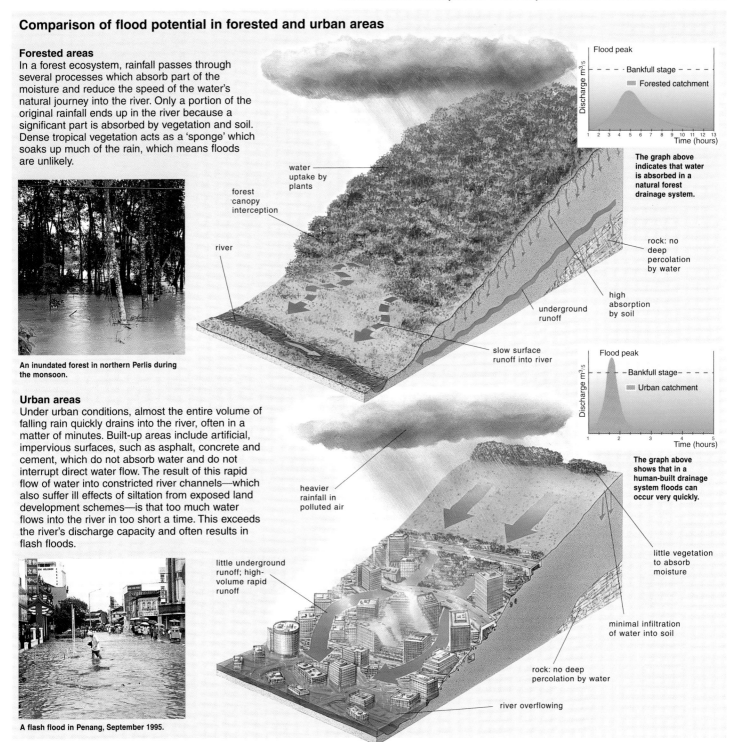

Flood peak
- - - Bankfull stage - - -
Forested catchment
Discharge m³/s
Time (hours)

The graph above indicates that water is absorbed in a natural forest drainage system.

water uptake by plants

forest canopy interception

river

rock: no deep percolation by water

high absorption by soil

underground runoff

slow surface runoff into river

An inundated forest in northern Perlis during the monsoon.

### Urban areas

Under urban conditions, almost the entire volume of falling rain quickly drains into the river, often in a matter of minutes. Built-up areas include artificial, impervious surfaces, such as asphalt, concrete and cement, which do not absorb water and do not interrupt direct water flow. The result of this rapid flow of water into constricted river channels—which also suffer ill effects of siltation from exposed land development schemes—is that too much water flows into the river in too short a time. This exceeds the river's discharge capacity and often results in flash floods.

Flood peak
- - Bankfull stage - - -
Urban catchment
Discharge m³/s
Time (hours)

The graph above shows that in a human-built drainage system floods can occur very quickly.

heavier rainfall in polluted air

little underground runoff; high-volume rapid runoff

little vegetation to absorb moisture

minimal infiltration of water into soil

rock: no deep percolation by water

river overflowing

A flash flood in Penang, September 1995.

Normal seasonal monsoon floods occur annually in Malaysia, usually during the northeast monsoon season. During these floods, the waters do not often exceed the stilt height of traditional Malay houses. However, extreme major monsoon floods do occur once every few years, rendering flood victims helpless. These floods are extensive, severe and often last for several weeks causing much damage to property and life. Major monsoon floods struck Malaysia in 1926, 1971 and 1988, when flood depths of 3 metres were recorded

Likewise, high tides coinciding with heavy rainfall increase the flow of water in an area vulnerable to floods. Spits and sand bars which form at river estuaries impede the free flow of river water into the sea. The river level is raised causing low-lying areas to floods.

## Human costs

Floods have a significant impact on both the national economy and the affected population. They cause damage to public infrastructure, property, businesses, crops and livestock, and can cause loss of life. There are around a dozen deaths due to flooding each year. It is estimated that the average potential flood damage each year in Malaysia is more than RM100 million at 1996 prices. The Malaysian Government incurs substantial annual costs in flood disaster alert preparations, rescue and relief operations, and post-flood rehabilitation of victims and public utilities. Every year millions of ringgit are spent on flood mitigation schemes in almost every state.

Enlarged drains are constructed, as here in Ipoh, to alleviate monsoon flooding in urban areas, at a cost to the public purse.

# Noise pollution

*Sound is a precursor to noise. It is all around us and has multifarious uses in everyday life. It is most people's direct form of communication. However, sound may sometimes interfere with normal activities and it is then that it crosses the boundary from sound to noise. In Malaysia, because of rapid industrialization and urbanization, noise is becoming an increasing problem, which government legislation seeks to control.*

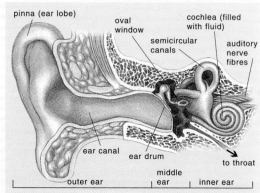

The tranquillity of the natural world, as typified by this scene in rural Raban, Perak, is a noise-free zone, a far cry from the industrial plants and bustling streets of urban centres.

### When is sound a noise?

Noise can be defined as any sound, independent of its loudness, that can produce an undesirable physiological or psychological effect on an individual, and which may interfere with his social needs, such as communication, work, rest and sleep. Noise is considered an environmental pollutant, which by definition categorizes it, along with the contributors to air and water pollution, as a waste product generated in association with various human activities.

The same sound can be music to one person's ears, but a considerable nuisance to another's. Whether a sound is noise or not is generally dependent on three factors: the quantity of the sound, the quality of the sound, and the attitude of the receiver towards the sound—the latter being dependent on location and time of day.

### Tuning into Malaysia's noise

The main causes of environmental noise pollution in Malaysia are the unsatisfactory planning decisions which lead to incompatible land use. Sources of such noise pollution include motor vehicles and planes, industrial and construction work, outdoor social and recreational events, and domestic activities such as noise from home appliances and pets.

Sound and noise are measured using a sound level meter and the intensity is recorded by decibels (dB). The sound level meter typically consists of a microphone linked to an electronic unit. The sounds picked up by the microphone are converted to electrical signals whose characteristics are then electronically measured. To take account of the frequency sensitivity of the human ear and so provide a better indication of nuisance induced by a particular sound, a weighting network is incorporated into the meter, referred to as A weighting and expressed in dB(A).

The World Health Organization recommends a maximum noise level of 55 dB(A) during the day and 45 dB(A) at night for residential areas. But, there are numerous examples of these guidelines being flouted. As cities grow larger, residential areas

## Limiting exposure to noise

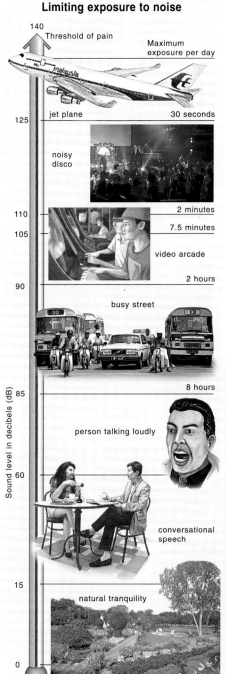

## Sounding out the human amplifier

In dry air, sound travels at the speed of approximately 1920 kilometres an hour or 331 metres every second. In its simplest form, sound can be described as a sensation or variation in pressure which enters, and is detected by, the ear. The level of pressure variation per second is called frequency and is measured in terms of cycles per second, or hertz (Hz). A healthy human being can detect sound made up of frequencies between 20 and 20,000 Hz.

The amplitude or loudness of sound essentially depends on the intensity, or the level of pressure, of the sound waves received by the ear. The ear is sensitive to an enormous range of pressures which are expressed by a logarithmic scale called the decibel scale named after the inventor Alexander Graham Bell. The immense range of pressures are compressed so that the entire amplitude range is contained within a sequence of values from 0 to 160. The human ear can safely be exposed to different levels of noise for varying lengths of time. The chart (left) indicates the approximate exposure time for common Malaysian sounds. The sound level is given in decibels (dB).

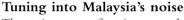

### How the ear works

The outer ear, or pinna, acts as a sound receptor that channels external sound down the ear canal to the ear drum. The ear drum moves in response to sound, causing vibration in the chain of adjacent bones and the opening of the oval window. The movement of the oval window membrane causes the fluid in the cochlea to move against sensory hair cells that change the sounds into signals. These signals get sent to the brain by the auditory nerve where they are processed and interpreted as sound.

sit close to factories or industrial activities. Schools, hospitals and libraries are situated near busy roads. In Malaysia, the noise levels in a general residential area may range from as low as 35 dB(A) during the night, to as high as 85 dB(A) during the day. Even though the night level is low and compares favourably with levels in developed countries, the daytime rate is rather high, and in some cases as high as the noise levels of a factory in operation. Continuous exposure at this level may cause adverse effects on the receiver.

In Petaling Jaya, for example, many residents in areas close to construction sites have actively protested to the local council about the level of noise they have experienced. The 65 dB(A) night noise level allowed by the council was considered too high by the residents. Even though the council prohibited the developer from carrying out piling and drilling works (which could produce noise as high as 90 dB(A)), noise from other construction activities, especially from construction vehicles and power generators, was enough to interfere with the sleep of local residents.

Taking readings of noise level using a sound level meter.

In 1994, Malaysia's Department of Environment received more complaints about noise pollution than for any other environmental problem with the exception of air pollution. In most residential areas, traffic noise has been identified as the main source of the problem, with motorcycles and heavy vehicles being the main contributors. In 1995, more than one-third of the complaints came from Selangor, followed by Johor and Kuala Lumpur. This is hardly surprising since these states are currently experiencing rapid development and a steady increase in the number of registered motor vehicles.

## The effects of noise pollution

Aside from being an irritant, noise pollution can be unhealthy and stressful. It may result in a temporary loss of hearing sensitivity if exposure to sufficiently loud noise (approximately above 85 dB(A)) occurs over a period of a few hours. The cumulative effect of exposure to repeated noise over many years may result in permanent, non-reversible loss of hearing sensitivity, a condition common among unprotected workers in a noisy factory. Acoustic trauma is loss in hearing, usually permanent, due to the injury of the ear as a result of a single exposure or relatively few exposures at a very high level, for example, an explosion. In addition, noise can interfere with domestic and social activities and can be dangerous when it interferes with communication or instructions, for example, when safety instructions

cannot be heard above the rumble of an operational machine or streams of passing traffic.

## Tackling noise pollution

In 1994, the Department of Environment commissioned a nationwide survey from the Universiti Teknologi Malaysia's Institute of Noise and Vibration on noise, its sources and people's perceptions of it. The results indicated that most Malaysians perceived noise to be an increasing annoyance. Most were unaware of the existence of legislation on noise and felt that the authorities should take action to establish noise level standards.

At present, the primary concern of the government is the effects of noise on school children. Through a nationwide monitoring programme, it was found that most schools in commercial areas are exposed to noise level in excess of 65 dB(A), which can be both disruptive to lessons and detrimental to the children's hearing. To alleviate the problem, all new schools are to be built in residential, not commercial, areas and existing schools are to be airconditioned and the windows glazed to help reduce excessive noise.

The Malaysian Government has passed several pieces of legislation to address the noise problem, including the Civil Aviation Act (1969), Environmental Quality (Motor Vehicle Noise) Regulations (1987) and Factories and Machinery (Noise Exposure) Regulations (1989). However, these do not specify exact limits or standards for environment noise for particular land use. New regulations are being drafted, which will explicitly establish the noise and vibration limits for industrial, commercial, noise-sensitive (schools and hospitals) and urban residential areas. Mandatory measures to mitigate noise, based on international specifications, will also be included.

### Reducing factory noise

New regulations to reduce factory noise were implemented in Malaysia at the beginning of 1997. The rules limit the time that workers can be exposed to specific noise levels. Extended exposure to loud noise can cause noise-induced deafness (NID), the most common occupational disease. To alleviate the situation, factories are required—they will incur heavy fines if they do not—to use quieter machines, build acoustic enclosures and barriers and keep noisy machines away from workers. Workers exposed to excessive noise are required to don hearing protection, and warning signs must be posted to alert workers to potential danger.

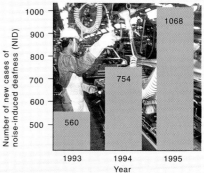

The number of factory workers suffering from NID has increased markedly over the years.

The Malaysian Government is taking steps to reduce the impact of noise on school children. School windows are to be glazed and new schools built in non-commercial areas.

# Municipal waste management

*Homes, commercial premises and industrial complexes in Malaysia's urban centres together generate an estimated 10 000 tonnes of garbage and 2500 cubic metres of sewage every day. As living standards continue to improve, expectations as to how the growing piles of waste should be disposed of rise. Malaysians more than ever expect a disposal practice which not only preserves public health and the environment, but also provides a higher degree of comfort in their daily life.*

## Waste water management

Municipal sewage is the biggest single source of pollution in Malaysian rivers. It is mainly domestic in origin, arising from personal sanitation, washing, laundry, food preparation and the cleaning of kitchen utensils. Fresh sewage is a grey turbid liquid containing solids (faeces, rags and toilet paper), colloidal (non-settleable) particles, as well as pollutants. In Malaysia's hot climate, the dissolved oxygen that breaks down the organic matter can quickly become exhausted, rendering the sewage 'stale' or 'septic' and thus unhealthy. Sewage can also carry organisms which thrive and increase in warm conditions and may lead to infections, such as cholera, typhoid and infectious hepatitis. It should therefore be adequately treated before its ultimate disposal in order to reduce the risk of disease outbreaks and to prevent the pollution of surface and ground waters.

Water treatment works at Pantai Dalam, Kuala Lumpur.

## Sanitation facilities

Malaysia's urban population generally has better access to hygienic sanitation facilities than rural dwellers. They have piped water supply and flush toilets which are treated using household septic tanks, communal treatment units or centralized sewerage treatment plants. Only a small minority located in squatter settlements are using less sanitary systems such as bucket and pit latrines. Household septic tanks are small, rectangular chambers usually located just below ground level,

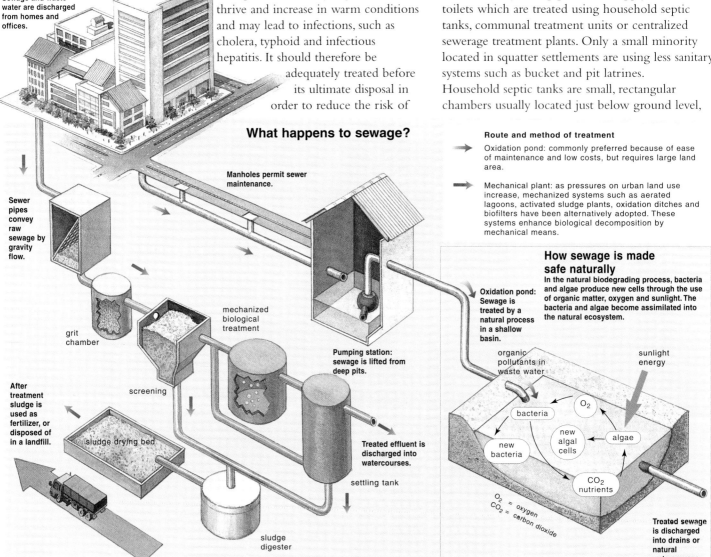

Sewage and waste water are discharged from homes and offices.

**What happens to sewage?**

Manholes permit sewer maintenance.

Sewer pipes convey raw sewage by gravity flow.

grit chamber

screening

mechanized biological treatment

Pumping station: sewage is lifted from deep pits.

After treatment sludge is used as fertilizer, or disposed of in a landfill.

sludge drying bed

settling tank

Treated effluent is discharged into watercourses.

sludge digester

**Route and method of treatment**

→ Oxidation pond: commonly preferred because of ease of maintenance and low costs, but requires large land area.

→ Mechanical plant: as pressures on urban land use increase, mechanized systems such as aerated lagoons, activated sludge plants, oxidation ditches and biofilters have been alternatively adopted. These systems enhance biological decomposition by mechanical means.

### How sewage is made safe naturally
In the natural biodegrading process, bacteria and algae produce new cells through the use of organic matter, oxygen and sunlight. The bacteria and algae become assimilated into the natural ecosystem.

**Oxidation pond:** Sewage is treated by a natural process in a shallow basin.

organic pollutants in waste water

sunlight energy

bacteria

$O_2$

new bacteria

new algal cells

algae

$CO_2$ nutrients

$O_2$ = oxygen
$CO_2$ = carbon dioxide

**Treated sewage is discharged into drains or natural watercourses.**

Places of natural beauty can fast lose their charm as a succession of litterbugs leave their mark. The piles of waste dumped in a river in Selangor reveal that Malaysia's waste management faces formidable challenges.

A pile of uncleared rubbish lies on a pavement in Kuala Lumpur. The city's authorities are trying to encourage people to dispose of their rubbish in a responsible manner.

## Reusing and recycling

The goals in Malaysia's modern waste management are to prevent pollution, to reduce consumption and to recycle. Reduction of waste at source is advocated, which in turn requires the public to be made aware of the environmental reasons for recycling and reusing so-called waste. Landfilling—burying rubbish—should be minimized.

Recycling programmes have been launched in several local authorities, but the recycling stations are far from widespread and support for those that exist has been variable. The major recyclable items include paper, cardboard, bottles, metals and plastics. There is great potential for small-scale resource recovery with the presence of informal recycling vendors and continual scavenging activities on landfill sites, but these are not credible long-term procedures to be advocated. People also need to be encouraged to use recycled products, since recycling can only be successful if there is a market for the products it produces.

School girls filling a recycling bin with used plastic bottles.

where sewage is retained for 1–3 days. Although the solids settle to the bottom of the tank, which requires desludging every few years, the effluent is still hazardous and is disposed of in permeable soil soakaways. In centralized systems, sewage is collected and conveyed, via sewer pipes and pump stations, to its place of treatment and disposal. The wet Malaysian climate favours a sewerage system that is separate from storm water drains. Voluminous storm water flow is kept apart in the surface-water drainage system, thus reducing sewage flows, and therefore sewer sizes and costs.

## Solid waste management

The safe and healthy storage, collection, transportation, processing and disposal of refuse constitute some of the main functions of municipal urban services in Malaysia, and take up a substantial share of manpower and financial resources. Before disposal, waste may be sorted in order to minimize the total amount to be disposed and to reduce costs. It may be sifted, so suitable materials and energy may be siphoned off for further use, and may undergo biological and thermal treatment.

The three most common solid waste processing options are composting and bioconversion, refuse-derived fuel, and incineration. With the exception of plastic, rubber and metals, the organic fraction of solid waste can be subjected to aerobic decomposition to produce a humus-rich compost. Solid waste can be processed to produce fuel to fire boilers that produce steam or electricity. Incineration involves the thermal transformation of waste into gaseous products which reduces its volume by about 85–95 per cent.

## How to handle waste: The Malaysian way

In Malaysia, the processing of solid waste before disposal is rarely performed. The prevailing practice involves the direct haulage of solid waste from collection point to disposal site without any intermediate treatment. Some local authorities are facing increasing difficulty in getting suitable land

for disposal sites due to public objections and the high cost of land acquisition. If the situation persists, intermediate treatment facilities such as incinerators and composting plants will be needed.

Open dumps are unsightly, smelly and unsanitary as they encourage debris to blow into the air, they attract birds and disease-carrying rodents, and liquids from the suppurating garbage may contaminate stream and ground water. In Malaysia, many of the landfill sites are now being upgraded using sound sanitary landfill principles which will ensure effective environmental protection. Suitable soil is used daily to cover deposited wastes to control pests, odour, fire and littering. A landfill should be sited to minimize its environmental impact. Biogas that is released by the rotting waste should ideally be removed to storage tanks from where it might be converted to electricity. Water percolating through waste creates a foul-smelling liquid called leachate, which needs to be safely treated to avoid contamination of drinking water by the pollutants in the liquid.

### THE CONTENTS OF THE NATION'S RUBBISH BINS

- 3% glass
- 3% cloth
- 7% wood
- 16.5% plastics
- 4% metal
- 0.5% other
- 2% rubber
- 37% organic matter (vegetable and garden waste)
- 27% paper and card

Biodegradable

Non-biodegradable: undergoes minimal breakdown with time

The high organic content of the waste means that it is high in moisture and bulk density.

The disposal of solid wastes in Malaysia is done almost solely through the landfill method. In many cases, the practice is crude dumping. Here, a compactor truck unloads at the working face of a sanitary landfill.

# Toxic and hazardous waste

*Malaysian industrialization brings with it the wonders of new technology and modern products. However, such riches are accompanied by dangerous wastes that can be extremely harmful to human health and to the natural environment. The main sources of such wastes in Malaysia are metal-based, textile and petrochemical industries. Current facilities for treatment and disposal are not sufficient, and as a result some wastes have been dumped illegally. Increased legal policing and a new integrated treatment facility are helping to cope with the problem.*

Scheduled wastes—those that appear on the Department of Environment's toxic and hazardous waste inventory—can poison air, water and soil, and therefore their safe treatment and disposal is critical. The photographs show a river in Selangor polluted with chemical waste (top) and a cement factory emitting fumes into the atmosphere (bottom).

## Manufacturing hazardous waste

As the Malaysian economic base has diversified from agriculture and natural resources to manufacturing, new product companies and industrial plants have emerged. For example, as a development of oil palm cultivation, consumable items, so-called 'value-added' products such as cosmetics and industrial additives, have been produced using the processed palm oil. Other plants manufacture a range of goods, from refrigerators to computers, which employ numerous chemicals to cleanse and process the raw materials. This, in turn, has seen the birth of a local chemical industry. The common result of both the primary and secondary industries is that industrial wastes are generated, some of which are hazardous to human health and safety and to the environment.

A waste is considered a hazard if it is corrosive, ignitable, reactive or shows toxic characteristics. Some waste components, although found at low concentrations, when accumulated in living tissues of plants can eventually lead to carcinogenic or other effects. To prevent disaster and environmental pollution, hazardous wastes

## How is waste hazardous?

The hazardous characteristics of wastes are based on the effects they have on the environment if there is spillage or improper use. An ignitable waste may lead to a fire, which in turn generates harmful volatile products. Corrosive, reactive or toxic wastes can burn skin upon contact, or harm aquatic life if waste leaks into a water body. Hazardous organics can accumulate and cause cancer or birth defects (mutagenic effects) years later.

ignitable    corrosive    toxic    reactive

## Industrial waste

The metal-based industries in Malaysia produce the greatest amount of hazardous waste and residues from burning (ash and clinker) are the main waste types.

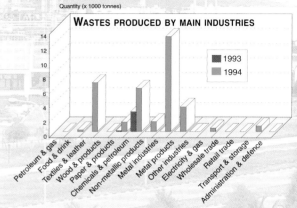

need first to be identified and then tracked to ensure that they are treated or managed so that they are dealt with in a safe way until they are rendered harmless.

## Hazardous waste in Malaysia

One of the main sources of hazardous wastes in Malaysia are metal-based industries, such as foundries and electroplating and acid leaching plants. Raw material cleaning, treatment and dyeing in the textile and leather industries also generate concentrated waste waters containing various chemicals and dyes, while the chemical, petroleum and petrochemical industries generate waters rich in chemicals and oils.

In Malaysia, there are only limited treatment facilities available for hazardous wastes. Existing landfill sites are not suitable to accommodate toxic wastes. Nor are they allowed to receive them. Although many large corporations have installed facilities to store their wastes on site, such individualized management of these by-products is both costly and not easily controlled by government agencies. Since the pace of industrial advancement shows no sign of abating, the amount of waste produced over the following decades will rise, particularly in the west coast region of Peninsular Malaysia.

Some companies currently subcontract the management of their wastes to other firms who may have neither the technology nor the knowledge to carry out the necessary treatment to render the wastes safe. At worst, an unscrupulous operator may simply dump the offending material. In 1995, an organization in Butterworth was apprehended for illegally dumping 41 drums containing deadly potassium cyanide. Traces of the chemical were found in the waters near Pulau Pangkor and are thought to have been responsible for the contamination of fish farmed there.

## Successfully managing hazardous waste

Under the terms of Malaysia's Environmental Quality Act Scheduled Waste Regulation (1989),

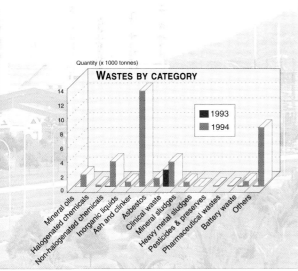

Quantity (x 1000 tonnes)

**WASTES BY CATEGORY**

- 1993
- 1994

Mineral oils · Halogenated chemicals · Non-halogenated chemicals · Inorganic liquids · Ash and clinker · Asbestos · Clinical waste · Mineral sludges · Heavy metal sludges · Pesticides & preserves · Pharmaceutical wastes · Battery waste · Others

## Stages of waste management

The guiding principles of waste management in Malaysia, which companies and government agencies are being encouraged to adopt, do not simply concern treatment of existing waste. The initial emphasis is on reducing waste production, of tapping it at source. The priorities (starting with the most important) are listed below. Once such a hierarchy is adopted, penalties and incentives can follow to motivate the successful implementation of policy in line with these priorities.

> avoid or eliminate waste in the production process
> ▼
> minimize waste in the production and waste treatment processes
> ▼
> recycle waste at its originating plant
> ▼
> reuse waste, or exchange it with compatible industries
> ▼
> treat or convert waste to non-hazardous residues
> ▼
> bury non-hazardous residues at designated landfills

Source: Scheduled Waste Regulation (1989)

The Bukit Nanas integrated waste treatment facility is a timely new project in Negeri Sembilan. In anticipation of an ever increasing amount of hazardous waste, this will be Malaysia's first comprehensive waste treatment plant, incorporating facilities for high-temperature incineration, physical and chemical treatment, stabilization, and a secure landfill.

toxic and hazardous wastes are categorized into 107 scheduled types. Waste-generating industries are obliged to notify the Department of Environment on the rate of production and waste characteristics of any output from their plants that falls within the defined categories. The waste generators are then bound by law to ensure that their scheduled wastes are well managed. This includes keeping an up-to-date inventory of scheduled wastes generated, treated and disposed of; labelling containers and storage areas properly; and not storing incompatible wastes together. The 'cradle to grave' strategy is advocated for waste care; that is, the concept of control of waste from its generation through to its disposal, with the waste generator responsible for the waste until it is rendered harmless.

## Storing and treating waste

The different ways in which hazardous waste is treated in Malaysia are shown in the illustration. Conditions necessary for the protection of human health and safety and the environment are imposed for each of the activities or options.

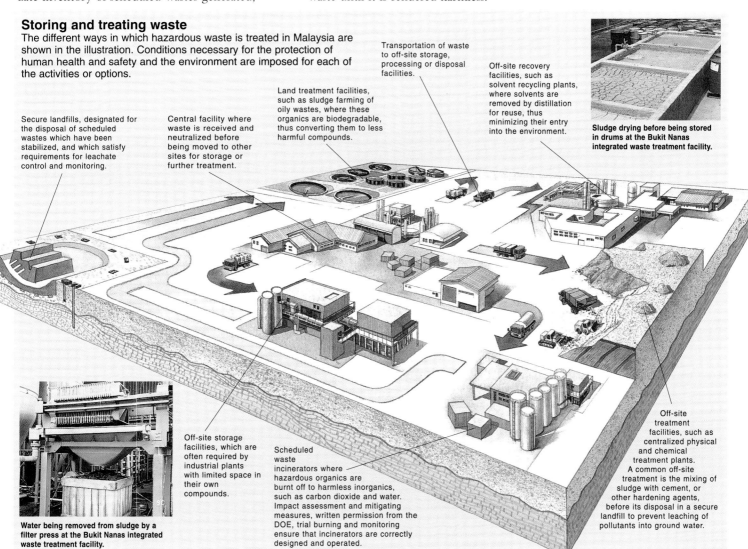

Secure landfills, designated for the disposal of scheduled wastes which have been stabilized, and which satisfy requirements for leachate control and monitoring.

Central facility where waste is received and neutralized before being moved to other sites for storage or further treatment.

Land treatment facilities, such as sludge farming of oily wastes, where these organics are biodegradable, thus converting them to less harmful compounds.

Transportation of waste to off-site storage, processing or disposal facilities.

Off-site recovery facilities, such as solvent recycling plants, where solvents are removed by distillation for reuse, thus minimizing their entry into the environment.

Sludge drying before being stored in drums at the Bukit Nanas integrated waste treatment facility.

Water being removed from sludge by a filter press at the Bukit Nanas integrated waste treatment facility.

Off-site storage facilities, which are often required by industrial plants with limited space in their own compounds.

Scheduled waste incinerators where hazardous organics are burnt off to harmless inorganics, such as carbon dioxide and water. Impact assessment and mitigating measures, written permission from the DOE, trial burning and monitoring ensure that incinerators are correctly designed and operated.

Off-site treatment facilities, such as centralized physical and chemical treatment plants. A common off-site treatment is the mixing of sludge with cement, or other hardening agents, before its disposal in a secure landfill to prevent leaching of pollutants into ground water.

# Agrochemicals

*The increasing need for food and cash crops by Malaysia's growing population has exerted pressure on land use, and has seen an acute shortage of workers, particularly in the agricultural sector. To maintain agricultural productivity, investment in mechanization, irrigation schemes and in agrochemicals has been necessary. Agrochemicals are compounds that protect and fertilize crops. The positive productive, and thus economic, results from their use must be balanced against the potential damage they can inflict on the environment.*

Despite urban growth and rural migration to cities, agriculture remains a crucial part of the Malaysian economy and the lives of its people. To improve crop yields—quantity, quality and value—agrochemicals are increasingly used.

## The use of agrochemicals

Agrochemicals affect our lives at the most basic level by providing growers with products which help them to achieve high-quality yields and to protect crops from pests, disease pathogens and weeds. They can protect during the seed dressing or pre-planting stages and, if applied after a crop is harvested, reduce damage during storage and transportation, helping to prolong its shelf life. Agrochemicals are often used in conjunction with other preventative or non-chemical agronomic practices, such as growing resistant plant varieties, pruning and burning diseased crop parts, managing irrigation and drainage, adopting crop rotation practices, and integrated pest management.

Despite evidence of toxicity to fish, birds and wildlife, some organophosphates and carbamates, common insecticides used in Malaysia, remain in widespread use because of desirable attributes such as cheapness, effective and quick action, relatively low toxicity to mammals and humans, rapid decomposition and their selective non-toxicity to insects that are beneficial to crops.

## Increased pesticide use

Increasing customer demand for high-quality crops and unblemished market produce may result in a high discard rate if crop protection is inadequate. Thus, growers may need to compensate by growing more on increased land areas and adopting new, innovative technology. Targeted use of new generation pesticides with more selective properties against specific pests or diseases, used in small amounts are highly effective and, toxicologically, pose little risk to users and non-targets.

### Agrochemicals used on Malaysian crops

The Malaysian agrochemical market is worth RM301 million.

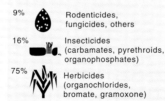

9% Rodenticides, fungicides, others

16% Insecticides (carbamates, pyrethroids, organophosphates)

75% Herbicides (organochlorides, bromate, gramoxone)

Source: Malaysian Agrochemicals Association (1996)

| MARKET SHARE OF PESTICIDES | |
| --- | --- |
| CROP | % |
| Cereals | 16 |
| Fruits | 14 |
| Vegetables | 11 |
| Rice | 10 |
| Maize | 10 |
| Soyabean | 8 |
| Cotton | 6 |
| Others | 25 |

Malaysia, 1993 Statistics

## Environmental risks

The judicious use of agrochemicals should mean reaching a balance between environmental risks and benefits. Good control can help in the management of aquatic weeds in irrigation canals, dams and reservoirs, and in sustaining Malaysia's forests—more efficient production per unit area, through agrochemical use, means fewer hectares are required for agriculture and thus more forest can be preserved. Pesticides are also needed in forest management to protect valuable timber species and weedicides or herbicides are used to control weeds.

However, abuse of agrochemicals can be extremely detrimental to the natural environment. Pesticide residues can enter water bodies through runoff, particularly liable after heavy rains, and pollute aquaculture and thus adversely affect the fishing industry. Such pollution may trigger fishkill—the mass death of fish—by reducing the amount of dissolved oxygen in a lake or river or induce algal bloom through enrichment of the nutrients in the water. Humans are affected if such residues enter and contaminate drinking water, and if they are exposed to too much pesticide they might develop toxicity-related illness. When used pesticide containers are employed as storage vessels for food or drinking water, poisoning of the food or water can result. The use of pesticides undermines the natural food chain patterns. Not only might there be a shift in prey–predator relationships, but some pests, might develop resistance to a chemical altogether.

## Good agrochemical use

Misuse of agrochemicals includes the improper choice of pesticide through ignorance or lack of guidance, wilful misuse of illegal pesticide in an effort to increase yield, adulteration of commercial pesticides by dilution or substitution, overapplication due to misinterpretation of label instructions, spraying immediately prior to crop harvesting, and inaccurate spraying methods. The marriage of environmental responsibility with the production and use of pesticides is starting to be achieved through awareness-raising projects and by harnessing advanced technology. Crop, site or species specific pesticide application, biotechnological products, ultra-low volume application and slow-release pesticide formulations—important in wet conditions where leaching can be a problem—are being used.

Control measures include the compilation of lists of pesticides prescribed for use on specified crops by regulatory authorities, audited stock checks of distributors and analysis of chemical residues in food. Distributors, salesmen and farm users are being educated to the potential danger of the chemicals they handle—both to themselves and to the wider environment. Manufacturers now label their products with safe disposal instructions, and different chemical formulations, which are biodegradable and harmlessly recycled, are being introduced. Advances in research

## Contamination of the food chain

The increasing and unregulated use of agrochemicals has caused major concern because of residue contamination in food, soil and water. Pesticide residues build up in the food chain as predators feed upon contaminated prey. The predators, such as fish, may then be caught and eaten by humans.

When animals are in contact with persistent pesticides through soil, air, water or their food, chemical residues will be found in their body tissues. The level depends on the duration and intensity of exposure, the type of pesticide, and the animal's ability to detoxify, metabolize or excrete the pesticide. Stable pesticides, such as organochlorines which accumulate in the fatty tissues of fish, will then accumulate in the body tissues of the predators that feed upon them.

In developed countries, there are already statutory regulations governing maximum residue levels permitted in produce for human consumption. But these do not yet exist in Malaysia, where pesticide and chemical fertilizer use in agriculture and recreation, such as for golf course turf management, is on the increase. The current casual reliance on shopkeepers to advise on pesticides is too localized and unregulated and training programmes in safe use of pesticides need to be intensified.

### An example of food chain contamination: Mercury from fungicides

Metal-based fungicides are especially used in the treatment of timber trees.

### Safe and unsafe spraying

In Malaysia, most agrochemical operators spray using backpack equipment without proper protective clothing or safety procedures (top). When powered sprayers and fogging machines are used, operators are at risk from drifting spray.

---

Raising awareness of the proper use of agrochemicals should be the responsibility of manufacturers, suppliers and users. CCMB Agrochemicals takes the initiative by promoting proper handling of chemicals.

provide a better understanding of disease processes and pathogenic organisms. Modern scientific techniques provide improvements to both chemical products and to the design of spraying tools to ensure maximum effectiveness and safety. For example, to avoid spray drift, a low-volume nozzle design has been manufactured. In short, every aspect of a product's life, from its manufacture, transport, storage and application to final disposal should be closely monitored and scrutinized to ensure safety.

## Maximum yield, minimum destruction

Crop production to ensure food quality and quantities, can be achieved through a combination of methods, and not merely by resorting to chemicals. These include plant breeding, the use of better machinery for planting, spraying and harvesting, better farming practices, fertilizer use, weather forecasting to predict disease or insect attack, assessing new genetic engineering techniques, introducing genes resistant to disease or insect attack, integrated pest management, insect sterilization, and gamma irradiation to protect

harvested produce. Organic farming methods are also being used. Agrochemicals will continue to play a significant role in Malaysian agriculture for the foreseeable future, but if used correctly they should pose minimal danger to the farmer, his crops, consumers and the environment.

## Integrated pest management

For all pesticides, overspraying can induce pest resistance, particularly of those pests with multiple generations in one cropping season. Resistance is minimized if chemicals are sprayed only against the target pests or are alternated with other products which have different modes of action.

Integrated pest management involves the coordination of cultural, biological, ecological and chemical aspects in food supply to obtain maximum cost-efficient production without detrimental effects to the environment and human health. When used in conjunction with other measures, low-rate pesticides provide good, economic control, by minimizing the development of resistance in important pest species. From the 1990s, the trend has been to use ultra-low volumes of active chemical to reduce costs and to protect the environment. Broad treatment of seeds and plants with pesticides has been largely replaced with band treatment, when a chemical is localized along crop rows or around the base of a plant.

Dayak women with their produce at a market in Kuching, Sarawak.

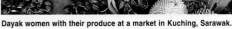

Persistent pests: Rodents attack crops in the field, or like the common rat (Rattus rattus) eat away at stored grain. Pests can be dealt with biologically as well as with chemicals. The barn owl (Tyto alba), for example, is very successful in helping to control rat populations in oil palm.

In the market gardens of the Cameron Highlands, synthetic pheromones are used to trap male diamond-backed moths (Plutella xylostella), whose larvae feed on cabbage leaves. The dearth of males of the species will reduce reproductive capacity, and thus control this pest population.

*Shorea faguetiana* dipterocarp seedlings being planted in reforestation programmes in Sabah by the Kinarut Japan International Cooperation Agency. International cooperation and discussion, at both the ASEAN and global levels, play an increasingly influential role in Malaysia's environmental policy.

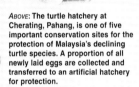

*ABOVE*: The turtle hatchery at Cherating, Pahang, is one of five important conservation sites for the protection of Malaysia's declining turtle species. A proportion of all newly laid eggs are collected and transferred to an artificial hatchery for protection.

*RIGHT*: Scientific research highlights the importance of Malaysia's natural heritage. In 1985–6, a major expedition in the Endau–Rompin State Park, involving 70 scientists, sought to document all plant and animal species in the Park and to study the geology and climate of the area.

Environmental education takes place through the state education system and in more informal atmospheres, such as at this alphabet hunt at the Malaysia Agricultural Park in Selangor.
*RIGHT*: Recycling glass bottles is one way Malaysians can help protect the environment.

Canopy walks allow visitors and researchers to view the upper reaches of Malaysia's rainforest. They are just one of the country's numerous ecotourist projects that attract increasing numbers of local and foreign visitors.

# ENVIRONMENT POLICY AND PROGRAMMES

Learning to investigate Malaysia's natural environment close up and from an early age is the best way to learn to appreciate it and thus to protect it for the future.

Posters, pamphlets and other brochures communicate the environmental message to target groups.

In Malaysia, in the years following Independence, environmental issues took a back seat to development priorities. In many development programmes, little or no consideration was given to the ways in which they might be detrimental to the environment. Although some 20 pieces of environment-related legislation had been passed by the end of the 1960s, these were not specifically designed to address environmental problems but rather concentrated on promoting sound housekeeping practices in specific sectors in line with government policies at the time. By the 1970s, it had become obvious that such legislation was inadequate to cope with the side effects, notably the pollution, from modern developments and industries.

At that time, the impact of development on the environment was becoming increasingly visible, with evidence of deterioration observable throughout Malaysia. Many concerned individuals, from both within the government circle and the general public, realized that environmental problems, then considered peripheral, were real and required redress. Environmental and consumer groups began to openly express their concern about uncontrolled pollution, and environmental issues were publicized in the media to increase awareness.

In 1974, the Environmental Quality Act (EQA) was passed, and a year later a Department of Environment (DOE) was created to administer the Act. In its first 13 years, the DOE concentrated almost exclusively on pollution control with some limited efforts on preventive measures. Following the introduction of Environmental Impact Assessment (EIA) procedures, the preventive approach became more prominent. Not all aspects of the environment are adequately covered by the EQA (1974). Issues such as forestry, water resources, mining, wildlife and fisheries are beyond its jurisdiction and that of the DOE. Currently there are more than 40 environment-related pieces of legislation on Malaysia's statutes, each being administered somewhat independently by various government agencies at the state and federal levels. In the case of environmental conservation, although the Federal Government enacted the EQA, management of basic resources (land and water) remain within the power of the states.

However, legislation alone is not enough: the will on the part of all citizens to protect the environment for a cleaner, greener Malaysia for the future is being fostered through education and awareness-raising campaigns.

# National environment policy

*Malaysia's policy on the environment aims 'to provide continued economic, social, and cultural progress of Malaysian people through environmentally sound and sustainable development'. The legal framework for such policy is the 1974 Environmental Quality Act (EQA) and its subsequent amendments, under whose auspices Environmental Impact Assessment (EIA) surveys are carried out. EIAs are important quality control documents that advise on how to prevent environmental degradation during the course of development projects.*

## Phases in Malaysia's environment management

Environmental law encompasses a wide range of activities and needs to anticipate advances in sociotechnological development that affect the environment. The three stages in Malaysia's management of the environment mirror those of the standard approach adopted by any developing nation.

**Phase One**
Curative action

1974 EQA Act

### 1970s
**Managing environmental problems once they have occurred.The Act emphasized remedial action to respond to emissions from new factories built at the start of Malaysia's period of rapid industrialization.**

**Phase Two**
Prevention

1986 Amendments
1988 EIA

### 1980s
**Preventative measures and the introduction of quality control in the form of EIAs of certain development projects.**

**Phase Three**
Self-regulation

1996 Amendments

### 1990s
**Management to achieve sustainable development where human and economic needs sit in harmony with environmental issues. Influenced by international standards.**

## Environmental legislation

Malaysia's National Environmental Policy (NEP) has three broad objectives: to maintain a clean, safe, healthy and productive environment for present and future generations; to conserve the country's unique and diverse cultural and natural heritage with effective participation by all sectors of society; and to ensure that lifestyles and patterns of consumption and production are consistent with the principles of sustainable development. These objectives are, in turn, based on seven principles which seek to harmonize economic goals with environmental concerns: responsibility for protection of the environment; conservation of nature's vitality and diversity; continuous improvement in the quality of the environment; wise use of natural resources; integration of the principle of sustainability in decision-making; commitment and accountability; and active participation in the community of nations.

The EQA of 1974 forms the basic instrument for achieving the policy objectives. The Act provides for an advisory Environmental Quality Council (EQC) whose functions are generally to advise on matters pertaining to the Act and those referred to it by the Minister of Environment. In addition, it led to the appointment of a Director-General of Environment whose duties include coordinating all activities relating to the discharge of wastes, preventing and controlling pollution, and protecting and enhancing the quality of the environment through the formulation of emission standards, issuing licences for waste discharge, coordinating pollution and environmental research, and orchestrating the dissemination of information and educational materials to the public. Under the terms of the legislation, the Minister, after consultation with the EQC, is authorized to endorse new rules to protect the environment. These regulations can prescribe standards to prohibit emissions or use of any equipment which is likely to endanger the environment, and they set the level of fines to be imposed on those who do not comply with the instructions.

Greening the city landscape: municipal flowerbeds along Jalan Kuching in Kuala Lumpur.

## Some activities subjected to EIA in Malaysia

Environmental Impact Assessments are concerned with maintaining ecological biodiversity, and aesthetic, functional and recreational values of the natural world. They are designed to predict the magnitude of environmental impact of proposed development projects so that adverse environmental effects may be avoided. EIAs report on and issue recommendations on the environmental matters they monitor, but their findings do not carry the power of veto over a project.

Nineteen categories of activities are subject to EIAs, including those depicted. For each category a specific area, weight or production capacity above which an EIA must be carried out is stipulated by law.

Petroleum: Oil- and gas-fuelled development; construction of offshore and onshore pipelines and oil and gas separation, processing, handling and storage facilities; construction of oil refineries. Above are oil storage tanks, Miri, Sarawak.

## Policy implementation

To assist the Director-General of the Environment to administer the EQA, a Division (now Department) of Environment (DOE) was established in 1975. A three-pronged strategy was developed which today forms the basis of environmental management in the country. The major elements of the strategy include the control of pollution and the taking of remedial action; integration of environmental dimensions in project planning and implementation; and provision of environmental inputs into resource and regional development planning. Under the first strategy, several regulations, of which there are currently 16, dictate enforceable emission limits for gas and smoke, sewage and industrial effluent discharges.

While the main objective of the first strategy is basically to ensure that the existing industries and other pollution sources are subject to direct controls, such remedial measures alone, without the support of some form of preventive controls, are inadequate. In view of this, an Environmental Impact Assessment (EIA) procedure, as an integral part of the overall project planning, was introduced. The DOE's third strategy is to incorporate environmental aspects into regional development plans. In this respect, the DOE has been proactive and plays an advisory role through its participation in the planning of projects by various state and federal government agencies.

To enhance the three broad strategies of policy implementation—pollution control, EIAs and land use planning—a number of support programmes are also developed and

Forestry: Conversion of hill land to other use; logging or conversion of forest in water catchment areas or adjacent to state and national parks; conversion of mangrove forests larger than 50 hectares for housing, agriculture or industrial use. Above, logging near Sibu, Sarawak.

Resort and recreational development: Construction of coastal resort facilities or hotels with more than 80 rooms, and clearing of land for recreation, as for a golf course, above.

Power generation and transmission: Construction of steam-generated power stations burning fossil fuels; dams and hydroelectric power schemes; construction of combined-cycle power stations and nuclear-fuelled stations. Temengor Dam in Perak is shown above.

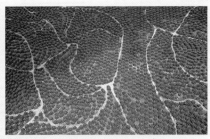

Agriculture: Land development schemes over 500 hectares; agriculture programmes necessitating resettlement of 100 families or more; development of agricultural estates over 500 hectares involving changes in agriculture use. An aerial view over an oil palm estate is shown.

Ports: Construction of ports and expansion involving an increase of 50 per cent in annual handling capacity. Penang harbour is shown.

Housing development: These apartments built in front of a steep hillside, Kota Kinabalu, Sabah, are at risk from landslides.

Fisheries: Construction or expansion of harbours; clearing of mangrove over 50 hectares for aquaculture. Above, prawn ponds in mangrove.

Transportation and infrastructure: Construction of new railway lines, airports, mass rapid transport projects (shown above) and roads.

implemented, very often with the cooperation of other government agencies, the private sector and non-governmental organizations (NGOs). These include education, information and awareness campaigns, environmental monitoring, research and development, federal–state cooperation, and bilateral, regional and international legal and institutional arrangements.

## Holes in the legal fabric

Not all aspects of the environment are adequately covered by the EQA of 1974 or the EQA (Amendments) of 1985 and 1996. Issues such as forestry, water resources, mining, wildlife and fisheries are beyond their jurisdiction. Each state in Malaysia is empowered to enact its own forestry laws. It is for this reason that federal–state cooperation is so crucial for any successful environmental management programme. While legislation and institutions to administer policies are important, public support is equally essential to ensure the success of such policies. At both the federal and state levels, efforts to educate the public need to be intensified, and since environmental education is basically aimed at community action, efforts to reach the different target groups need to be varied, involving not only government but also a wide variety of professional groups, the private sector and NGOs.

Currently, the environment is studied before a development project is conducted. The EIA consultants then make predictions as to what changes are likely to result from the intended development. These predictions are largely based on information from previous projects. To increase the credibility of EIAs, more extensive field studies would be advisable.

## Environmental Impact Assessment (EIA) surveys

The economic growth of many countries, including Malaysia, relies on renewable natural resources such as forest, water and soil. These natural systems are usually affected by development activities such as deforestation, urbanization and mass tourism. An EIA provides opportunities to use renewable resources to their optimum level. It is a constructive pro-development tool for management that improves the success and lengthens the life of a project. An EIA is a systematic process that examines in advance the potential environmental consequences of development to an area. It is thus a mechanism for preventive rather than curative action.

ENVIRONMENTAL IMPACT ASSESSMENT (EIA) PROCEDURE AND REQUIREMENTS IN MALAYSIA

1. Project screening narrows application of the EIA to those projects that may have significant environmental impacts.
2. Scoping identifies at an early stage all impacts of the project and its key issues.
3. Consideration of alternatives ensures that the project proponent has considered other feasible approaches: alternative locations, processes, operating conditions and the 'no action' option.
4. Description of the project clarifies its purpose and its development stages. This includes the present and future state of the environment in the absence of the project, and takes into account changes resulting from both human activities and natural events.
5. The prediction of impacts identifies the magnitude of impact over the long, medium and short term. Mitigation provides measures to avoid, minimize or remedy any significantly adverse impacts.
6. Public participation is important to ensure the quality, comprehensiveness and effectiveness of an EIA report and to take public views into consideration in the decision-making process.
7. EIA review involves appraisal of the EIA report made by an expert panel. Recommendations arising are transmitted to the relevant project approving authorities for consideration.
8. The approving authority is the government authority has the task of deciding whether or not a project should proceed.
9. Post-decision monitoring involves the recording of outcomes associated with development impacts. It can contribute to effective project management. Auditing involves comparing the actual with predicted outcomes and therefore can be used to assess the quality of predictions and the effectiveness of mitigation.

# Environmental education and awareness

*No environmental programme, however good, can be completely successful without public support, and such support can only be expected from citizens who are aware of environmental problems and who are committed to doing something about them. An effective education programme is therefore an essential part of Malaysia's long-term environmental management. Its primary objective is to enhance public awareness and commitment through the dissemination of environmental information, training seminars and educational campaigns and activities.*

The DOE has been at the forefront of dissemination of environmental information in the form of brochures, posters, books and videos, with the aim of educating the public, policy makers and the private sector.

*'Environmental education is a process of developing a world population that is aware of and concerned about the the total environment and its associated problems, and which has the knowledge, skills, attitudes, motivation and commitment to work individually and collectively toward solutions of current problems and prevention of new ones.'*

Source: UNESCO (1978)

## Formal environmental education

Throughout Malaysia's education system, from the primary through to the secondary and tertiary levels, pupils are introduced to environmental issues through a range of core subjects. In the first six years of the national education system, environment-related matters are introduced as part of the science, ecology and local studies curricula. In 1986, a new subject entitled 'Man and the Environment' was introduced in upper primary schools in a bid to promote a positive attitude towards the environment. At the secondary level, although environment and ecology are not taught as examination subjects, many environment-related themes are integrated into geography, biology, chemistry and other branches of science. Schools are also furnished with teaching resources pertaining to environmental matters. For example, the Marine Education Kit, a joint project by WWF Malaysia, the Department of Fisheries Malaysia and the Curriculum Development Centre of the Department of Education, highlights the functions of each of four habitats—mangroves, seashores, coral reefs, and oceans and seas—the threats to them and the urgent need for marine conservation.

In addition, the activities of some school societies are organized around environment

Malaysia's tree-planting campaign was formally inaugurated by Prime Minister Dato' Seri Dr Mahathir bin Mohamad in March 1997. He urged that all development projects include mandatory land rejuvenation. The campaign has a target of planting 20 million new trees by the year 2020, thus implicitly allying environmental concerns with economic development at the highest level. This Malaysian Timber Council poster promotes the campaign.

themes with students actively participating in improvement projects, such as tree planting, recycling and river-watch programmes. Nearly all the major Malaysian universities have either research institutes that carry out field work or departments with degree programmes on the environment, or a combination of both. This is in addition to the individual environment-related courses offered by other departments and faculties.

## The DOE education programme

The Environmental Quality Act (EQA, 1974) stipulates that Malaysia's Department of Environment (DOE) 'provide information and education to the public regarding the protection and enhancement of the environment', and that it publish an annual report on environmental quality and other information related to environmental protection. In line with this statutory requirement, the DOE established its Education Division and has since been active, not only in disseminating environmental information and thus promoting and enhancing public awareness, but also in educating the different sections of the public about the environment through seminars, educational campaigns, exhibitions and talks. Such activity complements the national educational efforts to inculcate values and positive attitudes towards conservation, and in the long run contributes to the Malaysian population's participatory process in achieving sustainable development.

Activities are continuously being organized either by the DOE alone or, more often, in collaboration with other government agencies, the private sector and non-governmental organizations (NGOs), to educate and inform specific target groups. Examples range from lectures in schools to environment video production, and from features in the print and broadcast media—to draw the public's attention to current and ongoing issues—to awareness campaigns. One of the best orchestrated activities is the annual Malaysian Environment Week which includes debates and environment camps.

## Policing the environment: NGOs active in Malaysia

In Malaysia, there are several active environmental NGOs. These include the Environmental Protection Society of Malaysia (EPSM), Sahabat Alam Malaysia (SAM), the Malaysian Nature Society (MNS), Ensearch, the World Wide Fund for Nature (WWF) Malaysia, Persatuan Ekologi Malaysia (PEM) and the Centre for Environment, Technology and Development Malaysia (CETDAM). These NGOs play an important role in complementing efforts by the government to promote environmental consciousness and responsibility among the Malaysian public. A number of the NGOs have contributed significant expertise and resources towards environmental programmes and activities organized by the Department of Environment. In addition, the corporate sector and other organizations in the private sector are also supportive of the environmental programmes. With the exception of perhaps the MNS, the number of registered members in the environment-based NGOs is relatively small. The NGO movements can become more effective if they receive more meaningful support from the community.

NGOs are involved in environmental education.

**WWF**

## The role of NGOs

NGOs have long been associated with environmental education. Their activities are aimed at effecting change and shaping attitudes, and so, both directly or indirectly, they are involved in education. The role of NGOs in providing a mechanism for feedback to the government and its regulatory agencies on negative side effects from programme implementation is one of their most important functions. In many respects, they fulfil a watchdog function on behalf of the public on the use and abuse of natural resources, conservation, professional practices and other activities of the government and the private sector which adversely impinge on the environment. The working relationship between the Malaysian Government and the NGOs is generally amicable. The government and development are very often intricately entwined and environmental NGOs may easily be dismissed as being anti-development or troublemakers. Like NGOs everywhere, they are vocal and often take an opposing stand to the government in environmental debates. However, while there have been differences and heated exchanges between them, the overall result is a positive one for the environment.

## Continued awareness and public support

A study conducted by the DOE in 1985 on the level of public awareness of environmental issues revealed considerable public apathy. As a public concern, it was ranked last but one of eight public issues. Over the years, the situation has improved, but still has a long way to go before the Malaysian population can declare itself truly environmentally friendly. The rise in the number of complaints about environment-related problems, the increase in media coverage of environmental issues, and an increasing number of questions and answers debated in both the Senate and Parliament suggest an increased awareness amongst the public, corporations and government bodies.

Increasing public awareness and engendering long-term commitment to the environmental cause are important aspects of future environment policy. While legislation and administration of policies and environmental management programmes are important, public support is equally essential in order to ensure the success of such programmes. At both the federal and state levels, efforts to educate the public and disseminate environmental information need to be intensified and verbal support followed by action.

Press coverage of environmental matters continues to increase. The number of newspaper cuttings on environment-related issues kept by the DOE since 1977 rose dramatically from about 1,000 to close to 36,000 in 1994.

Government ministers lead a convey of 20 trishaws decorated with environmental themes to signal the start of National Environment Week 1997, which was hosted by Penang.

## National Environment Week

To commemorate the adoption of the Langkawi Declaration on the Environment, which strengthens the framework of environmental management, by the Commonwealth Heads of Government Meeting held 18–24 October 1989, the Malaysian Government instituted National Environment Week. The first such awareness-raising week occurred in October 1991 and has subsequently taken place annually between the dates of the original Commonwealth conference. At the federal and local levels, seminars, exhibitions and activities are held. Each year the events are launched at a different Malaysian location and a theme is adopted. For example, in 1996 in Melaka, 'Healthy Environment for Healthy Living' was the week's slogan to help instil greater awareness and care for the environment among Malaysians.

Taman Negara, the location for nature study weekends for school children.

Nature games include the Blind Trail, an activity which is often carried out at night. Participants are blindfolded, led into the forest and left alone to listen to the sounds around them. Learning to appreciate the wonders of nature in this way can not only be fun, but also helps children overcome any preconceptions they may have about the dark, damp forests and the fearful creatures that lurk there.

## Studying nature

Since 1979, the Department of Wildlife and National Parks has conducted nature study programmes and weekend camping trips to encourage school children to get close to nature. One of their three study centres is located at Kuala Atok in Taman Negara and targets 14–18 year olds from urban areas. Taman Negara's 4 343 000 hectares provide participants with the opportunity to experience and appreciate the importance of pristine primary tropical rainforest and riverine ecosystems. The participants are encouraged to respond creatively to nature through writing poems and drawing, and are shown how caring for the environment can be both educational and fun through a series of ecology-related games. In one, 'Oh Deer', the children are divided into four groups representing deer, food, water and habitat (in this case forest), to highlight the importance of achieving ecological balance in wildlife management. In another, 'To Dam or not to Dam', groups take on the roles of opposing and proposing sides—dam construction company, travel agent, policy maker, NGO, local community—in a simulated debate based on a possible real-life scenario. This encourages the children to think about development impacts on their environment and that of future generations.

# Environmental awareness in action

*The number and variety of activities promoting the environment and good stewardship of it in Malaysia are growing. Between them official government agencies and non-government organizations are developing nature-related activities which render Malaysia's natural world more accessible, but at the same time seek to protect and develop it in sustainable ways.*

## Some environment-related educational, recreational and ecotourist activities

1. Arboretums and herbariums are like living museums. The herbarium at the Forest Research Institute Malaysia (FRIM) has over 150,000 plant species and functions as a central bank for plant specimens collected across the country.

2. Visitors are important for the financial wellbeing of parks and reserves. Visitor centres provide shelter and amenities to attract and cater for tourists and mount informative exhibitions. Some, like those at FRIM and the Kuala Selangor nature Park, house permanent museums.

3. Camping in the great outdoors is promoted as weekend getaways at parks such as Taman Negara and Endau-Rompin and on Malaysia's beaches. Chalet and A-frame accommodation is also available.

4. Boating, canoeing, rafting and other water sports are increasingly popular on Malaysia's lakes, such as Tasik Kenyir. Water is also the way to get about parts of Taman Negara, the Crocker Range Park (Sabah) and Batang Ai National Park (Sarawak).

5. Recreational fishing is one of the main environment-related activities. Malaysia's rivers and lakes are a magnet for both tourists and locals.

6. Outdoor classrooms introduce groups of school children to nature at close quarters. The Malaysian Nature Society runs Malaysia's first permanent Nature Education Centre, established at FRIM in January 1993 and the Department of Wildlife and National Parks organizes nature study trips.

7. Viewing stations, animal observation hides and lookouts permit closer access to various animal and bird species. In Taman Negara these include hides with overnight facilities to observe nocturnal animals.

8. Visitor-friendly and ecofriendly signs (they are usually made of wood that is itself recycled), give directions about all the activities on offer.

9. Paths, jungle walks and nature trails blend in with the environment whilst emphasizing the accessibility of nature. Some parks also offer safe and scenic routes for cyclists and horse riders.

10. Waterfalls help visitors to appreciate the value of clear water sources, and also offer a tranquil setting for family picnics and swimming.

11. Bird watching is a growing national pastime. In Malaysia, over 750 bird species have been recorded. Bird Sanctuaries already exist at Kuala Gula in Perak, Mantanani and Kota Belud in Sabah and at Sibuti in Sarawak.

12. Station markers highlight points of interest along nature trails and are usually fabricated from environmentally friendly materials.

13. Raised wooden walkways (broadwalks) give access to mangroves and their resident wildlife and to other forest types, such as peatswamp.

14. Canopy walks, such as those at Taman Negara, FRIM and Poring in the Kinabalu Park, permit visitors to observe the forest ceiling 60 metres up and, more importantly, allow scientists to carry out research into above ground flora and fauna.

15. Mountains and caves carved in limestone rock offer more adventurous exploration, including caving, abseiling, rock climbing and trekking.

# Ecotourism

*Since the 1990s, Malaysia's tourist industry has branched off into new areas, inviting local and international visitors to visit outdoor, natural attractions. The new brand of tourist is encouraged to learn how to protect the environment, and it is his money that in turn pays for the conservation projects in, for example, the country's national parks. The challenges ahead include successfully marrying environmental sustainability with the growth of the ecotourist sector.*

In the 10 years between 1985 and 1994, the number of overseas visitors to Malaysia grew at an average of 11.5 per cent a year. National parks, such as Bako National Park, Sarawak (shown above), experienced 9.6 per cent growth.

In the 1990s, ecotourism became the buzz word for marketing environmentally friendly excursions and holidays to both overseas visitors and Malaysians.

Pre-20th century precursors of modern ecotourism activities consisted of expeditions into little charted territories. Intrepid Englishwoman Isabella Bird ventured into the interior of late 19th-century Malaya mounted on an elephant. She marvels in her book *The Golden Chersonese* (1883) at the 'wandering about alone, and free, open air, tropical life'.

## What is ecotourism?

The term 'ecotourism' only appeared with any frequency in the late 1980s, and by the start of the 1990s had become the fashionable way to describe nature-based tourism. Despite its popular use, the term is still a vague one due to the ambiguous sense of the prefix 'eco'. Although, when combined with tourism, it may refer to an environmentally sound approach to tourism management, the term is used in a variety of ways in tourism literature. It is variously seen to be synonymous with 'green tourism', 'responsible tourism', 'sustainable tourism', 'nature tourism' or simply 'alternative tourism'. The emphasis in such usage is on the underlying principles of environmental sustainability, combined with the return of any significant profits to the local community. However, ecotourism may also refer to a particular category of tourism products, ones that depend on physical environmental resources without being ecologically sound. Hunting, for example, can be regarded as an ecotourism activity, but one which can be very destructive to wildlife populations.

## Ecotourism on the political agenda

Although ecotourism activities have been carried out in various parts of Malaysia since the turn of the century in the form of explorations into interior jungles, mountain climbing, hunting and scientific expeditions, it was only in the 1990s that the term first appeared in official documents. Prior to this, the primary interest among government planners and policy makers was mainly in capitalizing on nature-based tourism resources as a means of attracting more foreign tourists to the country. Thus, from the early 1970s the central administration started to focus on natural attractions as a principal strategy for promoting Malaysia as an international tourist destination.

With growing interest in environmental conservation issues, especially after the Langkawi Declaration of 1992, in which the heads of government of Commonwealth countries pledged to support activities related to the conservation of biological diversity and to promote environmental awareness, tourism authorities began to view the natural environment as a possible long-term base for the sustenance of the tourist industry as a whole. Sabah, in particular, began to pay increased attention to protecting its natural heritage. The priority it gives to conservation issues fits in well with the general agreement to focus tourism development efforts on nature-based resources by the four member nations of Brunei–Indonesia–Malaysia–Philippines East Asian Growth Area (BIMP–EAGA).

## The attractions of ecotourism

Ecotourism, as the world's fastest growing tourism niche with growth of about 20–30 per cent a year, means more ecodollars. The worldwide trend is mirrored in Malaysia, where the increasing number of overseas visitors who visited between 1985 and 1994, and particularly made trips to the main national parks, sugggests a rapid growth in Malaysia's ecotourism industry. Among domestic tourists, there is every likelihood that there will be equally swift growth in ecotourism participation, given the relatively rapid rise in dispensable income and mobility as a result of continued growth in the national economy. Furthermore, the growing trend towards widespread car ownership and urban congestion problems may make rural areas, including ecotourism sites, more accessible and

130

## Some ecotourism attractions

**Notable ecotourist sites in Malaysia**

### Gua Tempurung

The Tempurung Caves near Ipoh are relatively unknown as a speleological site in comparison to the well-orchestrated tourist trips to the Mulu Caves in Sarawak or the Batu Caves just outside Kuala Lumpur. The magnificent underground museum is now being developed as an ecotourism site. Internal walkways are being built and intricate lighting systems to show the features off to their best are being set up. Development of the cave will conserve the cave system, as unsupervised visitors will no longer be able to leave with stalactite and stalagmite souvenirs or to clamber indiscriminately across rocks, trampling on the ecosystems of rare trapdoor spiders and crickets in their path.

### Pulau Payar

The first marine park to be established off the west coast of Peninsular Malaysia, Pulau Payar, one of the islands in the Langkawi group, is rich in marine life, including many protected species. The broad, sandy beaches and shallow, clear waters are an obvious invitation, especially for those who want to experience the multicoloured underwater life at close range.

### Tasik Kenyir

Rapid expansion of Tasik Kenyir, an inland, man-made lake in Terengganu, as an ecotourist site has seen the construction of access roads and a host of new holiday facilities. One of the chief attractions are Kenyir's waterfalls, of which Lasir Waterfall, which is accessible by boat, is the most impressive. A rest house, jungle treks and camping sites are planned for the area, with other water sport facilities on the drawing board.

### Malaysia Agriculture Park, Selangor

This is the world's first agro-forestry park. Set up by Malaysia's Agriculture Ministry in 1986, the park displays the various types of agriculture—crop and plantation farming, animal husbandry and fish rearing—that are practised across the country. The 1295-hectare site, set against a backdrop of virgin jungle, aims to be a permanent showcase for new developments in agricultural methods. The park promotes sustainable agriculture and forestry, marrying production with conservation.

attractive than they have been in the past.

National parks and other protected areas make important contributions to human society by conserving the natural and cultural heritage for the enjoyment of people and by ensuring ecological balance. But conservation is not cheap. Such areas, however, can become self-financing through promoting tourism activities.

Malaysia offers a wide range of ecotourism attractions, which are mostly natural features such as beaches, marine and terrestrial parks, rivers, lakes, waterfalls, mountains and a variety of forest environments. In addition, there are countless hideaways, resorts, golf courses, kampong homestay facilities and fruit orchards. This variety of attractions and facilities is likely to increase as tourism expands. The risk of ecological damage does exist, however, which is why an adequate monitoring and protection system, in line with sustainable development policies, is being developed.

### Challenges for the future

The greatest challenge facing those in the tourism sector is to ensure that ecotourist activities grow with sustainable development and do not expand too rapidly. This means successfully coping with increased visitor numbers, ensuring that the environment is suitably protected during peak, holiday periods and at particular times in the natural cycle, for example, when birds are nesting or new seedlings have been planted. Combined with the mission to inculcate a healthy and environment-friendly attitude among users, due regard needs to be exercised in relation to the history and culture of local populations. How to sustain such sociocultural identity and ensure local control of ecotourist business and decision-making processes is as important as knowing how to protect indigenous plant and animal species.

The aim in developing new tourist sites is to maximize visitor enjoyment whilst minimizing environmental impact. Contrary to that premise, a tract of mangrove swamp is cleared to make way for a golf course on Pulau Redang, Terengganu. The important role of mangroves in maintaining coastal stability and productivity is frequently ignored.

# The global dimension

*The commitments made in Rio de Janeiro in June 1992 at the United Nations Conference on Environment and Development provided the international community with an opportunity to replace piecemeal policy making, which had characterized environmental awareness in the 1970s and 1980s, with integrated and sustainable management. The Rio accords held out an olive branch for developed and developing nations to create partnerships to compare experiences, examine opportunities for cooperation and strengthen informal networks.*

'Human beings are at the centre of concerns for sustainable development. They are entitled to a healthy and productive life in harmony with nature.'

**Principle 1 of the Rio Summit, which pledged US$125 billion a year in aid and drew up 27 environmental principles to influence government policy around the world. Precious few have been observed.**

## Regional environmental issues

While each of the ASEAN nations has its own share of environmental problems, the two major issues affecting the whole region concern the marine ecosystem and air quality. The escalating deterioration of the region's marine ecosystem results from rapid coastal development and land-based pollution discharges, the growing pressures on living and non-living resources from an expanding population, increased maritime traffic, and rapidly increasing amounts of industrial and urban waste dumped into the sea.

The problems may broadly be divided into two main issues: resource degradation and depletion, and pollution. The former are particularly serious in the case of coral reefs, mangroves, fisheries and endangered water species, such as giant clams, dugong and marine turtles. The biggest threat to marine pollution comes from heavy metals, especially contamination of shellfish by petroleum

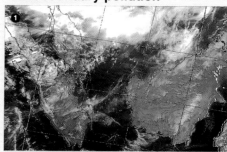

## Transboundary pollution

The US NOAA satellite monitored the 1997 haze.

1. 23 May 1997: Normal conditions for the time of year prevail, with a few localized 'hot spots' in Sumatra where small-scale fires (red dots) are burning.

hydrocarbons, including oil and grease, as well as dissolved petroleum and tarballs, chlorinated hydrocarbons in the form of pesticides, and sewage. Sewage from mainly human and domestic wastes represents the major source of organic pollution in the region. Some 60 per cent of the world's population lives within 100 kilometres of the coast and more than 3 billion people rely on marine habitats for food. It is easy to see why it is so important to preserve coastal areas, particularly in Southeast Asia where some of the most species-rich seas are and where some of the threats from pollution, and also from extensive tourist infiltration, are greatest.

## Regional management

All the ASEAN countries have established ministries or bureaus of the environment to deal with environmental protection and are implementing national and regional legislation. The main problem is ensuring that such legislation is enforced. At the regional level, there has been a growing awareness of the importance of marine resources. Efforts are being made to protect them through the Committee of ASEAN Senior Officials on the Environment (ASOEN), which also addresses other environmental aspects of common regional concern, including environmental information, public awareness and education, nature conservation, transboundary pollution (particularly haze) and environmental management. ASEAN cooperates with other international organizations and receives technical assistance from them.

## Malaysia in the global context

In the face of increased global concerns over environmental issues and the politics that have accompanied them, Malaysia appears to have taken a two-pronged strategy: a more organized approach towards environmental management to cope with problems at home, and a firm belief in the principle of an equitable share of responsibility in the management of global concerns at the international level. Malaysia expresses the views of many developing nations, maintaining that industrialized countries of the northern hemisphere (the North) must proportionately pay for the pollution and

## The ASEAN nations

The Association of Southeast Asian Nations (ASEAN) is a 'confederation' of nine nations that share similar patterns of economic and social problems. Cambodia remains the only Southeast Asian nation not to join; admittance was postponed in 1997 because of political upheavals at home. Originally established as a forum for economic and sociocultural cooperation, ASEAN has demonstrated an ability to induce and foster political cooperation. Differences are discussed and resolved through regional cooperation and regular consultation.

*Above*: ASEAN ministers present a united front at a meeting held in Singapore at the end of 1997 to discuss ways to prevent the haze. Standing from the left are representatives from Laos, the Philippines, Myanmar, Indonesia, Singapore, Malaysia, Thailand, the ASEAN Secretariat and Vietnam.

MYANMAR  LAO
THAILAND
VIETNAM
CAMBODIA
MALAYSIA  BRUNEI
SINGAPORE
INDONESIA
South China Sea
PHILIPPINES
Indian Ocean

 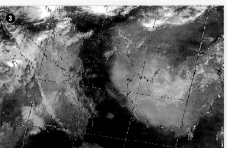

**2. 22 August 1997:** The number of fires have increased and winds start to carry smoke (yellow plumes) across the region.

**3. 19 September 1997:** The haze has intensified to engulf the region in thick clouds of smog (bright yellow).

Air pollution is particularly serious because regional and global wind patterns disperse pollutants far from their source. The levels of total suspended particulates in the air increase dramatically during September and October in many Southeast Asian countries because of forest fires in Kalimantan and Sumatra, Indonesia. The resulting haze cloaks the region in unhealthy smog almost on an annual basis, with particularly serious bouts experienced in 1991, 1994 and 1997.

## The Rio Summit

Five major agreements were ratified at Rio de Janeiro in 1992. These were an Earth Charter, which sets out fundamental principles for sustainable development, natural resource management and environmental protection; a blueprint for action (Agenda 21); a convention on climate change and one on biodiversity; and a set of principles for protecting and managing the world's forests. In addition, a Commission on Sustainable Development (CSD) was established whose function was to monitor and oversee the implementation of the commitments made at Rio.

Rio put environmental concerns firmly on the world agenda, but it was unable to follow up its rhetoric with action. The pledges at Rio to return carbon dioxide emissions to 1990 levels by the year 2000 look impossible to meet: in 1997, emissions had never been greater and they continue to rise. The number of newly extinct species in the world since Rio is estimated to be 130,000 and Third World aid, despite promises to the contrary, from rich, industrialized nations, is down.

other forms of environmental degradation they have created since the Industrial Revolution. The North, which consumes the greatest amount of energy per capita, has in effect grown rich on pollution.

As the world's population seeks to acquire wealth, and in many areas still strives for the basics of food and water, environmental issues frequently take a back seat. Problems lie embedded in the socioeconomic fabric of countries, and nationally and internationally the funds and political will are seemingly insufficient to halt further destruction. Though many developed nations have introduced environmentally sound technology, this is only a recent advance and has not kept pace with degradation or is unable to wipe out all the previous years of destruction.

At Rio, Malaysia pledged to maintain half its land as permanent forest cover, and suggested that other nations should establish similar greening targets. The effects of greenhouse gas emissions and the consequential global warming, combined with logging, make the Malaysian forests important on a global scale. Malaysia is involved in international

schemes to follow up words of commitment with action. The Sabah Foundation, for example, carries out major dipterocarp and rattan replanting funded by Dutch and US power companies.

## What hope for the future?

Perhaps the greatest challenge for Malaysia and the rest of the world in the 21st century will be the actual implementation of sustainable development principles, that is, development that meets the needs of the present generation without compromising the ability of future generations to meet their needs. The very principle of sustainable development requires that environmental management shifts from simply mitigating adverse environmental impacts to managing available resources for the present and future. Environmental regulations must move beyond mere safety regulations, zoning laws and pollution control enactments, and environmental objectives must be built into other areas, such as taxation and foreign trade incentives.

The Rio Summit included discussion of ways to prevent threatened species from becoming extinct. The seladang or gaur (*Bos gaurus*) is an endangered species in Malaysia.

## Tracking the growth of global environmental concern

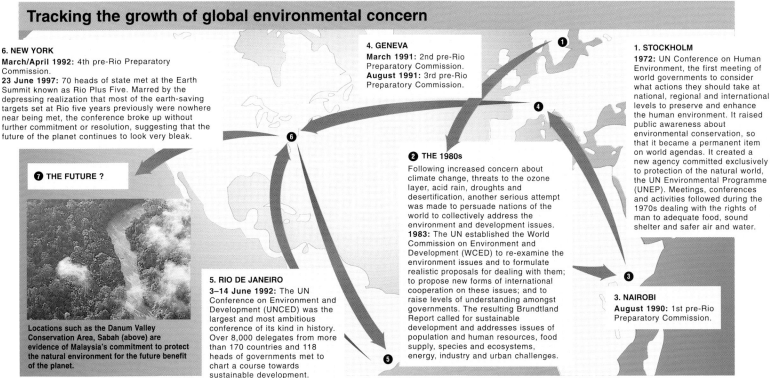

**6. NEW YORK**
**March/April 1992:** 4th pre-Rio Preparatory Commission.
**23 June 1997:** 70 heads of state met at the Earth Summit known as Rio Plus Five. Marred by the depressing realization that most of the earth-saving targets set at Rio five years previously were nowhere near being met, the conference broke up without further commitment or resolution, suggesting that the future of the planet continues to look very bleak.

**4. GENEVA**
**March 1991:** 2nd pre-Rio Preparatory Commission.
**August 1991:** 3rd pre-Rio Preparatory Commission.

**1. STOCKHOLM**
**1972:** UN Conference on Human Environment, the first meeting of world governments to consider what actions they should take at national, regional and international levels to preserve and enhance the human environment. It raised public awareness about environmental conservation, so that it became a permanent item on world agendas. It created a new agency committed exclusively to protection of the natural world, the UN Environmental Programme (UNEP). Meetings, conferences and activities followed during the 1970s dealing with the rights of man to adequate food, sound shelter and safer air and water.

**❼ THE FUTURE ?**

Locations such as the Danum Valley Conservation Area, Sabah (above) are evidence of Malaysia's commitment to protect the natural environment for the future benefit of the planet.

**❷ THE 1980s**
Following increased concern about climate change, threats to the ozone layer, acid rain, droughts and desertification, another serious attempt was made to persuade nations of the world to collectively address the environment and development issues.
**1983:** The UN established the World Commission on Environment and Development (WCED) to re-examine the environment issues and to formulate realistic proposals for dealing with them; to propose new forms of international cooperation on these issues; and to raise levels of understanding amongst governments. The resulting Brundtland Report called for sustainable development and addresses issues of population and human resources, food supply, species and ecosystems, energy, industry and urban challenges.

**5. RIO DE JANEIRO**
**3–14 June 1992:** The UN Conference on Environment and Development (UNCED) was the largest and most ambitious conference of its kind in history. Over 8,000 delegates from more than 170 countries and 118 heads of governments met to chart a course towards sustainable development.

**3. NAIROBI**
**August 1990:** 1st pre-Rio Preparatory Commission.

# Glossary

## A

**Accretion**: Accumulation of material, for example, sediment on a flood plain.

**Alluvial**: Of or relating to alluvium.

**Alluvium**: Fine-grained soil made up of silt, clay and sand deposited by flowing water.

**Altitude**: Vertical height of land above sea level.

**Anaerobic**: Without oxygen.

**Animism**: Belief system in which all material forms, such as plants and stones, are attributed with a living (animating) spirit.

**Anthropic, anthropogenic**: Relating to human beings; man-made.

**Anthropomorphic**: Attributing human characteristics to a non-human form, such as an animal.

**Aquaculture**: Artificial cultivation of water's natural wetland resources, such as fish farming.

**Aqueous**: Watery.

**Atoll**: Coral reef appearing above the sea as an island.

**Attrition**: Constant wearing down of rock material into finer particles through frictional grinding as they are moved by water, wind and waves.

## B

**Backwash**: Motion of water thrown or washed back to sea after a wave breaks on the shore.

**Basaltic**: Composed of or akin to basalt, a black, finely grained igneous rock.

**Basic rock**: Rock containing very little silica.

**Batholith**: Mass of igneous rock, usually granite, formed by intrusion of magma.

**Bedrock**: Solid rock beneath soil.

**Berm**: Low and narrow ridge at the top of a slope.

**Biodegradable**: Capable of being broken down by bacteria or by other natural means.

**Biodiversity**: Richness of species.

**Biogas**: Gas that is produced by the action of bacteria on organic waste and used as fuel.

**Biomass**: Amount of chemical energy in a group of growing plants at any given time, expressed by weight of dry matter per unit area.

**Biophysical**: Involving biological and physical matters or considerations.

**Bund**: Man-made embankment for containing liquid flow.

## C

**Calcite**: White or colourless mineral found in limestone.

**Caldera**: Large, basin-shaped crater at the top of a volcano.

**Capital goods**: Goods that are used in the production of other products and are not themselves sold direct to consumers.

**Carbon cycle**: Movement of carbon into the atmosphere as $CO_2$ and its return to the earth's surface, to be absorbed and stored in plants.

**Carbonation**: Form of chemical weathering of rocks by rainwater containing carbon dioxide in solution.

**Cash crop**: Crop grown for sale.

**Cassiterite**: Tin-bearing mineral found in igneous rocks.

**Catchment area**: Area drained by a single river.

**Chemical weathering**: Process of decomposition of rock exposed to air and water by chemical change.

**Chert**: Hard sedimentary rock composed of microcrystalline quartz.

**Compression, compressive**: Squeezed and reduced.

**Continental**: Of or related to a vast land area or continent; the opposite of oceanic.

**Convection**: Transmission of heat within a liquid or gas by the movement of heated particles. A convection storm is generated by hot rising currents on a sunny day.

**Crystalline**: Having the structure or characteristics of crystals.

## D

**Decomposer**: Organism, such as a fungus or bacterium, that breaks down dead matter into its constituent parts.

**Deforestation**: Clearance of trees, specifically on a large scale.

**Deposition**: Natural laying down of rock-forming material.

**Deposits**: Matter accumulated through a natural process, such as mud or sand laid down at the mouth of a river.

**Diapirism**: Process of formation of an anticlinal fold where brittle, overlying rock has been pierced by material beneath.

**Diurnal**: Daily.

**Domain**: Delineated geological area.

**Downdraught**: Large-scale downward movement of air, for example, down a hillside.

**Drip curtain**: Formation of calcium carbonate in caves created by the action of dripping water.

**Dripstone**: Collective term for calcium carbonate deposits in caves caused by the evaporation of dripping water over long periods of time.

## E

**Earthworks**: Work that involves the excavation of earth, as in engineering or construction activity.

**Ecology**: Branch of science that deals with the interrelationship between organisms and their environment.

**Ecosystem**: Organic community of plants and animals viewed within its physical environment.

**Effluent**: 1. Liquid discharged as waste, from an industrial plant for example.
2. Stream issuing from a lake.

**Eluvial**: Of or related to eluvium, sand and silt derived from eroded rocks that have remained

in their place of origin.

**Endemic**: Native or peculiar to a specific, localized area.

**Erosion**: Removal of weathered material by the action of water, ice, wind or gravity.

*Ex situ*: Off-site.

## F

**Fault**: Fracture in a rock along which displacement has occurred. An area of numerous, closely spaced faults is called a fault zone.

**Fauna**: All the animal life of a given place or time.

**Fibromat**: Covering of natural fibrous material used to control soil erosion.

**Fissure**: Hair-thin opening or crack, notably in rock.

**Flash flood**: Rapid, intense, localized flood that lasts for only a short time.

**Flood plain**: Flat area composed of sediment deposited during flooding that borders a river.

**Flora**: All the plant life of a given place or time.

**Floristic zone**: Area displaying particular flora.

**Flowstone**: Deposit of travertine where water flows over rock in a thin sheet. Chiefly found in caves.

**Food chain**: Sequence of organisms, each of which feeds on a form lower down the sequence.

**Food web**: Network of food chains.

**Forest canopy**: Uppermost spreading branched layer(s) of a forest.

**Fossil fuel**: Naturally occurring carbon fuel formed by the decomposition of prehistoric organisms, such as coal, peat, oil or natural gas.

**Fracture**: Crack or cleft in rock.

## G

**Gene pool**: All the genes (DNA unit of heredity) in an interbreeding population.

**Geomorphology:** Scientific study of landscapes and the processes that shape them.

**Glacial period:** Specific period of time that has been subjected to glaciation.

**Glaciation:** Effects formed by the action of huge sheets of ice called glaciers.

**Global warming:** An increase in the average worldwide temperature, believed to be caused by the greenhouse effect.

**Gondwana, Gondwanaland:** More southerly of two ancient landmasses that split from the supercontinent Pangea 180 million years ago.

**Graminoid:** Of or relating to grasses.

**Greenhouse gas:** Any gas, including carbon dioxide, nitrogen oxides and chlorofluorocarbons, that absorbs infrared radiation and may contribute to rising atmospheric temperature and thus to what is known as the greenhouse effect.

**Ground water:** Subsurface water in soil and bedrock. Opposite of surface water.

**Guano:** Dried excrement of cave-dwelling animals such as bats.

# H

**Habitat:** Place where flora and fauna naturally grow and live.

**Haze:** Reduced visibility as a result of condensed water vapour, dust and other pollutants in the atmosphere.

**Humus:** Mass of partially decomposed organic matter in the soil that improves its fertility and ability to hold water.

**Hunter-gatherers:** Peoples who exclusively depend on the forest and rivers for their food.

**Hydration:** Weathering process whereby minerals take up water and expand, causing stresses within rock.

**Hydrocarbon:** Organic compound that contains only carbon and hydrogen.

**Hydrologic cycle:** Circulation of water among sea, land and the atmosphere whereby water evaporates from the earth and oceans, rises to the atmosphere, condenses into clouds, falls as rain and finally flows in runoff back into the oceans.

**Hydrological cycle:** Another name for the hydrologic cycle.

**Hydromorphic:** Of or relating to a soil that has excess moisture, such as in a waterlogged bog.

# I

**Ice Age:** Period of extensive glacial activity.

**Igneous rock:** Rock formed by the solidification of molten magma.

*In situ:* Off-site.

**Inorganic:** Being composed of non-living material.

**Intermonsoon:** Two periods between the monsoon: from April to May, and from October to November.

**Intrusion:** Forcible entry of molten rock or magma into other rock formations.

**Intrusive rock:** Rock formed from molten rock that solidifies in other, pre-existing rock.

**Inversion:** Weather conditions that trap cold air with warmer air above, contrary to normal conditions.

# K

**Karren:** Ribbed limestone rock surface worn by water.

**Karst:** Type of topography formed on limestone and other soluble rock and characterized by caves and underground drainage.

# L

**Landfill:** Method of disposing of waste by burying it; the site where such disposal occurs.

**Landform:** Any natural feature on the earth's surface.

**Laurasia:** More northern of two ancient landmasses that split from the supercontinent Pangea 180 million years ago.

**Lava:** Magma emitted by a volcano.

**Leachate:** Concentrated liquid waste, such as produced as water reacts with rubbish in a landfill.

**Leaching:** Removal of soluble salts from the upper layer of soil by percolating soil-water in humid climates.

**Limestone:** Rock consisting mainly of calcium carbonate ($CaCO_3$). There are many types, defined by texture, mineral content, origin and age.

**Lithosphere:** Top 150 kilometres of the earth's surface comprising the rigid crust and the upper mantle of solidified rock.

**Littoral:** Zone at the edge of a lake or ocean that is temporarily exposed to air or immersed with water. Of the seashore.

**Logging:** Process of felling trees, cutting them up into logs and transporting the logs to sawmills.

# M

**Magma:** Molten rock that exists in liquid form inside the earth.

**Magmatic:** Intrusive and volcanic activity associated with subduction.

**Mantle:** Middle layer of the earth comprising the upper and lower mantle and containing silicate minerals.

**Mechanical weathering:** Process of rock disintegration by physical means that does not result in any change in the chemical composition of rock.

**Meiofauna:** Part of the fauna of the sea or a lake comprising small, although not microscopic, animals such as worms and snails.

**Metallic minerals:** Minerals from which metals can be extracted.

**Metamorphic rock:** Rock formed when other rocks recrystallize as a result of increased heat, pressure or chemical change.

**Meteorological:** Related to the study of the earth's atmosphere and in particular weather-forming processes.

**Mineral:** Naturally occurring inorganic solid with a definite chemical composition and a crystalline structure.

**Mogote:** Vertical-sided limestone hill.

**Monsoon:** Seasonal reversal of pressure and winds over land and neighbouring oceans.

**Mud flat:** Tract of flat, muddy land, especially near an estuary or along the coast, which is exposed at low tide.

# N

**Non-metallic minerals:** Minerals from which non-metals are extracted. These include oil, natural gas and silica sand.

**Non-target:** Organism which is not intended for elimination by a specific pesticide application.

**Nuclear settlement:** Small village or town with all basic amenities in a compact grouping.

# O

**Oceanic:** Of or relating to the sea or ocean. Opposite of continental.

**Orang Asli:** Literally 'original people', denoting the aborigines of Peninsular Malaysia.

**Organic:** Relating to or derived of living organisms.

**Organism:** Any living individual, plant or animal.

**Organophosphate:** Class of pesticide containing phosphorus and which acts by interfering with normal nerve transmission.

**Oxidation:** Process during weathering when a mineral reacts with oxygen.

**Ozone:** $O_3$, natural component of the upper atmosphere (stratosphere) that absorbs and filters out some of the sun's ultraviolet light.

# P

**Pangea:** Ancient supercontinent that existed 200 million years ago.

**Parent rock:** Any original rock before it is changed by weathering, metamorphism or other geological processes.

**Particle:** With reference to air pollution, any pollutant that is larger than a molecule.

**Particulates:** Any substance made up of separate particles.

**Pathogenic:** Able to cause or produce disease.

**Permeable:** Capable of being infiltrated by liquids such as water.

**Pesticide:** Chemical used to kill a pest. They include insecticides, fungicides, herbicides, rodenticides and termiticides which target specific pest groups.

**pH level/scale:** Measure of acidity. A solution with a pH less than 7 is acidic and more than 7 is alkaline. pH 7 is neutral.

**Photosynthesis:** Biological process by which plants make food energy through the use of sunlight, carbon dioxide and water.

**Phyllite:** Metamorphic rock with a silky appearance and a commonly wrinkled surface.

*135*

**Physiography**: Study of natural features in their causal relationships; synonymous with physical geography.

**Plate**: Rigid layer of the earth's lithosphere. The lithosphere is made up of eight major and several smaller such plates.

**Pluton**: Mass of igneous rock that has solidified below the earth's surface.

**Pollution**: Undesirable change in the quality of the environment: air, water or noise.

**Porosity**: Condition of being permeable to water, air and other fluids.

**Precipitation**: Falling of water from the atmosphere as rain, hail or snow.

**Predator**: Organism which kills and eats another organism.

**Prevailing wind**: Most frequent or conspicuous wind blowing at any one time in any one place.

**Primary consumer**: First level of animal or plant in food chain.

# Q

**Quartz**: Colourless mineral found in igneous, sedimentary and metamorphic rocks.

**Quartzite**: Very hard metamorphic rock consisting of a mosaic of quartz crystals and formed by recrystallization of sandstone.

# R

**Remote sensing**: Collection of data about an object by instruments that are not in direct contact with it.

**Renewable resource**: Resource that is replenished.

**Revetments**: Retaining walls erected to stem coastal erosion.

**Rift**: Zone separating two tectonic plates at a divergent plate boundary.

**Riparian**: Inhabiting or situated along the bank of a river.

**Runoff**: Surface water which carries dissolved and suspended matter into streams and rivers from the land.

# S

**Sand bar**: Ridge of sand built up by tidal action and often exposed at low tide.

**Sand cay**: Small, low island or bank of sand.

**Sand spit**: Long, narrow accumulation of sand with one end attached to the land, the other projecting into the sea.

*Sawah*: Wet rice cultivation.

**Schist**: Crystalline metamorphic rock composed of a series of thin rock layers and rich in minerals.

**Sea level**: Average midway position between high and low tides and used as the measurement of land height. Also called mean sea level.

**Sea stack**: Pillar of rock that remains when an arch collapses.

**Secondary consumer**: Organism in a food chain that is fed on by primary consumers and in turn feeds on lesser organisms.

**Secondary forest**: New forest that grows on land where (destroyed) natural forest once grew.

**Sediment**: Material transported and deposited by wind and rain and that accumulates in layers.

**Sedimentary rock**: Rock formed when sediment becomes solid.

**Selective felling and logging**: Method whereby only valuable mature trees are harvested and the rest remain untouched.

**Shale**: Dark, fine-grained sedimentary rock formed by the compression of successive layers of clay.

**Shaman**: Priest of Shamanism, a religious system that believes only the shaman can control the good and evil spirits that pervade the world.

**Shifting cultivation**: Movement of a community or of a community's farming plots when soil fertility cannot support further planting.

**Silica**: Silicon dioxide which includes quartz, opal and chert.

**Silt**: All sedimentary particles from 1/256–1/16 millimetres in size.

**Siltation**: Process in which loose material such as clay, silt and sands are deposited on river beds and lowlands, for example, making rivers shallow and more prone to flooding.

**Slash-and-burn**: Short-term method of cultivation in which land is cleared by burning trees and other vegetation for temporary agricultural use.

**Smog**: Smoky fog. Term loosely used to define visible air pollution.

**Soil creep**: Gradual downhill movement of soil and loose rocks on a slope.

**Soil horizon**: Layer of soil that has physical and chemical characteristics that are distinct from other soil layers.

**Solutioning**: Dissolving of solid in a liquid (thus creating a **solution**).

**Speleothem**: Any mineral formation in a cave created by water action.

**Stalactite**: Icicle-like dripstone that hangs down from the ceiling of a cave and has been deposited by dripping water.

**Stalagmite**: Formation of mineral matter that rises up from the floor of a cave and has been deposited by dripping water.

**Stylolites**: Small, columnar structures within limestone.

**Subduction**: Process in which one of the plates of the earth's surface (lithosphere) descends beneath another.

**Substrate**: Rock underlying the soil, also called bedrock.

**Sundaland**: Continental shelf in the south of the South China Sea.

**Sustainable development**: Development that is capable of being maintained at a steady pace without exhausting natural resources or causing severe environmental damage.

**Suture**: Mass of continental crust formed where two continents collide and weld together.

**Swale**: Damp depression in an area of land.

**Swallow hole**: Deep opening in the earth or a cave.

# T

**Tectonic**: Applied to all internal forces which build up or form the features of the earth's crust.

**Terrane**: Area or surface where a particular rock or group of rocks is prevalent.

**Till**: Sediment deposited by a glacial flow.

**Tombolo**: Sand or gravel bar that connects an island to the mainland.

**Topography**: Surface configuration or landforms of an area.

**Toxicity**: Property of substances which can pose danger to the environment or human health when received in sufficient amounts.

**Trade winds**: Winds that blow obliquely towards the equator from the northeast in the northern hemisphere and from the southeast in the southern hemisphere between latitudes 5 and 30 degrees north and south respectively.

**Transform fault**: Fault formed between two crustal plates that slide horizontally against each other.

**Transpiration**: Process whereby plants lose water to the atmosphere through their leaves.

**Travertine**: Porous rock consisting of calcium carbonate.

**Troposphere**: Lowest level of the atmosphere where most weather phenomenon occur.

# U

**Ultrabasic rock**: Rock composed mostly of the minerals iron and magnesium and which is low in silica.

**Ultramafic rock**: Another term for ultrabasic rock.

**Uplift**: Process by which part of the earth's surface is raised above the height of the surrounding area.

# W

**Watermark**: Line marking the level reached by a body of water.

**Water table**: Upper surface of the zone of saturation in permeable rocks that varies with the amount of percolation.

**Watershed**: Dividing line between adjacent river systems, such as a ridge.

**Weathering**: Process of rock and mineral disintegration at the earth's surface.

The following words in Bahasa Malaysia that denote geographical features are variously used throughout the book along with their English counterparts.

| | |
|---|---|
| **Gua** | Cave |
| **Gunung** | Mount |
| **Pulau** | Island |
| **Sungai** | River |
| **Taman** | Park |
| **Tanjung** | Headland |
| **Tasik** | Lake |

# Bibliography

Aiken, S. Robert et al. (1983), *Development and Environment in Peninsular Malaysia*, Singapore: McGraw-Hill.

Andriesse, J. (1968), 'A Study of the Environment and Characteristics of Tropical Podzols in Sarawak', *Geoderma*, 2: 201–27.

Appanah, S. and Weinland, G. (1993), 'Will the Management Systems for Hill Dipterocarp Forests Stand Up?', *Journal of Tropical Forest Science*, 3 (2): 140–58.

Azman Zainal Abidin (1994), 'The Haze of 1994: Have We Really Learnt Anything?', *ENSEARCH Newsletter*, December.

—— (1997), 'Haze Episodes in Malaysia', Paper presented to Institute of Engineers, Malaysia Petaling Jaya, 10 November.

Azman Z. A.; Yong, W. and Inouye, R. (1993), *The Occurrence of Haze in the Klang Valley, Malaysia: A Case Study of the October 1991 Haze Episode*, Proceedings of Conference on Regional Environment and Climate Change in East Asia, Taipei, 30 November–3 December.

Azman Z. A. et al. (1993), 'A Proposed Quality Air Index for Malaysia', Paper presented at ASEAN workshop on PSI, Singapore, 8–10 December.

Baas, P.; Kalkman, K. and Geesink, R. (eds.), *The Plant Diversity of Malesia*, Dordrecht: Kluwer Academic Publishers.

Benjamin, Geoffrey (1979), 'Indigenous Religious Systems of the Malay Peninsula', in A. L. Becker and A. Yengoyan (eds.), *The Imagination of Reality: Essays in Southeast Asian Coherence Systems*, Norwood, NJ: Ablex.

Braatz, Susan M. (1992), *Conserving Biological Diversity: A Strategy for Protected Areas in the Asia–Pacific Region*, Washington, DC: World Bank.

Briggs, John G. R. (1988), *Mountains of Malaysia: A Practical Guide and Manual*, Petaling Jaya: Longman.

Brookfield, Harold and Byron, Yvonne (eds.) (1993), *South-East Asia's Environmental Future: The Search for Sustainability*, Kuala Lumpur: Oxford University Press/UN.

Brookfield, Harold; Abdul Samad Hadi and Zaharah Mahmud (1991), *The City in the Village: The In-Situ Urbanization of Villages, Villagers and Their Land around Kuala Lumpur*, Singapore: Oxford University Press.

Brosius, J. P. (1992), 'Perspectives on Penan Development in Sarawak', *Sarawak Gazette*, 119 (1519): 5–22.

Burgess, P. F. (1971), 'Effect of Logging on Hill Dipterocarp Forest', *Malayan Nature Journal*, 33: 126–34.

Caldecott, J. (1987), *Hunting and Wildlife Management in Sarawak*, Kuala Lumpur: WWF Malaysia.

Chan Ngai Weng (1995), 'A Contextual Analysis of Flood Hazard Management in Peninsular Malaysia', Ph.D dissertation, Middlesex University, United Kingdom.

Chan Ngai Weng and Goh, B. L. (1995), 'Washed Up', *The Sun Magazine*, 23 November, pp. 4–9.

Cheang Boon Khean (1980), *Some Aspects of Winter Monsoon and Its Characteristics in Malaysia*, Kuala Lumpur: Malaysian Meteorological Service.

Cheang Boon Khean; Tan, H. V. and Yong, P. W. (1986), *Some Aspects of Wet and Dry Spells in Malaysia, 1951–1983*, Kuala Lumpur: Perkhidmatan Kajicuaca Malaysia.

Chuah, Donald G. S. and Lee, S. (1984), *Solar Radiation in Malaysia: A Study on Availability and Distribution of Solar Energy in Malaysia*, Kuala Lumpur: Oxford University Press.

Courtenay, P. P. (1986), *Geographical Themes in South-East Asia*, Sydney: Longman

Cheshire.

Cranbrook, Earl of (ed.) (1988), *Key Environments: Malaysia*, Oxford: Pergamon.

—— (1997), *Wonders of Nature in South-East Asia*, Kuala Lumpur: Oxford University Press.

Cunniff, Patrick F. (1977), *Environmental Noise Pollution*, New York: John Wiley & Sons.

Davies, Jon and Calridge, Gordon (eds.) (1993), *Wetland Benefits: The Potential for Wetlands to Support and Maintain Development*, Kuala Lumpur: Asian Wetland Bureau.

D' Silva, Emmanuel H. and Appanah, S. (1993), *Forest Management for Sustainable Development*, Washington, DC: World Bank.

Endicott, K. M. (1979), *Batek Negrito Religion: Worldview and Rituals of a Hunting and Gathering People*, Oxford: Oxford University Press.

English, Paul Ward (1995), *Geography, People and Places in a Changing World*, St Paul: West Publishing Company.

Gianno, R. (1990), *Semelai Culture and Resin Technology*, New Haven, Conn.: Connecticut Academy of Arts and Sciences.

Harrisson, Tom and Harrisson, Barbara (1971), 'The Prehistory of Sabah', *Sabah Society Journal*, 4: 1–272.

Hasan, Syed E. (1996), *Geology and Hazardous Waste Management*, Upper Saddle River, NJ: Prentice Hall.

Hill, R. D. (ed.) (1979), *South-East Asia: A Systematic Geography*, Kuala Lumpur: Oxford University Press.

Hood, M. S. (1978), 'Semelai Rituals of Curing', D.Phil dissertation, University of Oxford.

Howe, C. P. et al (1991), *Manual of Guidelines for Scoping EIA in Tropical Wetlands*, Kuala Lumpur: Asian Wetland Bureau.

Hu Hing Chong and Lim Joo Tick (1982), 'Solar and Net

Radiation in Peninsular Malaysia', *Journal of Climatology*, 3: 217.

Hutton, Wendy (1993), *Sabah and Sarawak with Brunei Darussalam*, Singapore: Periplus Editions.

IPT–AWB (1994), *Glimpses of Malaysian Mangroves*, Kuala Lumpur: Asian Wetland Bureau.

Ismail, A. B. (1984), *Characterization of Lowland Organic Soils in Peninsular Malaysia*, Proceedings of workshop on Classification and Management of Peat in Malaysia, Malaysian Society of Soil Science, pp. 109–26.

Jackson, J. (1995), *The Dive Sites of Malaysia and Singapore*, Singapore: New Holland.

Jackson, J. C. (1968), *Sarawak: A Geographical Survey of a Developing State*, London: University of London Press.

Jacobson, G. (1970), 'Gunong Kinabalu Area, Sabah, Malaysia', *Geological Survey of Malaysia*, Report 8.

Jacobson, S. K. (1996), *A Colour Guide to Kinabalu Park*, Kota Kinabalu: Sabah Parks.

Jensen, E. (1974), *Iban Religion*, Oxford: Clarendon Press.

Kapoor-Vijay, P.; Appanah, S. and Saulei, S. M. (1992), *Tropical Forest Ecology and Management in the Asia–Pacific Region*, London: Commonwealth Science Council.

Karim, Wazir-Jahan (1981), *Ma'Betisék Concepts of Living Things*, London: Athlone Press.

Kitayama, K. (1992), 'An Altitudinal Transect Study of the Vegetation on Mount Kinabalu, Borneo', *Vegetatio*, 102: 149–71.

Koopsman, B. N. and Stauffer, P. H. (1967), 'Glacial Phenomena on Mount Kinabalu, Sabah', *Geological Survey of Malaysia*, Bulletin 8: 25–35.

Langub, Jayl (1989), 'Some Aspects of the Life of the Penan', *Sarawak Museum Journal*, 40 (61) (New Series),

December, Special Issue 4, Part 3: 169–84.

Lim Jee Yuan (1987), *The Malay House: Rediscovering Malaysia's Indigenous Shelter System*, Pulau Pinang: Institut Masyarakat.

Lim Joo Tick (1976), 'Rainfall Minima in Peninsular Malaysia during the Northeast Monsoon', *Monthly Weather Review*, 104: 96–9.

—— (1979), 'Characteristics of the Winter Monsoon over the Malaysian Region', Ph.D dissertation, University of Hawaii, Manoa, Honolulu.

Lim Joo Tick and Ooi, S. H. (1985), *A Preliminary Investigation on Certain Large-scale Effects of Typhoons over the Equatorial Southeast Asia*, TOPEX Evaluation Meeting, Tropical Cyclone Programme Report 18, WMO: Geneva, pp. 19–20.

—— (1996), *Possible Typhoon Related Impacts on Malaysia*, Proceedings of the National Conference on Climate Change, Universiti Putra Malaysia, 12–13 August.

Lowry, J. B.; Lee, D. W. and Stone, B. C. (1973), 'Effects of Drought on Mount Kinabalu', *Malayan Nature Journal*, 26: 178–9.

Mastaller, M. and Howes, J. (eds.) (1997), *Mangroves, Forgotten Forests Between Land and Sea*, Kuala Lumpur: Tropical Press.

Needham, R. (1964), 'Blood, Thunder and Mockery of Animals', *Sociologus*, 14: 136–49.

Nieuwolt, S. (1982), *Climate and Agriculture Planning in Peninsular Malaysia*, Kuala Lumpur: Malaysian Agricultural Research and Development Institute.

Ooi Jin-Bee (1970), *Land, People and Economy in Malaya*, London: Longman, Green & Co.

Phillipps, A. (1988), *A Guide to the Parks of Sabah*, Kota Kinabalu: Sabah Parks.

Prentice, C. (1990), *Environmental Action Plan for the North Selangor Peat Swamp Forest*, Kuala Lumpur: Asian Wetland Bureau.

Rakmi Abd Rahman (1995), 'Towards a Comprehensive National System for Management of Chemicals', Evaluation of the UNEP/ UNITAR training programme on the implementation of the London Guidelines, United Nations/UNITAR, Geneva.

—— (1996), *Toxic Characteristics Leaching Procedure Test (TLPC) on Hazardous Waste Sludges*, Technical report, Waste Management Research Centre, Universiti Kebangsaan Malaysia.

Rakmi Abd Rahman and Abu Bakar Mohamad (1996), *Used Lubricating Oil and Availability for Rerefining*, Technical report, Advanced Engineering Centre, Universiti Kebangsaan Malaysia.

Ramage, C. S. (1971), *Monsoon Meteorology*, New York: Academic Press.

Sather, Clifford (1980), 'Symbolic Elements in Saribas Iban Rites of Padi Storage', *Journal of the Malaysian Branch of the Royal Asiatic Society*, 53 (2): 67–95.

Schebesta, Paul (1973), *Among the Forest Dwarfs of Malaya*, Kuala Lumpur: Oxford University Press; first published 1928.

Scrivenor, J. B. (1928), *The Geology of the Malayan Ore-Deposits*, London.

Sepakat Computer and Rakmi Abd Rahman (1995), *Revision of Scheduled Waste Regulation*, Department of Environment Malaysia.

Sham Sani (1977), 'An Index of Comfort for Kuala Lumpur: Petaling Jaya and its Environs', *Sains Malaysiana*, 6(1): 65–83.

—— (1979), *Aspects of Air Pollution Climatology in a Tropical City*, Bangi: Universiti Kebangsaan Malaysia Press.

—— (1993), *Environment and Development in Malaysia: Changing Concerns and Approaches*, Kuala Lumpur: Institute of Strategic and International Studies Malaysia.

—— (1997), *Environmental Quality Act 1974: Then and Now*, Kuala Lumpur: Institute for Environment and Development, Universiti Kebangsaan Malaysia.

Sham Sani and Badri, M. A. (eds.) (1979), *Environmental Monitoring and Assessment: Tropical Urban Applications*, Bangi: Universiti Kebangsaan Malaysia Press.

Sham Sani and Jamaluddin, J. (1990), 'Community Noise in the Residential Areas of Bandar Baru Bangi', *Tropical Urban Ecosystems Studies*, 7: 75–9.

Sharifah Mastura (1987), *Coastal Geomorphology of Desaru and Its Implication for Coastal Zone Management*, Bangi: Universiti Kebangsaan Malaysia Press.

Silvius, M. J.; Chan Hung Tuck and Shamsudin Ibrahim (1987), *Evaluation of Wetlands of the West Coast of Peninsular Malaysia and Their Importance for Natural Resource Conservation*, Kuala Lumpur: Asian Wetland Bureau.

Skeat, Walter William (1965), *Malay Magic: An Introduction to the Folklore and Popular Religion of the Malay Peninsula*, London: Frank Cass & Co.; first published 1900.

Solibun, J. C. (1987), 'The Role of NGOs in Conservation', in Sham Sani (ed.), *Environmental Conservation in Sabah: Issues and Strategies*, Kota Kinabalu: Institute of Development Studies, pp. 172–9.

Stauffer, P. H. and Lee, C. P. (1986), 'Late Paleozoic Glacial Marine Facies in Southeast Asia and Its Implications', *Geological Society of Malaysia Bulletin*, 20: 363–97.

Tan, M. L. (1978), 'Air Pollution in Malaysia: Problems, Perspectives and Control', in *Development and the Environment Crisis*, Penang: Consumers Association, pp. 213–21.

Teh Tiong Sa (1991), *Effects of and Responses to a Rising Sea: A National Assessment for Malaysia*, New Brunswick: Institute of Marine and Coastal Sciences, Rutgers, State University NJ.

Tho, Y. P. (1991), 'Conservation of Biodiversity: International and National Perspectives', in *Proceedings of the National Seminar on Environment and Development*, Kuala Lumpur, 9–11 July 1990, pp. 266–131.

Ti Teow Chuan (ed.) (1994), *Issues and Challenges in Developing Nature Tourism in Sabah*, Seminar proceedings, Kota Kinabalu: Institute of Development Studies.

Tjia, H. D. (1973a), 'Geomorphology', in D. J. Gobbett and C. S. Hutchison (eds.), *The Geology of the Malay Peninsula*, New York: John Wiley & Sons, pp. 13–24.

—— (1973b), 'Geological Observations of the Kinabalu Summit Region, Sabah', *Malaysian Journal of Science*, 2 (B): 137–43.

—— (1986), 'Geologic Transport Directions in Peninsular Malaysia', *Geological Society of Malaysia Bulletin*, 20: 149–77.

Tjia, H. D. and Sharifah Mastura (eds.) (1992), *Coastal Zone of Peninsular Malaysia*, Bangi: Universiti Kebangsaan Malaysia Press.

Tsen, Darrell N. C. (1993), *The Show Caves of Mulu Sarawak*, 2nd edn, Kuching.

UN (1995), *The Challenge of Urbanization: The World's Large Cities*, New York: UN.

UNDP–AGBP–HDP (1997), *Landuse and Landcover Change in Klang-Langat River Basin, Malaysia*, Technical paper, Remote Sensing and GIS Centre, Universiti Kebangsaan Malaysia.

UN/ESCAP (1995), *State of the Environment in Asia and the Pacific*, Bangkok: UN.

Valencia, M. J. and Abu Bakar Jaafar (1984), 'Malaysia and Extended Maritime Jurisdiction: The Foreign Policy Issues', *Malaysian Journal of Tropical Geography*, 10: 56–87.

Voon Phin Keong and Tunku Shamsul Bahrin (eds.) (1992), *The View from Within: Geographical Essays on Malaysia and Southeast Asia*, Kuala Lumpur: University of Malaya.

Whitmore, Timothy Charles (1990), *An Introduction to Tropical Rain Forests*, Oxford: Clarendon Press.

—— (ed.) (1984), *Tropical Rain Forests of the Far East*, 2nd edn, Oxford: Clarendon Press.

Wilford, G. E. (1964), 'The Geology of Sarawak and Sabah Caves', *Geological Survey of Malaysia Bulletin*, 6.

Williams, C. N. and Joseph, K. T. (1970), *Climate, Soil and Crop Production in the Humid Tropics*, Kuala Lumpur: Oxford University Press.

Wolters, O. W. (1970), *The Fall of Srivijaya in Malay History*, London: Lund Humpries.

Wong, K. M. and Chan, C. L. (1997), *Mount Kinabalu: Borneo's Magic Mountain*, Kota Kinabalu: Natural History Publications.

Wong, K. M. and Phillipps, A. (eds.) (1996), *Kinabalu: Summit of Borneo*, rev. edn, Kota Kinabalu: Sabah Society.

# Index

# Picture Credits

**Abdul Halim Mohd Noor/Halim Studio**, p. 78, bas-relief with floral designs (Terengganu Museum Collection); p. 79, weaver, *kain songket*. **Anizan Isahak**, p. 24, kaolinite plates under the microscope. **Antiques of the Orient**, p. 10, Ptolemy and Speed historic maps; p. 11, wood engraving of Borneo; p. 86, clearing jungle, engraving by C. J. Kleingrothe, in *Malay Peninsula (Straits Settlements & Federated Malay States)*, published by Messr. Kelly and Walsh Ltd., Singapore (undated). **Anuar bin Abdul Rahim**, p. 10, *Rafflesia*; pp. 18–19, Sundaland maps; p. 19, Rajah Brooke's birdwing; p. 22, pewter teapot, Chinese vase, how coal is made; p. 23, pewter teapot; p. 24, how soil is made; pp. 24–5, soil and vegetation types; p. 25, *periok*; p. 36, buttercup; p. 37, slow loris; p. 38, coral bed; p. 39, nest with swiftlets; p. 43, composition of the Wind and Lang Caves; p. 50, rainforest canopy layers; pp. 52–3, typical wetland types; p. 57, *temu/berus, pong-pong*; p. 79, Kudat basket, Melanau basket, batik; pp. 84–5, shifting cultivation; p. 85, rice plant; p. 94, bearded pig; p. 96, Sumatran rhinoceros, dugong, clouded leopard, Asian elephant; pp. 98–9 megadiversity composite; p. 99, white-handed gibbon; p. 106, three types of landslide; pp. 128–9, environmental awareness in action composite. **Auscape:** Jean-Paul Ferrero, p. 39, nest collection, p. 51, secondary forest, p. 95, over-logging, pre-felling inventory, setting minimum cutting limits, p. 96, logging, p. 99, plant nursery, p. 122, planting dipterocarp seedlings, p. 133, Danum Valley Conservation Area; Becca Saunders, p. 60, Layang-Layang. **Aw, Michael/OceanNEnvironment**, p. 11, marine life; p. 61, parrotfish; p. 103, oil spill; p. 131, marine life. **Bahruddin Yatim**, p. 75, drying cocoa. **BERNAMA**, p. 69, aerial view of Storm Greg devastation, burying the dead. **Briggs, John**, p. 42, the Pinnacles. **CCMB Agrochemicals Sdn Bhd**, p. 121, promotional leaflets and video. **Chai Kah Yune**, p. 39, cave artwork; p. 41, cycad; p. 43, sambar deer; p. 47, Rajang River artwork;

p. 91, phases of land use diagrams; p. 107, debris flow. **Chan Chew Lun**, p. 97, orang utan. **Chan Ngai Weng**, p. 67, Kota Bharu under floods (1988); p. 113, flash flood in Penang, enlarged drains. **Chan, Wendy**, p. 13, Malay girl, Orang Ulu woman, Dayak man; p. 85, Harvesting rice; p. 121, Dayak women at market. **Chang, Tommy**, p. 13, Kadazan boy; p. 35, Kadazan chicken sacrifice; p. 39, swiftlet nests; p. 79, *wakid* (Sabah Museum Collection); p. 82, Bobohizan; p. 83, Lotud Tantagas; p. 88, oil palm. **Chia Boon Kiang**, p. 27, impact of soil erosion on rivers; p. 29, stages in the weathering of granitic rock. **Chu Min Foo**, p. 22 & p. 114, MAS plane; pp. 44–5, river systems composite; p. 49, lotus flower; p. 103, sources of water pollution; p. 114, man shouting; p. 121, food chain, *rattus rattus*. **Department of Environment Malaysia**, p. 115, sound level meter; p. 125, EIA booklet; p. 126, water cycle poster, precious water poster. **Design Dimension**, p. 40, aerial view of Langkawi; p. 41, Tasik Dayang Bunting, Gua Langsiar; p. 45, Klang Gate Dam; p. 46, aerial view of peatswamp; p. 52, Tasik Bera; p. 53, disused mining pool; p. 56, mangrove forest; p. 57, Ibaj River, charcoal kiln; p. 60, Pulau Redang, Tioman; p. 61, Garuda, Manukan Island, Turtle Islands; p. 89, Petaling Jaya estate; p. 90, Bukit Merah; p. 91, Kuala Selangor landscape; p. 98, oil palm, Kenyir Dam; p. 104, house on Kelantan coast, Sabak beach; p. 116, water treatment works; p. 120, farming landscape; pp. 122–3, alphabet hunt; p. 123, children learning about nature; p. 124, Jalan Kuching; p. 125, Temengor Dam, oil palm estate. **Dew, Stephen**, p. 38, development of karst; p. 66, monsoon zones maps, land and sea breezes diagrams; p. 67, maps showing rainfall distribution during the monsoon seasons. **Duangdoa Suwunarungsi**, p. 32, Mount Kinabalu. **Falconer, John**, p. 10, engraving of Melaka; p. 19, Krakatau; p. 78, Sakai aboriginals; p. 79, basket weaving early 20th century; p. 86, rubber plantation; p. 87, Batu Caves Railway, Great Waterfall. **Geoff**

**Denney Associates**, p. 16, the earth's shells; p. 35, evolution of Mount Kinabalu; p. 64, convectional rainfall, orographic rainfall, cyclonic rainfall; p. 104, breakwater artwork, process of coastal erosion. **Geological Survey Department, Sabah**, p. 16, *Plesioptypmatis* sp. fossil. **Geological Survey Department, Sarawak**, p. 16, *Fusulinid* sp. fossil. **Girel, Stephane**, pp. 32–3, mountains artwork; pp. 60–1, islands artwork. **Harwant Singh**, p. 32, Mount Murud. **Hermann, Bernard**, p. 12, fisherman; p. 76, longhouse. **Hon Photo**, p. 29, weathered wall, house facade; p. 76, Bandar Sunway; p. 87, tin dredge; p. 108, traffic jam; p. 116, rubbish; p. 118, cement factory. K. S. Cheang, p. 120, carrots, p. 127, Taman Negara; Garry Leong, p. 114, disco; J. H. Voon, p. 130, Bako National Park. **Ibrahim Komoo**, p. 38, swallow hole; p. 40, rills, sea cave; p. 41, sea stack, ferns, plants of Pulau Anak Tikus; p. 42, Clearwater River, bats flying. **Isa Ipor**, p. 57, mangrove poles; p. 58, *Scaevola seriea*. **Jabatan Perhutanan (Forestry Department)**, p. 42, stalagmites, entrance to Deer Cave. **Jacobs, Joseph**, p. 39, drip curtain; p. 43, Lang Cave (photo); p. 51, upper montane ericaceous forest, montane forest; p. 92, oil palm factory; pp. 92–3, croplands; p. 99, tapir; p. 122, turtles, turtle hatchery at Cherating; p. 125, Penang harbour; p. 144, fishing boats at Kota Kinabalu. **Jansen, Jeffery Mark**, p. 56, milky stork; p. 99, orchid. **Kadderi Md Desa**, p. 28, three stages in weathered rock, roots penetrating soil, transformation of igneous rock. **Kratoska, Paul**, p. 77, colonial era railway. **Kyaw Han**, p. 52, weaving *atap*; p. 78, Malay house (artwork); p. 82, offerings and Bobohizan paraphernalia; p. 97, tiger. **Lau, Dennis**, p. 35, rice fields, Kadazan farmer; p. 53, paddy; p. 79, bark jacket; p. 82, traditional lifestyle; p. 92, Rajang River. **Lee Sin Bee**, p. 33, Kadazan woman; p. 48, lake ecosystem; p. 78, *bangau* boat prow; p. 84, Negrito Bateq; p. 101, FELDA plot. **Lelièvre, Olivier**, p. 80, Penan. **Lim Yew Cheong**, p. 78, ventilation

artwork (two pieces). **Lui Thue Wah**, p. 6, short-tailed magpie. **Maimon Abdullah**, p. 120, cabbages, p. 121, trap for male diamond-backed moths. **Malaysian Meteorological Service**, p. 69, satellite image, radar map. **Malaysian Timber Council**, p. 6, slipper orchid, sea stack; p. 7, poster, rattan weaver; pp. 75–6, weaving rattan; p. 89, urban trees; p. 91, logger; p. 94, flame of the forest; p. 99, plant nursery (close-up); p. 122, Endau-Rompin State Park; p. 123, posters (top three); p. 126, forest poster, tree-planting campaign poster. **Manoharan Sujithra**, p. 37, eagle; p. 133, seladang. **Massot, Gilles**, p. 29, Santiago Gate; p. 89, Kuala Lumpur; p. 109, exhaust fumes; p. 114, traffic, Lake Gardens; p. 115, school children. **Meteorological Service, Singapore/ United States NOAA14 Satellite**, pp. 132–3, three satellite photographs. **Mines Resort**, p. 49, Mines Resort. **Mohd Kassim Haji Ali**, p. 89, Kuala Lumpur in 1897. **New Straits Times Press (Malaysia) Berhad**, p. 5 and p. 117, school girls recycling cans; p. 68, fallen power cable; p. 71, haze over Kota Kinabalu; p. 100, destroyed home; p. 107, Genting Highlands landslide, landslide across East–West Expressway; p. 110, children in masks; p. 112, floods in Kuala Lumpur (1971), clear-up operation; p. 117, rubbish in Selangor river; p. 127, Ministers in trishaws during National Environment Week; p. 131, Gua Tempurung. **Noble, Chris**, p. 43, inside the Sarawak Chamber. **Ong Hean Chooi**, p. 120, oranges. **Osman Ashari**, p. 30, formation of the Titiwangsa Range; p. 48, lake zones. **Owen, Alysoun**, p. 75, Kek Lok Si Temple, municipal clock; p. 120, chillies. **Parnwell, Mike**, p. 46, longhouse; p. 47, longboat; p. 54, paddy; p. 101, FELDA houses (old and new). **Petronas**, p. 100, oil refinery. **Phillips, Karen**, pp. 54–5, peatswamp composite. **Photobank**, p. 11, Rajang River, Gunung Mulu National Park; p. 12, Kuching villagers; p. 13, Orang Asli; p. 18, Mount Kinabalu; p. 33, Mount Santubong; p. 34, cloud over Mount Kinabalu; p. 44, Sabah kampong, forest; p. 47, Pelagus

*143*

Rapids; p. 56, bar-tailed godwits; p. 59, Sandakan Bay; p. 78, Malay house (photo); p. 92, tin mine; p. 98, deforestation. **Alain Evrard**, p. 10, Mount Kinabalu, p. 34, glaciated surface of Mount Kinabalu; **Max Lawrence**, p. 42, Mulu Hills, p. 52, mangrove. **Picture Library**: David Bowden, p. 17, granite peaks, p. 51, lowland dipterocarp forest, p. 67, palm tree in the monsoon rain, p. 102, polluted Sungai Penchala, p. 117, garbage overflow, p. 125, clearing land for golf course; Chan Chun Keat, pp. 108–9, air pollution (back tint); Chin Fah Shin, p. 28, waterfall splash (back tint), p. 36, slipper orchid, p. 64, rain on leaf, p. 137, rhododendron; Eric Chin Wei King, p. 47, Shell station; S. K. Chong, p. 4 & p. 59, Cherating beach, p. 14, river, iron-stained rock, p. 17, Titiwangsa Range, p. 20, limestone pinnacle, p. 21, mud cones, metamorphic rock, p. 22, gravel pumping, p. 23, polishing and engraving pewter, p. 31, montane forest, dipterocarp forest, p. 32, mud volcano, p. 46, aerial view of Rajang, p. 47, Kapit, p. 58, breaking waves, p. 67, lorry in Perak flood, p. 73, two photographs of sunset over the Kuching River, p. 112, floods in Malay village, p. 114, Raban rural scene, p. 124, oil storage tanks at Miri; Goh Cheng Leong, p. 15, Titiwangsa Range, p. 26, slope near Simpang Pulai, granite work site, logging road, p. 27, rill erosion, sheet erosion, p. 29, heavily weathered surface in Ipoh, limestone landslide, p. 49, duck farm, p. 54, durians, p. 106, concrete protection wall; Goh Wooi Tuck, p. 27, gully erosion; Marlane Guelden, p. 65, Jalan Tuanku Abdul Rahman; Philip Hii Boh Tek, p. 107, Kundasang village; Kam Shee Meng, p. 25, paddy field, p. 46, Sibu; Rodney Lai, pp. 14–15, forest, p. 97, silvered leaf monkey, p. 102, clean water; Leong Yew Wah, p. 14, calcium deposits, p. 131, Tasik Kenyir; Christopher Liew, p. 17, limestone hills, p. 87, aerial view of tin mine; Lim Kheong Sen, p. 39, house in limestone; David Loh Swee Tatt, p. 46, washing in the river, p. 47, Iban along the Rajang River, river express; Loke Swee Ying, p. 31, Fraser's Hill, p. 38, limestone hills, p. 49, Semenyih Dam, p. 107, Lake View Hotel, p. 110, Kuala Lumpur during haze, Kuala Lumpur when haze has cleared, pp. 110–11, open burning (back tint); Stanley Loo, pp. 86–7, *dulang* washer; Manu Govindasamy, p. 58, sandy coast (photo); Ng Phoe Heng, p. 13,

Chinese man, Indian woman, Bajau man, p. 49, Tasik Chini, p. 68, uprooted tree, p. 108, open burning; Alan Ng Siew Hong, p. 45, waterfall; Teresa Ong, p. 59, mud flats on Langkawi; Pang Piow Kan, p. 35, picking tea; Tan Swee Lian, p. 25, rubber trees; Arthur Teng, p. 31, tree fern, p. 59, rocks on Pulau Gaya, p. 74, Kuala Lumpur; Wee Keng Bee, p. 48, Tasik Temengor, p. 107, Genting Highlands; Teresa Wong, p. 122, canopy walk; Wong Yoon Keong, p. 36, wild plants (back tint), p. 106, Bukit Melawati; Yap Kok Sun, p. 21, Gunung Tahan, p. 24, Bareo settlement, p. 31, Orang Asli settlement, p. 51, mangrove, peatswamp, beach forest, hill dipterocarp forest, limestone hill forest, p. 59, sandy ripples at Bako, p. 72, Stevensons screen inside and out, p. 118, chemical waste in Selangor river; P. K. Yap, p. 3, Abu Bakar Dam; Zain Noordin Daud, p. 121, safe spraying. **Raffles Hotel Singapore**, p. 7, Malay States Railway poster. **Rajanaidu, N.**, p. 25, oil palm plantation. **Remote Sensing and GIS Centre, Universiti Kebangsaan Malaysia**, pp. 8–9, three satellite photographs. **Rossi, Guido Alberto**, p. 18, Strait of Melaka; p. 47, Belaga; p. 91, landscape near Ipoh, Bareo Valley. **Royal Selangor**, p. 23, melting tin, buffing pewter with a 'stone leaf'. **Sarawak Museum**, p. 22, oil platform; p. 81, Iban ritual; p. 82, Iban seer; p. 84, hunters with game. **Sellato, Bernard**, p. 80, planting rice, dibbling; p. 81, shaman. **Seymour, Stephen (Bernard Thornton Artists)**, p. 27, principles of erosion; p. 40, Langkawi cross section; p. 41, Tasik Dayang Bunting cross section; p. 58, sandy coast (artwork), muddy coast (artwork); pp. 104–5, sources of coastal erosion; pp. 110–11, formation of haze; p. 113, flood potential in forest and urban areas. **Sharifah Mastura S. Abdullah**, p. 27, fibromat, crop cover; p. 105, revetments; pp. 118–19, petrochemical works (back tint). **Shekar, S. C.**, p. 6, solar-powered telephone, garbage collection; p. 122, recycling bin. **Soepadmo, E.**, p. 41, *Chinita calipinosa*; p. 59, *Rhodomyrtus tomentorus*. **Star Publications (Malaysia) Berhad**, p. 67, Kota Bharu under floods (1993). **Straits Times (Singapore)**, p. 132, ASEAN ministers. **Sui Chen Choi**, p. 36, lower montane forest; p. 37, mountain elevation, upper montane forest, subalpine forest. **Tan Hong Yew**, p. 16, plate activity; pp. 30–1, profile

of the Titiwangsa Range and its vegetation; p. 56, benefits of mangroves; p. 62, Kota Bharu under floods; pp. 62–3, sunshine over Danum Valley, ; p. 69, Storm Greg (artwork); p. 85, *tuai*; p. 94, charting forest destruction; pp. 94–5, the cost of forest destruction; p. 109, air pollutants; p. 114, video arcade, lunchtime conversation, the ear; p. 117, disposal at landfill; p. 118, how waste is hazardous; p. 125, EIA flow diagram; p. 132, leaf; p. 134, earthworks. **Tan, Freddie**, p. 139, silver-breasted broadbill (*Serilophus lunatus*). **Tan, Nelson**, p. 80, spirit figures. **Tan Swee Lian**, p. 120, sweet potatoes. **Tara Sosrowardoyo**, p. 83, Kuala Lumpur; p. 100, urban housing; p. 107, en route to Genting Highlands. **Taylor, Harold**, p. 14, sandy beach; p. 69, calm before the storm at Port Dickson. **Teh Tiong Sa**, p. 60, honeycomb weathering, Perhentian Islands; p. 61, Pulau Gaya. **Teo, Albert**, p. 77, *Sinningazanak*. **Tjia, H. D.**, p. 34, rock surface smoothed by glacial flow. **Tongkul, Felix**, p. 32, Mount Trusmadi. **Vidler, Steve**, p. 65, boat off Kota Bharu. **Villoo Surty**, p. 32, pitcher plant. **Wetlands International**, p. 54, tree species; p. 58, mud flats (photo); p. 105, mangrove; p. 123, *Wetlands Wonders* newspaper. **Wong Khoon Meng**, p. 36, *Rhododendron stenophyllum*. **World Wide Fund for Nature Malaysia**, p. 13, Kelabit man; p. 85, buffalo plough. Ahmad Lutpi, p. 26, pepper cultivation; Azwad M. N., p. 11, Tasik Kenyir, p. 26, hillside near Kampung Sungai Penchala, p. 36, *Nepenthes lowii*, p. 53, mangrove roots, p. 57, clam collection, p. 75, telephone, p. 76, harvesting rice by

machine, p. 92, bridge under construction, pp. 92–3, housing construction in Petaling Jaya, p. 107, landslide behind Highland Towers, landslide at Fraser's Hill, p. 109, damaged trees, p. 115, woman in factory, p. 125, mass transit transport project, p. 126, educational trip, p. 127, blind trail, p. 131, Agriculture Park, clearing mangrove; Balusubramaniam Perumal, p. 15, *Rhododendron wrayi*, p. 21, Main Range; David Bowden, p. 121, unsafe spraying; Ishak Ariffin, p. 93, erosion on Fraser's Hill slope; Rodney Lai, p. 1 and p. 90, *petai* pods gatherer, p. 12, Bateq, p. 97, bearded pig, p. 108, factory smoke; D. J. W. Lane, p. 97, hawksbill turtle; Lee Kup Jip, p. 86, opencast mining; Isabelle Louis, p. 101, model of the Bakun Dam; S. H. Oon, p. 31, tea plantation, p. 72, Cameron Highlands, p. 92, logging, p. 125, logging; Dionysius Sharma, p. 105, Sungei Dungun, p. 113, inundated forest; S. Sreedharan, p. 9, Orang Asli settlement, p. 76, harvesting rice by hand, p. 85, planting rice, p. 125, prawn ponds; S. Summerhays, p. 67, fishermen on Pulau Redang; TRAFFIC South-East Asia, p. 97, wildlife products; Sylvia Yorath, p. 125, housing in Kota Kinabalu; Yusof Ghani, p. 75, drying paddy. **Yahaya Ahmad**, p. 74, traditional Malay house. **Yeap Kok Chien**, p. 11, Malay man; p. 21, evolution of Taman Negara; p. 34, major peaks of Mount Kinabalu; p. 50, carbon cycle; p. 71, El Niño and normal year life cycles, boy with mask; p. 74, source of solar energy; p. 75, water heater, photovoltaic cell; p. 116, treatment of sewage; p. 119, storing and treating toxic and hazardous waste.